Learning in the Making

Disposition and Design in Early Education

Margaret Carr
Wendy Lee
Carolyn Jones
University of Waikato, New Zealand

Anne Smith
Kate Marshall
University of Otago, New Zealand

And

Judith Duncan
University of Canterbury, New Zealand

SENSE PUBLISHERS
ROTTERDAM/BOSTON/TAIPEI

D0265643

A C.I.P. record for this book is available from the Library of Congress.

ISBN 978-90-8790-965-9 (paperback)
ISBN 978-90-8790-966-6 (hardback)
ISBN 978-90-8790-967-3 (e-book)

Published by: Sense Publishers,
P. O. Box 21858, 3001 AW
Rotterdam, The Netherlands
http://www.sensepublishers.com

Printed on acid-free paper

CONTENTS

CONTENTS

ABOUT THE AUTHORS

Margaret Carr is a Professor of Education at the University of Waikato, New Zealand. She was one of the co-Directors of a curriculum development project that developed Te Whāriki, the national early childhood curriculum in New Zealand, and her academic career has continued to focus on curriculum in action: especially pedagogy and assessment practices in early childhood and the early years of school. She has written a book on Learning Stories as a narrative mode of assessment, and her research has included being a research associate for projects where the teachers are researching their own practice; recent completed projects include: ICT in early childhood, transition to school, question-asking and question-posing, and key learning competencies across place and time. She was a co-Director, with Anne Smith, of the Dispositions in Social Context project that forms the basis for the fourteen case studies in this book.

Anne Smith is an Emeritus Professor at the University of Otago, New Zealand. She returned from Alberta, Canada where she did her PhD in Educational Psychology in 1974, to a position in the Education Department at Otago University. She was the first Director of the Children's Issues Centre, from 1995 until 2006. During her tenure as director, the centre carried out applied research related to children's well being and rights – for example in families after parental separation, and in early childhood centres and schools. In her role as director, Anne initiated many advocacy and outreach education activities to disseminate research to professionals working with children, and to impact on policy and practice. Her books include *Understanding Children's Development*; and (with colleagues) *Children's Voices, Research, Policy and Practice*; and *What does it mean for children to be citizens? International perspectives*. Anne continues to work on research in the field of Childhood Studies.

Judith Duncan is an Associate Professor in Education, School of Māori, Social and Cultural Studies at the University of Canterbury College of Education, Christchurch, New Zealand. When this study was carried out Judith was employed at the Children's Issues Centre, University of Otago, New Zealand, where for 9 years she researched and taught in the area of early childhood education and children's participation. Judith is an established researcher with over 15 years of research experience, predominantly using qualitative research methods in a range of education settings. Her research and teaching interests include early childhood education, children's voices, gender and education, and education policy and practice. Since her doctoral studies, which examined teachers' perspectives of education reforms in the kindergarten sector, she has been involved in a range of projects that examine early childhood from multiple and interdisciplinary perspectives, placing central to each research project the perspectives of children and their families.

Carolyn Jones is the Research Manager at the Wilf Malcolm Institute of Educational Research at the School of Education, University of Waikato, New Zealand. Her particular research interests are in early childhood education, transition to school and the involvement of the families in education. In 2009 she co-authored a series of 20 booklets in a professional development resource for teachers: Kei Tua o te Pae Assessment for Learning Early Childhood Exemplars. Currently, her work as Research Manager involves working with staff across a wide range of contexts within education, assisting them with the design and implementation of research projects, and developing both a deeper and a broader knowledge of a variety of education research approaches.

Wendy Lee is the Project Director of the Educational Leadership Project which provides professional development for early childhood teachers in New Zealand and contributes to the teacher education programme at the University of Waikato. She has been a co-researcher with Margaret Carr on two 'Centres of Innovation' action research projects, investigating the role of ICT in pedagogy and practice in the early years, and question-asking and question-exploring by children in the early years. Between 2001 and 2007, she co-directed the ECE Assessment and Learning Early Childhood Exemplar Project with Margaret Carr. In 2008 and 2009, she and Margaret also worked together on a research project entitled Learning Wisdom. Working with teachers from nine early childhood centres, they explored dialogue between teachers and children using Learning Stories as a catalyst. Wendy is a passionate advocate for ECE and has a strong commitment to strengthening the leadership capacity of the ECE sector.

Kate Marshall was an early childhood teacher before she took up a research position at the Children's Issues Centre at the University of Otago, New Zealand. Through her work in early childhood centres in Wellington, Palmerston North, and Dunedin, she has had considerable experience of working with young children and families. Kate has been engaged in a range of research projects focusing on family discipline, children's participation in community decision-making, the place and meaning of health in young people's lives and, the contribution of Playcentre to building social capital. Involvement in the research that contributes to this book represents the culmination of a passion for research and practices that value the experience and voices of children. She has completed a Bachelor of Arts, a Bachelor of Design (interiors), a Master of Education (Counselling) and is currently juggling interior design projects with qualitative research at Dunedin's School of Medicine. As an educator, researcher, parent and grandparent, she draws on both personal and professional expertise and interest in her contribution to this book.

ACKNOWLEDGEMENTS

The authors are grateful to the Marsden Grant fund, administered by the Royal Society of New Zealand, which allowed this research to be carried out. We would also like to thank the children, parents, extended families, early childhood teachers and primary school teachers who participated in the research, for the privilege and pleasure of talking to them, observing them and writing about them. Their stories of 'learning in the making' have fascinated and delighted us. We hope that we have conveyed some of the richness of their stories for the readers of this book.

JACQUELINE GOODNOW

FOREWORD

It is a rare experience to find a book that moves us forward on three fronts: theories, research methods, and links to policy and practice. This book does so.

The questions tackled are major. What do we – as children or as adults – learn in the course of various kinds of experience? How does learning take place? How can we encourage effective and rewarding learning ?

The focus is on the years usually covered by "early education". These are times when children are in day care centres and kindergarten, often tagged as "pre-school" contexts. These are important times. This is when we acquire what this book calls "learning identity": an identity that includes views of ourselves as learners, approaches to learning, and decisions about the best courses to take. Shall we, for example, turn in a safe performance, take up a challenge and risk failure, ask questions and look for alternatives or just go along with what others suggest, see ourselves as competent, perhaps one of those "at the top" or as always a good second, perhaps even always an "also-ran"? "Learning identity", the book reminds us, is not fixed. It is, however, often acquired early and carried forward: one aspect – to take part of the book's title – to "learning in the making".

Offered, however, are insights that apply throughout life. These years are a kind of spotlight or test case for our understanding of learning through years of schooling and outside school. Here is a time marked by a first transition to formal learning. Here is also a time of rapid changes that enable us to track the kinds of change that occur and the way those are shaped by what children bring into this learning situation and what they encounter. That makes all the more appropriate and rewarding, the longitudinal accounts of changes and encounters for a varied group of children that are a major part of this book.

That broad relevance was one of the reasons for my enthusiastic reading. I found it also a refreshing break from some often restrictive but popular views of early education and of school learning. Here was a different view of what learning covers, and of how it takes place: part of a shift that others are also making but also expanding on what they have offered.

Rewarding, to start with, are the approaches to the question: *What does "learning" cover?* We are in the midst of emphases on the need for a "skills-centred" approach to early education. Our society, it is often said, needs citizens with particular kinds of competence: "literacy" and "numeracy" especially. Schools are where these kinds of competence are acquired, and those kinds of competence are all that schools should aim for.

"Learning", however, covers far more than those kinds of competence. Schools need to aim at more than this important but narrow range. And schools do in fact have an effect on more than these kinds of competence. Here, to repeat a phrase used earlier, is where we acquire major parts of our "learning identity". Here is where—to take some phrases cited from Vivian Paley's work – we learn a great deal about "reading the environment" and take major steps toward being able to step into "the mental shoes of others": critical skills for any life with others or any progress in understanding the work of others that are a constant part of schooling.

Ability and knowledge, the book points out, are an essential part of learning. But they are not a sufficient account of what happens or of what we should aim for. We can, to borrow from some other analyses of learning, end with children who are "able" in school terms and are physically present but have no sense of "engagement" with what is happening in class or with any "learning" situation.

Out of these broader concerns with learning, there has emerged an emphasis on the importance of children acquiring some particular characteristics, often with the names "reciprocity", "resilience" and "imagination". One of the major steps that this book makes consists of translating these nouns into verbs. With that translation, one can pin down what these terms mean. We can begin to see what children do that indicates moves toward reciprocity, resilience, or imagination, And we can begin to see – by way of those specific activities – what we ourselves can do or can foster.

To take one example, "reciprocity" is turned into "establishing a dialogue" and "being and becoming a group member". "Resilience" becomes "initiating and orchestrating projects" and "asking questions", "Imagination" becomes "exploring possible worlds" and "storying selves" (e.g., stories of who one is and might become).

Charting what children and teachers do along those specific lines, and how children change in what they do, then becomes the major target not only conceptually but also in practice. Charting the nature of those activities, the changes that occur in them, and the ways in which the contexts they encounter encourage or constrain them, is the task at the centre of the book's six research chapters. They are highly informative. They also offer clear examples of what we may all begin to notice and to aim for in our interactions with children.

Rewarding also are the approaches taken to the question: *How does learning take place?* Some of the approaches taken have already been signalled in my comments on what learning covers. A first added feature, however, is the shift away from regarding children as solitary learners, with all the relevant changes occurring in their minds. The book offers an informative account of several shifts from this view of children, or of learners at any age. Learning takes place, we are reminded, in the course of social relationships and social interactions, both with teachers and with peers. Critical in those interactions is the establishment of a sense of shared goals, shared meanings, shared attention, and a sense of really "working together": a further part of what is covered by the book's phrase "learning in the making". Offered here is not only a review of those conceptual positions, but an expansion on them and wonderfully explicit examples of what they mean in practice and how they might be encouraged.

Learning always takes place, to take another feature of the book's approach to how learning takes place, within contexts. Those contexts may be of several kinds, and pinning down how they vary has become a strong line of interest in analyses of development. Highlighted by the book, and again added to, are the ways in which various contexts restrict or open up what is possible. Highlighted also are contexts often forgotten: the worlds outside classrooms: playgrounds and home. I liked especially the emphasis on home and community as containing "funds of knowledge" that schools may tap into and use as a building base and as prime sources for the kinds of "learning identities" we develop. In a world increasingly marked by cultural diversity and population flow, the book reminds us, we need to recognise and to build on the way parents especially perceive their children's needs and abilities, and the work of teachers and schools, and to be alert for changes in those views as well as changes in children.

One last comment on why I hold such a positive view of this book. It is a rare example of work that has two firm bases. One is in the conceptual analyses of learning. The other is in what one learns from the longitudinal following of individual children and particular aspects of change. The two bases are well described in themselves. They are also well integrated. Here then is an unusually rewarding volume for those interested in one or other of the two bases, for those who ask how they can be brought together, and for those who ask about the implications of both for how we might "design" early education.

Jacqueline Goodnow
Emeritus Professor
Macquarie University
Sydney, Australia
May 2009

WHERE IT ALL BEGAN

> I soon discovered that whoever forays into this exciting territory
> dooms herself to an uneasy life. The first predicament of the student
> of human development is her being torn between two conflicting
> wishes: the wish to be scientific, whatever this word means to her,
> and the desire to capture the gist of those phenomena that are unique
> to humans. (Sfard, 2008, p. xiv)

This book is about one aspect of human development. It considers the relationship
between learning and educational environments for fourteen children over eighteen
months of their early education. The learning that is emphasised is what we have
called learning *disposition* and the educational environments that we have emphasised
form the educational *design* that was the reciprocal and responsive partner in the
formation and transformation of learning dispositions and learning identities. To
tell our versions of these children's journeys we have zoomed in on learning
episodes in educational settings, and zoomed out on our understanding of their
dispositional *learning in the making* to suggest connections and continuities. And
we have been assisted in this by conversations with the major players in these
stories: the children, the teachers, and the families.

Anna Sfard, quoted at the beginning of this chapter, has provided a reminder of
the difficulties in embarking on such a project. She adds:

> Whenever one of these needs is taken care of, the other one appears to be
> inherently unsatisfiable. Indeed, across history, the tug-of-war between the
> two goals, that of scientific reproducibility, rigor, and cumulativeness, on the
> one hand, and that of doing justice to the complexity of the "uniquely
> human", on the other, resulted in the pendulum-like movement between the
> reductionist and the "gestaltist" poles. (Sfard, 2008, p. xiv)

We knew already, from our previous work, that we were working in a very
contested and well-populated field, attempting to do justice to the complexity of
the uniquely human, and to present a trustworthy theoretical and empirical account.
Our response to Sfard's pendulum has been: to work in the borderland between
paradigms, to build narratives from 'pieces', and to argue that the development of
learning dispositions is about identity work in an interactional space 'in the middle'
between individual disposition and curriculum design.

WORKING IN THE BORDERLAND BETWEEN PARADIGMS

The six authors of this book had become interested in the ways that the big ideas of
learning *disposition* are constructed and provide what we might call navigation

tools as children navigate with and around people, places and things over time in early childhood settings, move from home to early childhood centre (and back again), and travel from early childhood centre to school. We come from a number of learning and teaching pathways in order to do this. Anne has had a long-term commitment to identifying and re-cognising spaces for children's voices and children's rights; Margaret's focus has for some time been the exploration of ways in which curriculum, pedagogy and assessment practice can enhance children's identities as learners; Judith's interests have included the discourse frames that position children and teachers in inclusive or excluded ways; Carolyn has developed and extended her interest in the opportunities that enhance reciprocal connections between the cultures of home and educational setting; Wendy has been immersed in researching and working towards settings in which teachers and children develop mindsets of agency and resourcefulness; and Kate came to this project with a passion for research and practices that value the experience and voices of children. Our philosophical backgrounds were diverse as well: education and sociocultural geography, psychology and human development, poststructural and critical inquiry, community action and professional development, sociology and demography, and education and counselling. Nevertheless, we came together with a collective experience of researching on, and a common interest in, young children and their learning. We also all brought a common commitment to researching and writing about the design of educational environments that contribute to the development of useful and mindful learning dispositions that concern themselves with ethics of care, competence, connection and critique. We had all worked with – and found them to be fruitful contexts for discussion – episodes or stories of children's participation in their early childhood or school environments.

Writing about research from a narrative paradigm, Jean Clandinin and Jerry Rosiek (2007) commented that:

> As researchers we find ourselves drifting, often profitably, from one paradigm of inquiry into another. We do not cross borders as much as we traverse borderlands... (W)e play with the idea of borderlands, those spaces that exist around borders where one lives with the possibility of multiple plotlines. This way of understanding the spaces around the philosophical borders we have described fits with a view of a landscape that does not have sharp divides that mark where one leaves one way of making sense for another. (Clandinin & Rosiek, pp. 58–59)

There is a sense in which we have worked towards what we might call a critical sociocultural (Lewis, Enciso & Moje, 2007) approach, or a sociocritical stance on the data we have collected with children. We did not begin with a sociocritical frame already worked out, but as we have wrestled together with interpreting the data, we have shaped a methodology that we hope will be interesting for readers. Kris Guttiérrez describes a similar process by the authors of a book entitled 'Reframing Sociocultural Research on Literacy'. She describes it as anchoring one foot inside a sociocultural frame, while allowing the other foot to move around into other conceptual terrain:

Throughout the set of chapters, the authors draw on a number of theoretical perspectives, largely practice-based views, to extend their own conceptual, methodological, and empirical work. ... In an effort to capture the complexity, the multimodality, the spatial, temporal, and cultural dimensions of literacy activity we argued the need for a better way of studying learning environments and individual learning within. As we described it then, a syncretic approach allowed us to anchor one foot firmly in cultural-historical activity theory, while allowing the other foot to move around in principled, deliberate, and strategic ways into other conceptual terrain to help make visible our theoretical and methodological blindspots. (Guttiérrez, 2007, p. 117).

These borderland metaphors describe our process of collaborative work on the *learning in the making* project, and the writing of this book, rather well. Our discussions for the sociocultural 'home' frame began not with cultural-historical theory (as the chapters referred to by Guttiérrez do) but with ideas about *belonging* from Etienne Wenger (1998), and the work on *affordance networks* and ecological frameworks from James Gee (2008), Sasha Barab & Wolff-Michael Roth (2006), James Greeno (2006) and Uri Bronfenbrenner (1979). But as our 'other foot' moved around, we recognised the important role of positioning and agency in the design of the educational settings in which we sited our research. Pierre Bourdieu (e.g. 1990), read in less determinist mode (Albright & Luke, 2008), provided one of the bridges we needed. His connection between *disposition* and *position*, also elaborated by Dorothy Holland, William Lachicotte, Debra Skinner & Carole Cain (1998), has provided a guiding theme to the argument that this book makes about learning. Holland et al. describe this theme as being about identity and agency in cultural worlds, so this is the territory into which we have ventured as well. We take the view that agency extends "beyond the skin" (Wertsch, Tulviste & Hagstrom, 1993, p. 337), sited in the ways in which children are positioned by their social and physical environments and the tools they share with others (including language). "The spark of agency", according to Peter Johnston (2004, p. 29), "is simply the perception that the environment is responsive to our actions." In this study we explore some aspects of the spaces in which that spark was kindled and kept alive.

BUILDING NARRATIVES FROM 'PIECES'

Many writers have researched the ways in which learners construct, and make their own, the big ideas of *subject knowledge*: for instance in physics (Roth, 2001), mathematics (Wagner, 2006) or linguistics (Gee, 2008). We have been interested in the ways in which learners are, at the same time, apparently developing the big ideas of *learning disposition*. We are therefore foregrounding learning disposition, learning orientation (Dweck, 2006), habits of mind (Costa & Kallick, 2000) or learning power (Claxton, 2002), keeping in mind that in the background, closely tethered, are the subject knowledges and the domain-specific expertise. James Greeno combines the two when he writes about "aspects of classroom practice that involve both interpersonal and subject matter aspects of interaction" (Greeno, 2007 p. 21).

We are also straying into the topic of transfer of learning, and one idea about transfer that has resonance with our interest in the tethering of learning disposition to context is the notion of 'transfer by pieces' (Wagner, 2006). Joseph Wagner develops this idea to theorise a student's growing understanding of 'big ideas' in mathematics; he describes Maria and the researcher revisiting a number of mathematics education episodes in which Maria participated and where the same idea appeared in different guises. He writes about the value of Maria seeing the 'pieces' as a sequence, and of the opportunity for reflection on the similarities and differences in situations. Carlina Rinaldi (2006) writes similarly about children and adults making meaning from a 'dictionary of experiences' which helped them to reflect, infer, hypothesise and understand (p. 76).

Our research followed this notion of building narratives from 'pieces' by using *episodes* as conceptual units (the pieces or building blocks of a repertoire of dispositions) and as units of analysis for the research data. We started the search for dispositions in social context and their affordances by observing and recording children's activities in episodes of learning in their early childhood centres and schools.

Jay Lemke (2000) writes about researching 'across the scales of time', and sets out a table of 'representative timescales for education or related processes'. The scale includes: an utterance (one-ten seconds), an exchange (seconds to minutes), an episode (about fifteen minutes), a lesson (an hour), a school day, and so on up to a planetary change of 3.2 billion years and a universal change of thirty-two billion years. In this research we zoomed in on episodes of ten minutes or more ('thematic, functional units'), and the research considered the construction over time of dictionaries of 'episodes of joint attention' in early years settings.

Our interest in observing children's episodes of joint attention developed from a study by one of the authors (Smith, 1999) of infant and toddler experiences at their early childhood centres. Joint attention is "an encounter between two individuals in which the participants pay joint attention to, and jointly act on some external topic" (Schaffer, 1992, p. 101). Joint attention episodes have long been regarded as important early learning contexts and experiences during infancy (Bruner, 1995; Schaffer, 1992; White, Kahan & Attamucci, 1979). Much of the early work tended to look mainly at infants and their mothers. Looking for an explanatory hypothesis about the effectiveness of particular teacher practices in early childhood centres, the Effective Provision of Preschool Education (EPPE) study (Sylva, Sammons, Melhuish, Siraj-Blatchford & Taggart, 1999) categorised joint attention episodes between teachers and children. This was a qualitative extension to a five-year longitudinal study of the effects of preschool education on children's attainment and social development at entry to school and beyond. The authors developed a category that they called 'sustained shared thinking' with sub-categories of 'child initiated' and 'adult initiated' (Siraj-Blatchford & Manni, 2008 p. 6). In that research, sustained shared thinking "came to be defined as an effective pedagogic interaction, where two or more individuals 'work together' in an intellectual way to solve a problem, clarify a concept, evaluate activities or extend a narrative" (p. 7). In our study, we extended our concept of episodes to include engagement with activities or tools in the material world as well as joint attention activities with other people.

At the same time we reflected together and then zoomed out on what we interpreted as longer-term narratives, processes and patterns. We traced these episodes over time, analysing repeating patterns (Lemke, 2000, p. 278) and the social contexts that had apparently afforded, invited, provoked or inhibited the strengthening of learning dispositions over time. The clues we followed included those moments when learning dispositions in action appeared even when the social context was unfavourable, calling on children to resist the norms of the moment and therefore, in a sense, to refer back to their dictionary of facilitated experiences. On those occasions it appeared that the children themselves were 'zooming out', as Maria had done for the big ideas of mathematics in the Wagner study. In the following example, Joseph, one of the children in our study, appeared to be constructing an opportunity to zoom out from a particular and local conversation in his school classroom to a big picture of contexts that concern themselves with fairness and justice. This looked to us like a disposition in action, working against the grain of a worksheet activity which was mainly concerned with matching pictures and colouring in between the lines.

> Joseph is colouring in a work sheet; the episode turns into a discussion amongst the children about who is the fastest. Joseph reminds the group that this should not be a race and adds: "If I win a race and all of you are trying, it's not...What if I was ten and you were five?". (Field notes. Joseph, phase three)

We shifted from the literature to the data and back again to begin to build narratives over time, in the same way as researchers "moved to and fro between the gradually unfolding stories of our young people and our emerging conceptual models and tentative theorizing" in a longitudinal study focusing on the continuity and change in young people's dispositions to learning for seventy-nine year eleven pupils from secondary schools in the west of England (Bloomer & Hodkinson, 2000, p. 586). These researchers argued that although there was an extensive literature on learning, very little had been written about how children's dispositions to learn changed over time. Our study will, we hope, make a contribution to this field.

LEARNING 'IN THE MIDDLE'

In our rejection of the stages of development that had traditionally set out a normative pathway of learning and development, we were influenced by John Morss's account of the way Rom Harré turned the notion of stages on its side, changing a hierarchical account of children's development into a set of alternatives (Morss, 1996). In this way, a sequence becomes a conceptual network, retaining the historical conceptual work but inviting the analysis to recognise diverse learning journeys and trajectories. Jerome Bruner (1986, p. 155) also commented on his change of mind about the three stages of representation that he had advocated in 1971:

You represented the world in action routines, in pictures, or in symbols, and the more mature you became, the more likely you were to favour the after end of the progression than the starting end. At the time we thought that the course from enactive through iconic to symbolic representation was a progression, although I no longer think so. But I do still find it useful to make a threefold distinction in modes of representation, although not on developmental grounds.

Seymour Papert in his 1993 book *Mindstorms* celebrated 'concreteness' and criticised what he called the 'perverse commitment to moving as quickly as possible from the concrete to the abstract' (p. 146). The value of Piaget's work, he maintained, is that he gave us valuable insights into the workings of a non-abstract way of thinking, and he pointed out that concrete thinking was not confined to "underdeveloped societies" or to children, but that people everywhere (from Paris to African villages) used it (Papert, 1993, p. 151).

Our observations and the literature insisted that we incorporate the opportunities to learn, or the design of the educational environment, into this study of learning dispositions over time. The notion of learning as a situated and 'relational matter' was expressed by Jean Lave in 1996:

> Why pursue a social rather than a more familiar psychological theory of learning? To the extent that being human is a relational matter, generated in social living, historically, in social formations whose participants engage with each other as a condition and precondition for their existence, theories that conceive of learning as a special universal mental process impoverish and misrecognize it. (Lave, 1996, p. 149)

Situating learning means that "Learning is not separated from the world of action but exists in robust, complex, social environments made up of actors, actions and situations" (Pitri, 2004, p. 6). Our focus has been on what we have perceived as the relationship between the disposition and the design, and we have called on the literature on affordance networks to assist us in the quest for a framework for theorising the continuity and development of this relationship for the fourteen children in our study. Barab & Roth define an affordance network as resources or aspects of an educational design that are *viewed as* necessary or useful, depending on the purpose at the time:

> An affordance network is the collection of facts, concepts, tools, methods, practices, agendas, commitments, and even people....that are distributed across time and space and are viewed as necessary for the satisfaction of particular goal sets. (Barab & Roth, 2006, p. 5)

James Wertsch (1998) writes about 'living in the middle', between the individual and the context, focusing on action mediated by people, places, and things. He has said that "a focus on mediated action and the cultural tools employed in it makes it possible to 'live in the middle' and to address the sociocultural situatedness of action, power and authority" (Wertsch, 1998, p. 65). The space *in the middle* is occupied by the relating: the recognising, adapting, editing, recontextualising, improvising, constructing, enjoying, puzzling about, and taking up of (or ignoring) opportunities in the environment. This middle space is where identity work takes place. Cultural brokers and boundary objects – the recontextualising agents (Walker & Nocon, 2007; Lemke, 2000) – do their work there, and it is this space that is the focus of this book.

RECONCEPTUALISING AND REFORMING EDUCATION

Underlying all of this was a commitment to reconceptualising the major outcomes for education and to contributing to policy and practice discussions. We wondered what learning *in the making* might look like when we foreground learning dispositions, and what policy and practice can learn from this interpretation of the educational experience of a number of children over time, searching for continuity and dissonance over eighteen months in early childhood and after they had completed their first few months of schooling.

We had been aware for some time of the curriculum focus in many school curriculums – including our own in New Zealand when we began this study – on subject area knowledge and skill as the key outcomes for education. Our awareness that this is not the only way to conceptualise learning has been sharpened by a very different New Zealand early childhood curriculum in which the learning outcomes are summarised as working theories and learning dispositions (Ministry of Education, 1996 p. 44). There is a recognition in this early childhood curriculum that much knowledge is couched as 'working theory' with the implication that it is uncertain and that it may look different depending on one's prior experience and the context. The curriculum also states that learning dispositions are important learning outcomes. Referring to the five strands of the curriculum (well-being, belonging, contribution, communication and exploration) the document states:

> Dispositions to learn develop when children are immersed in an environment that is characterised by well-being and trust, belonging and purposeful activity, contributing and collaborating, communicating and representing, and exploring and guided participation. (Ministry of Education, 1996, p. 45)

After we began our study, a new *school* curriculum was published in New Zealand, with the significant inclusion of dispositional outcomes that have been called 'key competencies':

> More complex than skills, the competencies draw also on knowledge, attitudes, and values in ways that lead to action..... The competencies continue to develop over time, shaped by interactions with people, places, ideas and things. Opportunities to develop the key competencies occur in social contexts. People adopt and adapt practices that they see used and valued by those closest to them, and they make these practices part of their own identity and expertise. (Ministry of Education, 2007, p. 12)

The cultures that develop in early childhood centres and school classrooms can be described as 'dispositional milieux'; they may be overt and public, or subtle and covert; they may support the spirit and intent of a curriculum document or they may not. Jo Boaler and James Greeno (2000), for instance, analysed the different 'ways of knowing' that had developed in two school mathematics classrooms with different dispositional milieux. They argued that 'ways of knowing' (after Belenky, Clinchy, Goldberger & Tarule, 1986) could be a characteristic of classrooms or places.

In the same way, we suggest that learning dispositions are features of places, in this case of early childhood centres, school classrooms and homes. These dispositional milieux are affordance networks: networks of useful resources, including people, that provide, *or appear to provide*, opportunities and constraints for the learning that the individual has in mind.

THE CHILDREN AND THE RESEARCH

We will meet the children – Aralynn, Buzz, David, Henry, Jack, Jeff, Joseph, Lauren, Leona, Lisa, Yasin, Ofeina, Samuel and Sarah[1] – and aspects of their learning journeys, in chapters three to nine. When we first met these children they were attending two kindergartens[2] and three childcare centres, located in three New Zealand cities. One research team worked in the North Island of New Zealand, the other in the South Island. These early childhood centres were selected on the basis that they met agreed criteria for quality: they all employed qualified (three-year degree) staff, provided stimulating environments (according to local advisors and our own knowledge), and had positive reports from the Educational Review Office.[3] The children and families who participated in the study were chosen because the children's birthdays met the criterion of going to school over the same three-month period in 2003. We invited all the families whose children met this criterion to participate, and all of them accepted[4].

Five of the families of the fourteen children in this book had moved to New Zealand from China, India, or the Pacific Islands during the previous five years. For four of them, English was an additional language for both parents[5]. For two of those children the grandmother or grandparents had moved to New Zealand to be with the family, looking after the child outside the early childhood centre sessions and after school, speaking the first language to them.

Of the fourteen children, five were the only child in the family, two were in re-constructed families with a stepfather, and there was one solo parent. On or around their fifth birthdays the children made the transition from the early childhood settings to ten new entrant school classrooms[6].

Because we were interested in learning as the relationship between disposition and design, we wanted to observe the children's engagement with other people, and the places and things in their learning environments, as well as to talk to a variety of participants in their learning settings – the children themselves, and their parents and teachers. A number of aspects of a critical sociocultural approach determined the ways in which we went about researching the space "in the middle" (to address the "sociocultural situatedness of action, power and authority") that Wertsch (1998, p. 65) had described. These were: an interest in what was going on in joint attention episodes, a view of children as capable co-authors of their own learning, and a concern for multiple perspectives.

An interest in what was going on in joint attention episodes

We observed each of the children over three different periods of time, or *phases*. Phase one observations were at the early childhood centre, close to the children's fourth birthdays; phase two observations were also at the early childhood centre, a month or so before they turned five and would go to school; phase three observations were after a few months at school.

Children were observed for from four to 12 hours at each phase, twice in their early childhood centres (phases one and two), and once at school (phase three). We attempted to sample each portion of the day when the child was attending, and for any one phase of observation there were usually at least three days when the child was observed. We kept a continuous written running record of the children's activities, and interactions, writing field notes at the end of the day. At the same time we were recording the children's conversations via remote microphones placed inside 'research jackets' worn over their normal clothes by the children. The 'research jackets' were sleeveless jackets sewn with adjustable side straps to enable them to fit a range of young-children sizes. A pocket was also sewn onto them into which a small transmitter for the microphone was able to be easily inserted and removed. This process for recording the data was slightly different in the North Island from the South Island project (see Jones, 2009 for the North Island process, and Smith, Duncan & Marshall, 2005, for more details from the South Island). In the North Island, fifteen base calico jackets were sewn, and a variety of decorative jackets were available to be attached with velcro over the plain base jacket. The children were particularly interested in the fabrics of these over-jackets: the most popular were bright orange with silver tape, pink sequins, Pasifika (Pacific nations) designs, and silver stars on a black background. There was a demand by many of the children in the centres to wear the jackets; this meant that at any one time there were many children wearing the decorated 'research' jackets, while only one or two were being recorded. By phase two in the North Island, we introduced the novelty of placing the transmitters in belt packs or 'bum bags', and these were popular as well. In the South Island, a number of coloured base jackets were available, and the children chose from a collection of attractive badges (with pictures of trains, insects, angels etc) to decorate the jacket for the day. Occasionally the case study children decided to remove the jackets; then, we observed without the recording. In phase three, in the school classrooms, the North Island researchers used table-top voice recorders to provide data on the conversations, while the South Island researchers continued to use the jackets. We took digital photographs of children as they were engaged in activities at their early childhood centres or new entrant classroom.

We chose up to ten episodes for transcription and analysis for each phase of observation for each child (occasionally, if all the episodes were short, we included

9

more than ten). An episode was defined as a period of sustained involvement or joint attention with people (peers or teachers) or objects, having a clear beginning and end. Below is an example of an episode in phase two where Leona is engaged in her favourite activity: making things, in this case making a necklace from string and a shell. This after-lunch necklace project had begun before lunch, when Lizzie had the idea of making a necklace with shells and wanted to make a hole in a shell; Leona joined her in this enterprise. They could not figure out how to make a hole in the shell, and asked a teacher who suggested a drill might be the right tool – but said they did not have the right sort of drill at the centre. The teacher then suggested using the centre's hot glue gun – but they had run out of glue. She said she would go to the shop at lunch-time to get some more glue. Leona commented on how she liked the smoothness of the inside of the shell, and talked to the researcher about the shellfish that lived in there. They found a safe place for their shells and then went off to play on climbing equipment and wait for a pre-lunch mat time where they would listen to a story.

Making a necklace: Leona (phase two)

After lunch .... Leona has her shell and string all ready. Lizzie goes first, using the glue gun to glue her shell to the string (with assistance from the teacher). The teacher starts to tie a knot in the string but Leona suggests that Lizzie put it on before the knot is tied (to get the length right). Leona asks the teacher what the (glue) stick in the gun is, and the teacher explains how the glue stick works.

Leona: What are they? (points to glue sticks)

Teacher: That is actually the glue. That is it in a really solid form and then when it goes through this gun it gets really hot inside and it melts it and that is how it sticks,.

Leona: Oh.

Teacher: So that is actually glue in a real hard solid form. It goes through the gun and then it melts it with the heat. Neat eh.

Leona: Yes.

Leona then measures her string by holding it up to her neck: "Shall we size it?", she says. Teacher: "Shall we size it? That's a good idea". She assists Leona to measure the length for the necklace. ....

Then Leona uses the glue gun very competently and, after two attempts, joins the shell to the string. She puts it on, and asks the researcher "I want a picture of it on me". A photo is taken.

A view of children as capable co-authors of their own learning

The notion of agency is threaded throughout the study. We viewed children as social actors with opinions and views of their own, as experts and agents, rather than as incompetent and passive recipients of what adults do to them (James, 2007; Mayall, 2002), so we devised ways in which to hear their voices in everyday activities, and to listen to their views on their learning. We had worked previously on research which attempted to get close to children's thinking and perspectives

(Carr, 2001a, 2002; Smith, Taylor & Gollop, 2001), and, like Mariane Hedegaard (2009), we have been interested in everyday local settings as the site for researching children's development and learning. In this project, the recording of the everyday learning episodes in the centres and the schools provided much of this data.

The observations and recording were one part of the mosaic of data in this study. A 'mosaic approach' was introduced to the research literature by Alison Clark and Peter Moss to explore ways of listening to young children. This approach describes a range of ways to research the views of young children in early childhood provision on "What is it like to be here?" and "Do you listen to me?". The latter question was adapted from an evaluative framework developed in New Zealand for the early childhood curriculum (Clark & Moss, 2001 p. 12; Carr, May, Podmore, Cubey, Hatherly & Macartney, 2000). The mosaic approach includes observation and narrative accounts, child conferencing, children's photographs and mapping of the place using photographs and drawings, tours led by the children, and role plays. Parents', practitioners' and researchers' perspectives were added. In our project we talked informally to the children during the participant observations of everyday activities, took photographs and asked children for comments about the episodes around the photographs. We also invited teachers and families to discuss the photographs with the children, and invited children and their families to take photographs at home. Here is an example of a one-to-one interview with Jeff at his early childhood centre.

Jeff attends a parent co-operative community childcare centre and the researcher is showing him photographs of a group of children who have climbed up on the climbing equipment and are singing "I'm the King of the Castle". Jeff is not present in the first photograph but in the second photograph, he is shown climbing up to join the other children. Jeff (at that phase) was not often involved with a group of peers. This extract, however, shows that he is aware of his role in the peer group of the centre and does not want to be excluded.

Researcher: Okay, right let's see what you did next (Picture of children – not including Jeff – on climbing equipment singing "I'm the King of the Castle") PAUSE. You aren't in this one.

Jeff: No, I came up you see. (The next photograph in the sequence is another one of the group after he had climbed up to join them).

Researcher: You did too – look (shows next picture which includes Jeff). But what were they doing?

Jeff: They were singing a song up there.

Researcher: They were, they were singing "I'm the King of the Castle".

Jeff: Yeah.

Researcher: They were having a good time weren't they, and you decided you'd join them.

Jeff: Yeah, I didn't want them to tease me so I just came up.

Researcher: Oh I see you didn't want them to tease you. Do you worry about [*inaudible*] teasing you?

Jeff: I don't want to be the Dirty Rascal sometimes.

Researcher: You don't want to be the Dirty Rascal.
Jeff: Yes.
Researcher: That's a bit mean isn't it? So you wanted to be the King of the
              Castle too. (Shows another picture) (Interview with Jeff, phase
              one)

A concern for multiple perspectives

Families' perspectives and stories from home contributed to our interpretations. Andrew Pollard and Ann Filer's research on patterns of learning orientation concluded that parents of young school children played a significant role in discussing, mediating and interpreting school experiences and new challenges (Filer & Pollard, 2000, p. 141; Pollard & Filer, 1999). The EPPE study also found that home learning environments predicted child outcomes at pre-school, but socio-economic status and parent qualifications were not the whole story. Iram Siraj-Blatchford concludes: "In other words; EPPE found that it is what parents did that is more important than who they were" (Siraj-Blatchford, 2004 p. 9). We interviewed the families at each phase of the research, sharing our ideas with them, and inviting them to write down their children's comments about photographs of the children in action at the early childhood centre. We gave the families a disposable camera for the children to take photos of home activities and we used these photographs as a catalyst for discussions. We asked the parents for their perspectives about their children's learning. David's mother, for instance, contributed her thoughts about the continuity of David's learning:

In some ways I was probably disappointed [that the school didn't ask about his interests], especially because he was a sandpit child, and the concern that he may not have settled into the classroom. This is a boy who's never sat down for half an hour. ... Friends would say "Oh, you know, David, he won't sit on the mat". But I thought, well, I always thought that he would, because he's got good concentration. (Interview with David's parents, phase three)

We also recorded conversations with the teachers (often in a group at the early childhood centre), asking whether what we observed was fairly typical for the case study children's participation in the centre or the classroom. The school teachers often wanted to talk about the constraints on their teaching. One of the teachers commented on what she called the 'crowded curriculum' in the early years of school:

In the olden days we had what was called 'Developmental'. Probably when I first started teaching [over ten years ago]. When I first started teaching, you'd have a developmental time in the morning, and like a kindy [kindergarten], you'd have set-up stations. You'd have water play and play dough, and they could roam around and go, like, an easier transition to school from kindy. And while they were doing that, you could withdraw little groups, and do some writing with them, or.... But as the curriculum became more crowded, we had to fit in more coverage of subjects, and we don't have time to let them play. It seems dreadful. The only time they have for free choice is when they finish their work. (Teacher interview, phase three)

These discussions with the teachers made it clear that, as Bronfenbrenner would have reminded us, there is another level of actual and perceived affordance operating here: the ways in which mandated curriculum and school-wide or early-childhood-service-wide policies and practices can enable or disable the teachers' perceived (and actual) ability to design and provide opportunities to strengthen learning dispositions for the children in their centres and their classrooms. There was a wider system of influence for at least five of these families too. These New Zealand families had left their homelands for a better life and a good education for their children; they were accountable to an extended family overseas.

Chapter two will introduce the three learning dispositions that became the focus of this study: reciprocity, imagination, and resilience. The six chapters that follow chapter two tell stories about *learning in the making* for the fourteen children who began their early-childhood-centre and school educational journeys in five early childhood centres and shifted to new entrant classrooms in ten different schools. In each of those chapters, two or three case study children illustrate a facet of one of the three learning dispositions.

DISPOSITIONS AND POSITIONS

Mapping the Field

> How shall we deal with Self? ... I think of Self as a text about how one is situated with respect to others and towards the world – a canonical text about powers and skills and dispositions that change as one's situation changes from young to old, from one kind of setting to another. (Bruner, 1986, p. 130)

Learning dispositions, as described here, are complex units of educational input, uptake and outcome. We are more or less disposed to notice, recognise, respond to, reciprocate with, author, improvise from, and imagine alternatives to, what we already know and can do. Dispositions act as an affective and cultural filter for trajectories of learning in the making, and they can turn knowledge and skill into action. They can often be traced back through generations of families and students, and are strengthened, adapted, transformed or interrupted by circumstance and experience. They are the source of the recognition (or misrecognition) of learning opportunities and provide strategy and motivation for the inevitable improvisation that is learning.

But this notion of 'they' is a reification, turning dispositions into things that we can ring-fence, move about and nail down. This objectification is a typical trick of language (Sfard, 2008) and might do well in an introductory paragraph about dispositions, but as researchers and teachers it is more helpful to think of dispositions as units of participatory action, as verbs with qualifying adverbs (Claxton & Carr, 2004). This chapter will oscillate between the noun and the verb, but our stance is that a disposition is a process of overt and covert decision-making about a course of action. These decisions, consciously and unconsciously, are made in relation to the perceived affordances or opportunities in the environment; and in relation to particular purposes, desires and intentions by the individual or the collective at the time. The literature that we have found useful comes from two different, but intersecting, directions. We describe these directions as *Dispositions for the individual: being ready willing and able* and *Dispositions in social fields and communities.*

DISPOSITIONS FOR THE INDIVIDUAL: BEING READY WILLING AND ABLE

Dispositions that focus more on the 'mind' than the 'environment' appear in the literature under various names, and in various guises: as intellectual habits (Sizer, 1992), mindsets (Dweck, 1999, 2006) or habits of mind (Costa & Kallick, 2000), thinking dispositions (Perkins, Jay & Tishman, 1993; Ritchhart, 2002), learning dispositions (Bloomer & Hodkinson, 2000), ways of knowing (Belenky, Clinchy, Goldberger & Tamle, 1986; Boaler & Greeno, 2000), key competencies (Rychen & Salganik, 2001, 2003), and learning power (Claxton, 2002). In 1987, Lauren Resnick commented on the disposition to be a good thinker, pointing out that much of that is learning to recognise, and even search for opportunities to apply one's capacities. Later, in 1993, a three-part analysis of thinking dispositions was outlined by David Perkins, Eileen Jay and Shari Tishman at Harvard University's Project Zero: inclination, sensitivity to occasion, and ability. They argued that:

> It would be easy to see dispositions mainly as an effort to honor the role of motivation in complex cognition, and certainly this is one of the objectives. However, to treat dispositions as solely about motivation would be to take too narrow a view. Instead, we propose a conception of dispositions that includes attention to habits, perceptual sensitivities, and even abilities themselves. This conception puts forth dispositions as a unit of analysis for a broad and fruitful conception of mind. Specifically, a *disposition* in our sense is a psychological element with three components: inclination, sensitivity, and ability. (Perkins et al., 1993, p. 4)

These were later summarised as attitude, alertness and ability (Perkins, 2001). We have widened the focus by calling them *learning dispositions,* but we still find the three components the most helpful description, making it very clear that dispositions are different from (but incorporate) skills or strategies. In the final chapter we will shift this triad of components into the "middle" space between the individual and the educational design or environment.

One way of describing this triad was to say that learning includes knowing why, knowing when and where, and knowing how, to use knowledge and ability – later described as being ready, willing and able (Carr, 2001b; Claxton, 2002), an idea which has been incorporated into the New Zealand school curriculum, in the construct of key competencies:

> As they develop the competencies, successful learners are also motivated to use them, recognising when and how to do so and why. (Ministry of Education, 2007, p. 12)

Knowing why: the inclination

People often don't apply or practise their skills if they are not inclined to do so – if they don't recognise why, or feel that, they should. Inclination is usually associated with the learners' intentions, interests, goals and commitments. Opportunities to learn in the classroom may – or may not – connect with intentions and commitments from prior experiences, or in communities outside the classroom (Goodenow, 1992; Nasir & Saxe, 2003). Margaret Donaldson (2002 p. 259) has reminded us, however:

> That people should not be forced into activities that seem pointless to them is, I am sure, the intuition underlying the claim that all education must be

relevant to pupils' lives. And this basic intuition is sound. But education is about *changing* lives – about enlarging the scope of relevance. It is about changing the modal repertoire for one thing. It is about suggesting new directions in which lives may go (p. 259).

In a story about the curriculum in a high school in Harlem, five 'habits of mind' were phrased as questions posted on the wall of every classroom. Deborah Meier, the principal, commented: "But the most important of all is the 5th "habit": Who cares? Knowing and learning take on importance only when we are convinced that it matters, it makes a difference" (Meier, 1995, p. 41). Interest is part of this. Mihaly Csikszentmihalyi (1996) interviewed ninety-one 'creative' people (including fourteen Nobel prize winners) and concluded that in their early years those innovative thinkers had at least one strongly developed interest (even if this was not the interest that they became known for later in life).

Knowing when and where: sensitivity to occasion

An aspect of all learning is, in a sense, learning to 'read' situations: recognising when to speak, when to be silent, when to ask questions. We bring our prior experiences to these 'readings', and this may enhance or constrain our interpretations. Barbara Comber's (2000) work on early literacy highlighted the children's disposition to 'read the environment', and Barbara Rogoff has commented (2003, p. 253) that generalising experience from one situation to another involves knowing "which strategies are helpful in what circumstances". Of course, our intentions, interests and passions – knowing why – also contribute to our understanding about *knowing when and where*: they influence the opportunities that we notice and recognise.

Barab and Roth (2006 p. 3) have emphasised the importance of the 'attunements' that an individual can enlist to realise an affordance network and Helen Haste, writing about competencies for the OECD *Definition and Selection of Competencies: Theoretical and Conceptual Foundations* (DeSeCo) project, says that "It (competence) implies effectiveness not only in performance, but in the interpretation of context and meaning" (Haste, 2001, p. 94). Philippe Perrenoud (2001, p. 132) argues that: "Learners need to be able to mobilise resources and to orchestrate them, at an appropriate time, in a complex situation". Outlining a 'situative' view of learning and making a connection between *attunement* and transfer of learning, James Greeno and colleagues say that:

> *Learning*, in this situative view, is hypothesized to be becoming attuned to constraints and affordances of activity and becoming more centrally involved in the practices of a community (Lave & Wenger, 1991), and *transfer* is hypothesized to depend on attunement to constraints and affordances that are invariant or modifiable across transformations of a situation where learning occurred to another situation in which that learning can have an effect. (Greeno and the Middle School Mathematics Through Application Project Group, 1998, p. 11)

We have become interested in the ways in which learners might *perceive* constraints or affordances to be invariant or modifiable across situations, and which curriculum or pedagogical designs can afford the recognising or constructing of constraints or affordances – with learning dispositions in mind. Where learning dispositions are fragile, we assumed that designs for 'sensitivity to occasion' will require more powerful mediation than material affordance can offer: the environment may need to *invite* learners to participate, *actively engage* them and include their prior knowledge in conversations and interactions of joint attention, or *provoke* them to recognise opportunities that are unfamiliar and new (Claxton & Carr, 2004). We have extended the definition of 'affordance' and an 'affordance network' to include these processes.

Knowing how: the ability

Although Perkins and colleagues write about dispositions as 'beyond abilities', they argue for including dispositional ability as one of the three components: the ability to 'follow through', to take another point of view, for instance. In our triadic model of disposition, actual *and perceived* ability is part of the learning disposition. Lorna Hamilton (2002) argues, for instance, that conceptions of ability are part of the work of classrooms and that classroom organizational patterns are reflected in pupils' perceptions of their ability. Her research explored the ways in which pupils from different schools "chose to deal with competing or complementary constructions of ability" (Hamilton, 2002, p. 591). She researched the nature of ability conceptualisation from a range of perspectives – teachers, parents, and pupils – in four case study schools. Her discussion included ideas of fixed capacity, and the influence of 'setting' (streaming), and grading. She noted the role of families on the negotiation of what she has called 'pupil ability identity', adding that: "the impact of those in power may be challenged or reinforced by parental constructs of ability and schooling". (p. 593).

In chapter one we commented on the tethering of dispositions with subject knowledges and domain-specific expertise. Subject-matter ability and knowledge domains interact closely with learning-disposition ability and knowledge domains. For instance, our children's knowing in the domains of concrete making, cooking, gardening, writing, and the protocols for dramatic play were closely tethered to what they knew about relating to others, responding to set-backs with resilience, and imagining alternatives inside dispositions towards reciprocity, resilience and imagination.

Being ready willing and able

We have retained this triadic definition of learning disposition throughout the book. When we came to analyse the children's dispositions-in-action, with reference to "living in the middle", we described inclination, sensitivity to occasion and ability (being ready, willing and able) as *authoring, recognising opportunity* and *connected knowing*.

DISPOSITIONS AND COMMUNITIES: IDENTITY WORK IN THE MIDDLE

What is sought is an understanding of society and individuals that avoids the twin hazards of 'individual constructivism' and 'social determinism'. The one emphasizes the individual to such an extent that minimal attention is given to the way objects are socially defined, actions are socially constrained, and the acquisition of some forms of knowledge is promoted and of others is restricted or prohibited. The other sees the social context as shaping the individual to such an extent that attention to choice, resistance, or intention becomes minimal. Both of these extremes are avoided when the person-participating-in-a-practice is taken as the unit of analysis. (Miller & Goodnow, 1995 p. 8)

We developed a broad base of three dispositions: reciprocity, resilience and imagination, constructed as a framework from sociocultural theory. This chapter describes the conceptual journey that took us there. A second layer of six disposition-in-action was then constructed from our research on children's activities and conversations in real-life social and cultural contexts.

Authoring and authoritative positioning

A number of writers have been interested in the interactive space between the design of environments that contribute to dispositional work and the development of dispositions. James Greeno (2006), for instance, writes about authoritative and accountable positioning, and connected general knowing, as 'progressive themes in understanding transfer'. In a 2006 commentary he is reviewing papers in an issue of the Journal of the Learning Sciences on the topic of the transfer of learning. One of the authors in that issue of the journal (Randi Engle) uses the concept of sociolinguistic framing and Greeno writes in response about 'authoritative and accountable positioning' (p. 538, italics in the original):

The sociolinguistic concept of framing is a close conceptual relative of some other concepts in the study of interaction, such as agency, positioning, and positional identity. Accounts that use these concepts draw attention to aspects of interaction such as crediting individuals with authorship, initiating ideas and topics, and challenging or questioning what others have to say. I refer to this collection of concepts here as *authoritative and accountable positioning*.

"Authoritative, accountable positioning" is a collection of aspects of interaction that includes crediting individuals with authorship. This notion of positioning as a key construct for disposition was introduced in chapter one. Greeno concludes that 'To act effectively in a way that counts as transfer, therefore, involves having or taking authority to go beyond what has been taught" (Greeno, 2006, p. 546).

Linked to this notion of crediting learners with authorship, the New Zealand early childhood curriculum sets out a framework of outcome strands, introduced in chapter one, that align with five domains of 'mana': a Māori concept that can be loosely translated as agency, authority, power or prestige. The implications of the

Māori constructs of these strands of belonging, well-being, contribution, communication and exploration, is that they are sources of authoring or agency, sited in: place, spiritual mental and physical well-being, people (the community or the collective), language, and knowledge of the world. Bourdieu has the following to say:

> In short, the art of estimating and seizing chances, the capacity to anticipate the future by a kind of practical induction or even to take a calculated gamble on the possible against the probable, are dispositions that can only be acquired in certain social conditions.... Economic competence, like all competence (linguistic, political etc.), far from being a simple technical capacity acquired in certain conditions is a power tacitly conferred on those who have power over the economy or (as the very ambiguity of the word 'competence' indicates) an attribute of status. (Bourdieu, 1990, p. 64)

It is not possible to consider dispositions without using as a platform the theoretical work of Pierre Bourdieu, who insists on a wider scope for disposition and a longer time frame, and imbues them with a less tractable character. He writes about conditions of existence that produce *habitus*: "systems of durable, transposable dispositions"; they define responses by inscribing "things to do or not to do, things to say or not to say, in relation to a 'probable' upcoming future" (1990, p. 53). Bourdieu emphasises motivation and attunement: "[the habitus acts as] a system of cognitive and motivating structures... – procedures to follow, paths to take" (Bourdieu, 1990, p. 53).

James Albright and Allan Luke make a connection between James Gee's notion of 'primary discourses' of early cultural socialisation and Pierre Bourdieu's habitus, and comment that this has "refocused attention on the interaction of habitus with the social field of the school" (Albright & Luke, 2008, p. 7). In his 1992 book, *The Social Mind,* Gee has also outlined the features of what he calls Discourse (with a capital D); they would include Bourdieu's 'things to do or not to do, things to say or not to say, in relation to a 'probable' upcoming future'.

> Discourses [with a capital "D"] are composed of people, of objects (like books), and of characteristic ways of talking, acting, interacting, thinking, believing and valuing, and sometimes characteristic ways of writing, reading, and/or interpreting (offering translations of oral and/or written texts sensitive to the cures these texts present for interpretations to these practices).... Long before the child can decode print, she has become a member of one or more school-based Discourses – ways of thinking, acting, valuing with words and objects – that undergird school-based and mainstream literacy practices. (Gee, 1992, pp. 20, 123)

These ideas connect with New Zealand research by Stuart McNaughton on the ways in which literacy practices from diverse homes can be incorporated into school literacy practices, and research on 'funds of knowledge' in households, communities and classrooms, taken up in research projects by Pat Thomson and Christine Hall (González, Moll & Amanti, 2005; McNaughton, 2002; Thomson & Hall, 2008). The assumption behind González et al.'s "funds of knowledge" is that families have valuable competence and knowledge from their life experiences, and that knowing about these family resources opens up new possibilities for learning and effective classroom teaching. Prior experience provides the foundation for interpreting new information, and discourse and practice together form the basis for an approach to viewing households. Pat Thomson and Christine Hall's research explores the ways in which curriculum design can ignore or thwart opportunities to connect with funds of knowledge (or 'virtual school bags'). They comment on the respectful ethnographic studies of González and colleagues, and their utilisation of students' experiences and understandings at home as a bridge to the learnings that count as school success. Thomson and Hall (2008, p. 100) believe that it is necessary to open the 'virtual school bags', but *also* to change what counts as important knowledge. They conclude that the prescribed and privileged "sets of knowings and doings" within the UK English national curriculum are not easily permeable for children who have a diverse range of community pedagogy and knowledges.

Research in classrooms inspired by Bourdieu has focused on identity work. Jessica Zacher (2008, p. 252), for instance, researched what fifth grade students in an urban Californian classroom '*did* with discursive practices for talking about difference that they gleaned from assigned multicultural texts'.

> My analysis takes place at the intersection of habitus, "that product of history [that] produces individual and collective practices" (Bourdieu 1977:82), and social space, where such practices are formed and reformed.... In this sense, students' identity and affiliation choices were mediated by both their habitus-histories and their sense of what kinds of identity claims were permitted to them by their position in the classroom social hierarchy. (Zachner, 2008 p. 254)

Writing about 'positional identities', and echoing Bourdieu, Dorothy Holland et al., (1998, p. 143) have suggested that children have relational identities, "a set of dispositions toward themselves in relation to where they can enter, what they can say, what emotions they can have, and what they can do in a given situation". In a discussion of 'Identity and Agency in Cultural Worlds', they use the term 'figured world' to refer to a cultural world or space (p. 60). Figured worlds refer to meaning and action contexts in which social positions and relationships take place; we have also called them 'dispositional milieux'. They provide the spaces in which people fashion their identities, so there is a connection between identity and trajectories of participation:

> (Identities) remain multiple, as people's trajectories through figured worlds neither take on one path nor remain in the ambit of one cultural space, one figured world. Nonetheless, identities constitute an enduring and significant aspect of history-in-person, history that is brought to current situations. *They are a pivotal element of the perspective that persons bring to the construal of new activities and even new figured worlds.* (Holland, et al, 1998, p. 65, our italics)

Bourdieu described habitus as "embodied history, internalized as a second nature and so forgotten as history" (Bourdieu, 1990, p. 56). And, although a reading of Bourdieu is that he favours structural determinism over agency (Albright, 2008 p. 18), we take the stance that dispositions are durable but not fixed, a view supported by Albright and Luke (2008) and the work of Dorothy Holland and her colleagues, who view habitus as a fundamental but not finally determinating aspect of identity and personhood. Bloomer and Hodkinson's research (2000) on the learning careers of English secondary students, argued that dispositions can transform in a short time. They write about "the complexities of relationships between positions and dispositions, and between contexts, meanings, identity and learning" (p. 593), and comment on the connection with Bourdieu:

> He [Bourdieu] talks of a person's *habitus*: a portfolio of dispositions to all aspects of life, largely tacitly held, which strongly influence actions in any situation – familiar or novel. The habitus is, in turn, influenced by who the person is and where in society they are positioned, as well as by their interactions with others. (Bloomer & Hodkinson, 2000, p. 589)

In the 21st century, early years figured worlds and dispositional milieux beyond the home – early childhood centres – play an increasingly significant role, wittingly and unwittingly, in mediating students' identity and affiliation choices. Children now spend longer hours in early childhood programmes, and at increasingly younger ages. In our view, dispositional design in early years educational programmes should be implemented more wittingly, more deliberately, and this book provides research and reflection to inform such a project.

Linking clusters of disposition to modes of belonging and conceptions of culture

Three messages from Bourdieu are relevant to the *learning in the making* discussion here.
– Dispositions inform us about who we can or ought to communicate with, how to do this, and what language we should use.
– Habitus is a life-style, a 'world view' (Bourdieu, 1979/1984, p. 173). It develops in early experiences and social fields, and it invites us to choose familiar pathways.
– It implies certain commitments, responsibilities, expectations and possibilities (and ignores others).

The work of Etienne Wenger (1998) parallels these ideas, but takes us directly to agency and designs for change. Wenger suggests that identity work resides in the development of *belonging* to a community of practice and that there are three distinct but necessarily connected modes of belonging: mutual engagement, alignment and imagination.
– On educational *engagement* he says that a learning community, in contrast to traditional learning institutions (which often ignore these), should view social relationships and interests as essential ingredients in maximising members' engagement.

- On educational *alignment* he says that education should engage communities in broader contexts in purposeful activities which have consequences beyond their boundaries, in order to help students become more effective in the world.
- On educational *imagination* he says that imagination is an integral part of education, and that education should not be confined to teaching specific capabilities but instead make students aware of a variety of possible trajectories.

Another parallel can be made with Martin Packer and Mark Tappan's (2001) analysis of conceptions of culture. They distinguish between three types of culture. Firstly culture as mediational means and the arrangements of artefacts, events and practices into an intentional world. Secondly culture as the use of power in division, exclusion and domination. Thirdly culture as the semiotic messages and texts of human communication. The three forms of culture are not mutually exclusive, and influence children as power "enacted in messages circulating through one or more forms of life. But the threefold division is a helpful one, in part because parallel to these conceptions of culture we can anticipate three broad strategies of critique" (Packer & Tappan, 2001, p. 13). In this last sentence, Packer and Tappan (p. 13) are referring to researcher critique, and they set out three parallel critical aims for research. These are:

- to read communication messages critically;
- to diagnose the operation of power and its consequent exploitations and coercions;
- to disclose how culture provides conditions for a possible way of life.

Just such a critical stance can be envisaged as a long-term dispositional goal for learners.

We therefore saw synergies between (i) Bourdieu messages: habitus informs us about who we can/ought to communicate with and how to do this, it invites us to choose the familiar, and it suggests possibilities, (ii) *Wenger modes of belonging*: engagement, alignment and imagination, (iii) *Packer and Tappan conceptions of culture*: the semiotic forms of messages and texts in human communication, the play of power, and artefacts, practices, and events that make up an intentional world, and (iv) *Packer and Tappan's foundations for critical disposition*: reading the messages critically, understanding who and what is recognised as being of value here, envisaging possible selves and possible worlds. From these synergies we constructed three dispositions as our conceptual frame, aligned with these three frameworks: reciprocity, resilience and imagination (see Table 2.1).

Table 2.1. Conceptual frameworks for a study of disposition

Dispositions in this study	Reciprocity	Resilience	Imagination
Bourdieu messages	Habitus informs us about who we can/ought to communicate with and how to do this	It invites us to choose the familiar	It suggests possibilities
Wenger modes of belonging	engagement	alignment	imagination

Packer & Tappan conceptions of culture	the semiotic forms of messages and texts in human communication	the play of power	artefacts, practices, and events that make up an intentional world
Packer & Tappan's foundations for critical disposition	reading the messages critically	understanding who and what is recognised as being of value here	envisaging possible selves and possible worlds

We then interrogated our data to select two actions, or facets, for each learning disposition. These broadly described actions do not in any sense 'cover the field' of the three dispositions: they might be described as examples that provide the opportunity for us to analyse learning identity at work "in the middle" and for the reader to reflect on and critique these ideas. They are the verbs that make visible the nouns of disposition. And all three learning dispositions are intertwined and interlocked, so the case studies written up here do not encompass all aspects of each child's learning journeys. They provide a framing for each of the fourteen children's stories, to inform the discussion of disposition and design.

RECIPROCITY: THE LEARNING DISPOSITIONS AND THE LEARNING DESIGN

Developmentally effective proximal processes are not unidirectional: there must be influence in both directions. In the case of interpersonal interaction, this means that initiatives do not come from one side only; there must be some degree of reciprocity in the exchange. (Bronfenbrenner & Morris, 1998, p. 996)

It is a central aspect of learning that we are social beings. A sociocultural perspective suggests that learning develops from, and is embedded in reciprocal and responsive relationships and interactions with other people, who share meanings and understandings (Bruner, 1986; Lave & Wenger, 1991; Vygotsky, 1978). Children perform more capably in collaboration with others and learning changes how people belong, participate and negotiate meanings with each other. Collaboration stretches children's thinking, and invites them to learn more difficult things. Human beings are able to learn collaboratively when they put themselves in the 'mental shoes' of other people (Tomasello, 1999).

Multiple individuals create something together that no one individual could have created on its own. These special powers come directly from the fact that as one human being is learning 'through' another, she identifies with that other person and his intentional and sometimes mental states. (Tomasello, 1999, p. 6)

A disposition towards reciprocity includes engaging in dialogue with others, negotiating mutual sense and interest, communicating with others (both adults and peers), giving an opinion, taking into account the perspectives of others, sharing responsibility, communicating ideas, and valuing being and becoming a group member. The absence of reciprocity is characterised by ignoring the viewpoints of others, not taking advantage of others as resources for learning, not engaging in collaborative role-taking, and not sharing responsibilities and activities (Bronfenbrenner, 1979; Carr & Claxton, 2002). Reciprocity emerges out of warm, trusting relationships during infancy when babies are surrounded by "prompt, contingent and consistent responses" to their signals (Clarke-Stewart, 1973, p. 4). The characteristics of social interactions which provide ongoing momentum for learning are reciprocity, a balance of power and warmth (Bronfenbrenner, 1979). Bronfenbrenner's famous statement that learning is facilitated by "the participation of the developing person in progressively more complex patterns of reciprocal activity" (Bronfenbrenner, 1979, p. 13) highlights the centrality of reciprocity in learning. Language increases the possibilities for reciprocity because it extends dialogue and provides a shared means of encoding experience. Toddlers as they are beginning to learn language, engage in talk with parents and other people about everyday activities, the past and the future (Nelson & Fivush, 2004). These conversations and stories are crucial in strengthening dispositions towards ongoing learning. Peer conversations are a source of extending learning for preschool children.

> Experience with different forms of narrative, in play, in stories, and especially in talk about personal episodes, provides a model for organizing one's own episodic memories into the kinds of narratives that emphasize personhood, motivations, goals, outcomes, emotions and values. (Nelson & Fivush, 2004, p. 8)

The engagement of the participants in this study in joint attention episodes (Moore & Dunham, 1995) was a focus of interest in our research from the beginning. Joint attention involves an individual paying attention to some external object or topic with one or more other people (Schaffer, 1992), and requires shared experience of scripts, objects or events. Many researchers regard early episodes of joint attention between infant and caregiver as the crucible for the development of later reciprocal relationships. Bruner (1995, p. 3) describes joint attention as a way for children to 'know other minds', which first becomes evident when children realise that other people are agents with different perspectives and goals from their own. The realisation that other people are also intentional beings is the foundation for communication, language and identity (Bruner, 2002; Nelson & Fivush, 2004; Tomasello, 1999) and marks the beginning of a disposition towards reciprocity. The "dawning of the idea of 'me' has ramifications for how the child sees himself or herself in relation to the views of other people" (Nelson & Fivush, 2004, p. 8). In joint attention between an infant and an adult:

> ... as the child begins to monitor the adults' attention to outside entities, that outside entity sometimes turns out to be the child herself – and so she begins to monitor adults' attention to her and thus to see herself from the outside, as it were. She also comprehends the role of the adult from this same vantage point, and so, overall, it is as if she were viewing the whole scene from above, with herself as just one player in it. (Tomasello, 1999, pp. 99–1000)

A shared focus of attention helps to sustain reciprocity. From a study of joint attention in under two-year-olds in early childhood centres (Smith, 1999), the following example of a joint attention episode between a toddler and his teacher illustrates its important features.

> ### Putting Socks, Boots and Hat on
>
> A is sitting by carer. 'Es a my socks', says A. 'Your socks, these yours?', says carer, kneeling. A points 'Dat sockey'. Carer says, 'You've got socks, he's got socks'. They laugh together. 'Where's your foot?' says carer. A. points. Carer says 'Put gum boots on?' A replies 'yes'. Carer says 'You want to fix it, good girl'. Carer tries hood. 'I had a hat', says A and pats head. A walks aside outside, puts foot in boot as she holds the wall, vocalises 'Ah, ug'. Carer asks 'Can't get it on'? A replies 'I push it'. (Joint Attention Episode,17 month-old, Smith, 1999, p. 94)

The episode shows how the teacher supported the child's growing language at the same time as helping him to put his socks, boots and hat on. The teacher was able to co-construct meanings with the toddler because of her familiarity with what the child knew and understood, including his idiosyncratic language, and their shared context and focus of attention. At the same time as the teacher engaged in reciprocal interaction with the child and called on his existing skills, she was extending his language and understanding and contributing to successful achievement of his goal. In this example, the teacher supported the child's actions and showed sensitive responsiveness and intersubjectivity (or shared focus of understanding and purpose) with the child. While the adult played an important part in the episode, it is initiated by the child, but the adult was attuned to the child's actions and intentions. The shared affect and warmth of the exchange was also a key feature in establishing and maintaining reciprocity. The child was not simply absorbing an adult perspective but was self-regulating his own activities in an interactive context.

The characteristics of the disposition of reciprocity that we found in our current research, however, differs to some degree from what was observed in Smith's study of infants and toddlers, because of the different ages and contexts of our participants. Research on joint attention has focused on adult-child interactions. While these are of ongoing importance and power, we expected joint attention with peers to be much more influential and central to the learning of the four and five-year-olds in our study. Moreover in searching for dispositions we are looking, not just for episodes, but for ongoing 'habits of mind' (Carr & Claxton, 2002), and for the affordances which encourage these habits of mind to develop. We also had the opportunity in looking at our data, to see the trajectories of children's dispositions, since we observed their learning in context over eighteen months between the ages of four and five-and-a-half. We looked at the changing patterns of how and with whom children engaged, the expectations and demands of their social partners, and the extent to which children were able to understand and accommodate to the viewpoints of others.

We traced two facets of reciprocity: establishing a dialogue (chapter three), and being and becoming a group member (chapter four).

RESILIENCE: THE LEARNING DISPOSITIONS AND THE LEARNING DESIGN

For the purposes of this study we have defined resilience as an individual's and family's ability to: appraise the demands of different situations and to apply a set of skills and knowledge that enable the individual or family to 'cope' with and 'recover' from significant adversity or stress, in ways that are not only effective, but may result in increased ability to 'respond' to and 'protect' their families from future adversity. (Duncan, Bowden, & Smith, 2005, p. i)

Resilience, as a concept, has been well researched over the years. Often this research has examined how individuals who encounter risk or harm manage to keep their health and well-being intact while other individuals, who are described as not being resilient, succumb to the crisis (Coordenacao De Estudos E Pesquisas Sobre A Infancia (CESPI-USU), 2001; Duncan, et al., 2005, 2006; Gellert, 2002; Gilligan, 2001; Kalil, 2003; Masten, 2001; Walsh, 1996, 1998). For example, Masten (2001, p. 228) describes resilience as " a class of phenomena characterized by good outcomes in spite of serious threats to adaptation or development". In a theoretical overview of family resilience, based on a clinical orientation to family functioning, Walsh (1998) has outlined key family processes in family resilience. She examines the role of family belief systems, organisational processes and communication processes. Walsh (1998) sees "family resilience" as being significantly influenced by family belief systems. Resilient families are characterised as having beliefs that enable them to:

– make meaning of adversity (for example: normalising or contextualising adversity and distress; seeing the crisis as meaningful or comprehensible; having a sense of coherence)
– affirm strengths and possibilities (for example: maintaining courage and hope; optimism)
– encourage transcendence and spirituality (for example: seeking purpose in faith, rituals, creativity).

We have looked at resilience, in this project, as a disposition which is afforded or constrained by the children's experiences and environments (i.e. their social contexts) rather than as an individual psychological trait, or belief system, in isolation. This approach to resilience has emerging support from researchers who are working in social constructionist approaches to resilience (see Ungar, 2004a) where they argue that in contrast to a developmental or ecological approach, a constructionist approach "defines resilience as the outcome from negotiations between individuals and their environments for the resources to define themselves as healthy amidst conditions collectively viewed as adverse" (Ungar, 2004b, cited in Ungar, 2004a).

Affordances and constraints in educational settings include this access or lack of access to resources. With our case study children we used a contextual examination of features of resilience within a learning setting, and we explored the role that the affordances and constraints played on children's enactment of 'resilience'. In this way our study shares much in common with constructionist studies of resilience and less with traditional developmental approaches. Mike Ungar (2004a, p. 354) poses a challenge to the traditional ecological model of resilience, arguing that its causal linkages and predetermination of health outcomes "is simply unable to accommodate the plurality of meanings individuals negotiate in their self-constructions as resilient". He summarises the debate between approaches to resilience:

> While there is agreement that certain factors put children at risk and others mitigate risk, there is no universal set of conditions that can be said to protect all children. In part, this is because no one set of causal risk factors has been found, or is likely to exist. ... Understood [in a constructive] way, " resilience is the outcome of negotiations between individuals and their environments to maintain a self-definition as healthy". (Ungar, 2004b, cited in Ungar, 2004a, pp. 350, 352)

Addressing resilience in learning outcomes enables us to shift our gaze to learning challenges and successes. Carol Dweck's (2000, 2006) extensive research on what she calls *performance* goals and *learning* goals are relevant here. One of the goals that students enter school with, and that have consequences for the type of learner students become is: looking competent and performing well. Carol Dweck (1985) and Carole Ames (1992) called this a 'performance' goal or orientation and contrasted it with a 'learning' (Dweck) or a 'mastery' (Ames) goal or orientation. Research by Dweck and colleagues has indicated that many four-year-olds are sacrificing valuable learning opportunities in order to 'look good' (Smiley & Dweck, 1994). Task-involvement in learning or mastery goals is contrasted with ego-involvement in performance goals. Learning goals are associated with an incremental belief about intelligence (a growth mindset), while performance goals are associated with an entity belief about intelligence (a fixed mindset) (Dweck, 2006). We can argue that 'learning goals' are never appropriate for all occasions (nor are performance goals), but that an aim of education is for children to be sensitive to occasion, to be able to 'read' the environment, and to be therefore equipped to deploy strategies and goals appropriate to the occasion. Although Dweck does not allude to Bourdieu, we can make a connection via the following comment by James Collins:

> Bourdieu and Passeron's *Reproduction* had attributed to class habitus the disposition to assume that you are simply expected and entitled to higher education versus the pre-conscious fear that you will probably fail, leading to dropping out and other forms of educational self-exclusion. (Collins, 2008, p. 366)

In a research project in an early childhood centre Margaret Carr argued that learning and performance goals can become embedded (often covertly) over time in the design of activities by participants – adults and children – in particular places. For instance, in an early childhood centre, discourses of performance had become attached to screen-printing while discourses of authoring had become attached to an activity that had begun as ritualistic and routine: marble painting (Carr, 2001c). This project moved Dweck's ideas into "the middle", into the relationship between the individual and the environment, interpreting places and activities as dispositional milieux, while children's entering dispositions formed 'default settings' for interpreting and taking up, or ignoring, affordances. The children in the *Learning in the Making* study were constructing resilience within a multiplicity of social contexts. Viewing resilience as sited 'in the middle' enabled us to see it as children *negotiating* with others (people), the environments (places) and the resources (things) they need to position themselves as authoritative within adverse difficult or challenging circumstances (Ungar, 2004a).

We traced two facets of resilience: initiating and orchestrating projects (chapter five), and asking questions (chapter six).

IMAGINATION: THE LEARNING DISPOSITIONS AND THE LEARNING DESIGN

Imagination is no mere ornament; nor is art. Together they can liberate us from our indurated [durable] habits. They might help us to restore decent purpose to our efforts and help us create the kind of schools our children deserve and our culture needs. Those aspirations, my friends, are stars worth stretching for. (Eisner, 2005 p. 214)

Elliot Eisner, an artist himself, is an eloquent and passionate advocate for the recognition of imagination in education. He argues that the ability to remember without the ability to imagine would leave us with a static culture, and that imagining should be one of the basics of education: "to create new images, images that function in the development of a new science, the creation of a new symphony, and the invention of a new bridge" (Eisner, 2005, pp. 107–108). He describes people with imagination as 'boundary breakers' who reject accepted assumptions, make the "given" problematic, and imagine new possibilities.

Karen Gallas (2003), Gunther Kress (2003) and Carey Jewitt (2008) have reminded us that human expression is multimodal, and imaginative multimodal representations enable us to recognise and construct new understandings and ideas. Gallas (2003, p. 4) argues that play is a critical part of learning and that wonder feeds our desire to understand the world. Paul Harris (2000, p. 8), reviewing the research on imagination, says that early pretence "offers a way to imagine, explore and talk about possibilities inherent in imagination". In an essay entitled 'What Happened to imagination?' Maxine Greene, like Eisner, was troubled by the neglect and distortion of imagination in education:

It is not simply the idea of confinement [to one of the multiple realities available to human beings] that troubles me. It is the idea that young people are not encouraged to look through the windows of the actual on occasion, to regard things as if they could be otherwise. (Greene, 1988, p. 45)

Dorothy Holland et al. (1998, p. 272) also write about a context of identity as 'making worlds' or 'newly imagined communities'. Imagination is about creating images of the world and seeing connections through time and space by extrapolating from earlier and other experience. The disposition of imagination relies on making connections with the past, present and future; exploring possibilities; being playful and creative; connecting with cultural artefacts such as stories, characters, and shared knowledge from the past or from other places. The affordances for imagination include: opportunities for playing out stories of moment, connections with families, and conversations between adults and children that make these imaginative shifts and leaps. Barbara Rogoff (2003) links reciprocity and imagination, and argues that when social partners suggest connections between one situation and another, this enhances the creative role of individuals.

Imagination and play has been a theme of Vivian Paley's teaching and writing for many years. Her books form a major research project into imagination, play and identity. She recognises that early childhood and school classrooms can be a safe place to re-run imaginative stories about fears friends and fantasy, stories that have personal and, frequently, collective, meaning. In Paley's early years' settings, dramatic play – with the children as authors, directors, and players – enables children to explore sense-making and to re-cognise events, making the connection between imagination and resilience. A London theatre director wrote to Paley describing young children in a reception class playing out the September 2001 attack on the New York Trade Centre, and part of that letter is published in the book *A Child's Work: the importance of fantasy play*: "For all my years in the theatre and my belief in its value, I feel that right now I'm able to see its truest and deepest value. How amazing that this lesson comes from the age group listened to the least" (Paley, 2004, p. 109). In *The Girl with the Brown Crayon* (1997), Paley's class spends much of the year exploring the books of one author, Leo Lionni, and she writes about how children use these imaginative stories to shape their lives. She describes the engagement of two-year-olds with making stories: "They are 'doing' stories. Doing goes beyond pretending and telling; doing is the final process, or at least the sum of events up to a particular moment" (Paley, 2001 p. 5). It is multimodal, embodied imagination, like dance. She sees story and play as 'nourishing the ground and opening the seed packets' for growing ideas and identities.

If readiness for school has meaning, it is to be found first in the children's flow of ideas, their own and those of their peers, families, teachers, books, and television, from play into story and back into more play. It was when I asked the children to dictate their stories and bring them to life again on a stage that the connections between play and analytical thinking became clear. The children and I were nourishing the ground and opening the seed packets, ready to plant our garden of ideas and identities. ... (Paley, 2004, pp. 11–12)

Considerations of identity connect with the idea of 'possible selves', introduced to the literature from psychology by Hazel Markus and Patricia Nurius (1986). They write about the selves we (think we) could become, and the selves that we are afraid of becoming.

> An individual's repertoire of possible selves can be viewed as the cognitive manifestation of enduring goals, aspirations, motives, fears, and threats.... Possible selves derive from representations of the self in the past and they include representations of the self in the future. They are different and separable from the current or now selves, yet are intimately connected to them (Markus & Nurius, 1986, pp. 954-955).

Markus and Nurius argue that possible selves are important because they function as incentives for future behaviour, and because they provide an evaluative and interpretive context for the current view of self (p. 954). Jerome Bruner takes a more cultural view, linking identity to story and comments that we are, from the start, expressions of our culture, and that culture is "replete with alternative narratives about what self is or might be" (2002, p. 86).

We traced two facets of imagination: exploring possible worlds (chapter 7), and storying selves (chapter 8).

WHAT MIGHT WE ASK OF AN EDUCATIONAL SYSTEM OVER TIME?

There are at least two reasons why we should pay attention to dispositions-in-action in the early years. One reason is that learning dispositions enable children (and adults) to go beyond what they have been taught, to improvise in new contexts, to re-cognise the past, to learn in the present, and to imagine the future. Ability and knowledge are part of this 'going beyond'; they are necessary, but not sufficient: inclination (commitment) and attunement (to circumstances) are needed as well. A second reason is that there is research evidence that they appear at an early age, and we can argue that noticing recognising and responding to them in the early years is wise practice. Patricia Smiley and Carol Dweck (1994) concluded from their research on learning goals and performance goals (and associated incremental and entity beliefs about intelligence) that even very young children have developed mindsets about whether it is a good idea to risk failure (and one's reputation as capable) by engaging with challenge, or better to play it safe and only engage with learning opportunities that will probably be successful. Bourdieu had maintained that "early experiences have particular weight" (1990 p. 60) in the social trajectories of dispositions as *habitus*: they develop from an accumulation, a 'dictionary' of episodes of joint attention.

What might we ask of an educational system over time? Gordon Wells (2002, p. 205) has said that it was the process of his and his colleagues' research and reading on interaction in classrooms that made them recognise "the critically important role of dialogic knowledge building in fostering the dispositions of caring, collaboration and critical inquiry that are at the heart of our vision of education." This project has worked in the same field of endeavour. The above discussion has also suggested

that for all three of the dispositions we focus on in this book, critical inquiry or a critical stance can be envisaged as a long-term dispositional goal for learners: to be attuned to, to critique, and sometimes to resist or change the affordances and constraints in the environment; to choose from a repertoire or dictionary of discourses, communication strategies, positions, social intents and possible ways of life, depending on the circumstances. In order to tackle this project we have shifted our perspective from nouns of disposition (reciprocity, resilience and imagination) to the following verbs:
– establishing a dialogue
– being and becoming a group member
– initiating and orchestrating projects
– asking questions
– exploring possible worlds
– storying selves
   These facets of learning disposition are the topics of the next six chapters.

CHAPTER THREE

ENGAGING RECIPROCALLY

Establishing a Dialogue

> Understanding the role of spoken dialogue in learning and development
> must involve consideration of children as social actors, and not just as
> developing individuals. (Mercer & Littleton, 2007 p.2)

One important part of establishing a disposition to engage reciprocally with peers, is finding a common language. A common language and focus of interest and attention is a starting point for dialogue, which helps children to orient themselves with respect to the utterances of others, and is the basis for understanding. A focus on dialogue implies that children's learning is not about the exclusive efforts of the individual child but emerges from mutual interdependence, recognition and respect (Fitzgerald, Graham, Smith & Taylor, 2010). Dialogue within a shared language opens up endless future opportunities for play and learning. Joint attention can be focused, plans can be made and shared, scripts and stories created and enacted, and past experiences reflected on. Language allows children to achieve collective intentionality and extend and co-construct their understanding of cultural institutions such as parenthood or money (Tomasello & Rakoczy, 2003). It is the tool through which children can achieve intersubjectivity, recognise a different opinion and effectively scaffold each other's play. A shared history and a common language "becomes the glue that binds the group jointly creating meanings, relationships, collective rituals and routines". (Brennan & Hayes, 2007, p. 18)

> With the availability of formal language come possibilities for shared meaning in regard to events and objects that are not present, and with increases in children's knowledge and perspective come engagement that is less closely supported by their partners and more tuned to the skills and understandings of society. (Rogoff, 1990, p. 78)

Within reciprocal engagement in dialogue, children achieve mutual interdependence and recognition, and a degree of independence from adult control. They often develop fluency and expertise in languages of their own which are beyond the boundary of adults' awareness or understanding. The common language and verbal strategies which children use in these narratives are a way of constructing a sense of togetherness. Togetherness is associated with forming and maintaining groups, and with affective feelings of belongingness. The concept is very appropriate to collaborative learning in communities of practice, and helps children to constantly maintain a zone of proximal development for each other (van Oers & Hannikainen, 2001). Children affirm togetherness by complimenting and greeting each other, noting similarities to each other ("we're all eating"), using the language of co-operation ("we", "let's"), and offering each other help, care or friendship (de Haan & Singer, 2003). Dorian de Haan and Elly Singer suggest that in establishing togetherness, children move from common ground to common goals where they negotiate a shared orientation within activities.

Peer (and adult) conversations, nonverbal communication, the routines and rules of social interaction and even the arrangement of space and furniture, continually reinforce dispositions or *habitus* towards engaging reciprocally within prevailing discourses (Thomas, 2007). Together with Holland and colleagues (p.27) we reject versions of essential selves as "stable and enduring characters set in place (by the end of childhood)".

> Socially constructed selves, in sharp contrast, are subject to positioning by whatever powerful discourses they happen to encounter – changing state policies that dictate new ways of categorizing people in the census, educational diagnostics that label some children "at risk", or new forms of racist discourse taken up from right-wing talk shows. Perhaps they are resistant to such social forces; they nonetheless remain provisionally at their mercy. (Holland et al. 1998 p.27)

Holland et al. add that discourses and practices are the tools that "build the self in contexts of power, rather than as expressions of the world". This book will argue that opportunities in early years' educational contexts to experience a range of discourses and practices provides children with alternative interpretations that they can call on as they set about making sense of the world in new contexts and developing multifaceted learner selves.

LISA

Lisa was the youngest of two children, whose parents were well educated. Lisa's mother is a European immigrant and her father was born in New Zealand. At the beginning of the study when Lisa was just four, her parents and teachers saw her as a very shy child, who often lapsed into 'baby talk'. Both teachers and parents thought that Lisa was very competent academically but not very sociable. Lisa's brother, Ted, is two years older than her and was attending the school that Lisa would attend. Lisa's parents provided encouragement and resources, and supported her interest in Ted's school work. Lisa was unusual in that she was the only child in the study who was observed in two different early childhood centres (which she was attending simultaneously during phase one: a kindergarten in the afternoon and a parent cooperative childcare centre in the morning).

When the researcher[7] first started to observe Lisa, her mother was concerned at her "retrograde speech" (speaking like a baby). She described her as "quite a private person" and one who "likes things done in a certain way." She said that Lisa got very upset if things did not go right and she recalled a recent incident at the supermarket when she (the mother) had told a lady at the supermarket that it was Lisa's birthday, and Lisa had blushed in response to the lady's attention. The incident had made her realise the extent of Lisa's shyness. She did say, however, that Lisa engaged in extended play and talk with her older brother and two younger girls in the neighbourhood. Her parents had originally sent Lisa to preschool because "we really want her to make more friends." They had moved the previous year from another city and Lisa had changed quite markedly after that move and Lisa's mother thought that the move had been quite traumatic for her.

> Before she was talking, you know, as we left [city] at Easter last year, she was talking quite freely before that, and then she nearly stopped talking... You know she wouldn't talk to people for ages.. She talked to us but not you know... (Parent interview, phase one)

Lisa's teachers as well as her parents were worried about her lack of peer interaction. Her kindergarten teacher said:

> I'm not always successful trying to get her to talk, even just you know the 'hellos' and 'goodbyes' was a goal at one stage. But then it became a bit of an issue. Because dad would really, you know, stand there and want her to say it. And her body language is too much... yeah, yeah, did not like to be in eye contact. (Kindergarten teacher interview, phase one)

When the researcher talked to the kindergarten teachers about Lisa's interest and knowledge of stories, they said that she was just beginning to participate in conversations about stories in a small group, but that "often in those group situations, you know, somebody else will be louder and faster". They described her as a reflective observer.

> A lot of watching – see what's happening...she'll watch before she... and you know, and she'll, until she moves into somewhere she feels safe – listens and watches and she's drawing really well. She'll draw really well. (Kindergarten teacher interview, phase one)

The childcare teacher described Lisa, as follows:-

> It was just full-on shyness. She used to hang her head and yeah.... Yeah... which was interesting because listening to her talking to Theresa [friend], or when her mother came in, I could see all these things that she had all these skills that she was hiding under this shyness. (Childcare teacher interview, phase one)

Lisa's progress towards a disposition for reciprocity was interesting, because she participated in two early childhood programmes during phase one. Five episodes of play in the kindergarten and five in the childcare centre were observed in phase one (By the second phase of the study she only attended kindergarten and ten episodes were recorded at the kindergarten.) Her reciprocal engagement with peers and adults was very different in the two centres.

Trying to draw Lisa into dialogue in the kindergarten

Lisa showed almost no inclination towards reciprocity in the kindergarten during this first phase of the study. She very rarely talked or played with another child, did not initiate any conversations with teachers, and responded very reluctantly or not at all to teacher's questions. She engaged with the activities available at the centre, but usually alone or in parallel with other children. Lisa would, however, come and ask for help from a teacher – for example if she wanted water in the sandpit – and the teachers knew enough about her family to be able to chat to her about familiar things over quiet activities like collage. In the five episodes where the researcher observed Lisa in phase one at kindergarten, the teachers regularly tried to engage her in conversation or in play, but most efforts were unsuccessful. Lisa was involved in table activities (such as collage and dough) alongside other children in three of these episodes, listening to a story and answering teacher questions in one episode, and watching but declining to interact with a pet mouse being showed to her by a teacher, in another episode. Lisa did show some interest in the dough episode when a teacher suggested that they make a cake for a party and said a few words, and she correctly answered all of the questions the teacher asked in the Goldilocks story episode. She sometimes watched and stayed near Rika, a child from Korea, but the researcher did not observe any talk or sustained play.

The following episode (when Lisa was aged four years and three weeks) is a fairly typical example of Lisa's social interactions at kindergarten. She had not established patterns of conversation with other children (or teachers). Two teachers tried to draw her into conversation and she responded only with a few words or with nodding her head. She participated alongside a group of other children in the same activity of making a collage, but did not initiate any interactions with others and responded minimally when others initiated. She accepted teacher praise but did not initiate interaction with the other children or with the teachers.

Pasting at Collage Table (phase one, kindergarten)

Lisa is pasting at the collage table. She is sitting beside Catherine (a teacher) and a small group of children at a table with collage material, making a collage. She watches as Catherine interacts with other children. She smiles and watches her mother talking to Jo (another teacher). Jo comes over to where Lisa is making her collage. Jo asks "Is that a boat?" L. says "No it's a ?? [inaudible]" Jo says "Putting lots of things on there? Mmmh?" Lisa. says "Yeah". Jo says "Are you talking to me now? Did you do this too?" Lisa says: "Yeah". Jo says "Wow! What's this colour? What's this colour in the background?" (No answer.) "Is it yellow?" Jo: "No. Is it red? Mmmh?" (No answer.) "Let's put your name on here." "Lisa did you write your own name today? Mmm?". Lisa nods her head. "You did?" Lisa watches Jo talking to another child. Jo writes Laetitia's name on her collage. Jo: "There's a pen Lisa. You could write your name on this one." Lisa writes her name on the collage. Jo: "That's lovely writing." (Jo later says that Lisa wrote her own name but that she helped her with some letters.)

This next episode, however, shows Lisa being drawn into conversation over afternoon tea with one of the teachers about a forthcoming overseas trip to visit her mother's family. The teacher was a little more successful this time in getting a response from Lisa.

Going on a Plane (phase one, kindergarten)	
Teacher:	I heard you are going to [European country]. Who are you going to see there?
Lisa:	Um, I am going to lots of places.
Teacher:	Are you, where are you going to?
Lisa:	Singapore too.
Teacher:	How are you getting there?
Lisa:	Um in a plane.
Teacher:	A great big airplane, will you sit on a seat? When you go on the airplane will you have a seat by your self, who will you sit beside?
Lisa:	I think I am going to sit next to Ted (brother).
Teacher:	Next to Ted, I will show you on the map of the world where you are going. You're going to fly here to [European country], who lives there?
Lisa:	Um, Uncle Werner.
Teacher:	And do you have a Grandma and Grandad that lives there?
Lisa:	There is only Uncle Werner there.

At kindergarten Lisa played alongside other children but during phase one was never observed in sustained reciprocal interaction with any peer. Any language she used was in response to teachers' questions. In all episodes she had some interaction with teachers (who were trying to encourage her to talk), but she was usually responding to teacher questions and often contributed one-word answers.

Sharing common goals in the childcare centre

At the childcare centre, Lisa had a friend, Theresa, with whom she played a great deal. The two children knew each other well, as outside the centre they lived in the same street and went to the same Sunday School and playgroup. Lisa and Theresa had both been attending the centre for a year. Lisa was the quieter partner but did not allow Theresa to take complete control and was a relatively equal partner in play. The two girls were particularly involved in family play and all kinds of pretend around mothers and babies. The childcare head teacher talked about how crucial Theresa was in helping her to engage Lisa with activities at the centre. The teacher said that during the first few months at the centre, Lisa did not open her mouth and hung her head when spoken to. She would actually move away when other children approached her. The teacher spoke of her efforts to build a relationship with Lisa, and the importance of Theresa in these efforts.

So the first thing – I did not push myself onto her, but I actually sort of tried to make a friendship with her. I think to actually build up her courage so that she had one special person. Luckily she had Theresa, which is her special friend here, to play with. So it was a matter of this little girl who had all this knowledge and things inside her and so many skills, but she wasn't using them because of her shyness. (Teacher interview, phase one)

During each of the five episodes at childcare, Lisa was engaged reciprocally and in a sustained way with Theresa (and from time to time the teacher). Three of the five episodes involved extended pretend play around family themes, one was at an afternoon tea birthday party involving conversation with Theresa (and others), and one involved Lisa and Theresa taking turns 'reading' a story to each other. Lisa talked to teachers as well as peers at childcare, although most of her interaction was with one peer, Theresa. In contrast to the previous kindergarten episode, the following episode, a day later in childcare, showed Lisa engaging and conversing very actively in pretend play. The teacher also played a role in the children's pretend play.

> *Shopping and Feeding Baby (phase one, childcare)*
>
> Lisa and her friend Theresa are playing a family game together – both are mothers and have their babies (dolls). The teacher is involved from time to time and 'visits' them as they play with their babies. The episode starts with a plan to go shopping and ends with morning tea after the children have fed their babies mashed potatoes. At the start Lisa says: "Let's go for a walk and show (teacher's name) what we are playing", and the two children chat to each other and to the teacher about going shopping with their babies to get food. The teacher asks if she can come to visit later for a cup of tea and Lisa says that she can. The teacher says that she will bring her baby and asks if they want her to buy milk. Theresa says that they are going to buy milk and that she should bring her baby. The children play with the babies and take them shopping. Theresa says that the 'baby' is sick and that they are taking her to the doctor. They get food for the babies, and some milk and sugar for the teacher's visit, on their shopping trip. Lisa says that she is making a cake and Theresa says that she is making muffins. They discuss birthdays and how old they are. The teacher 'knocks on the door' and says her baby is sick. Lisa says that the baby needs medicine and that she has some from the doctor. There is a discussion of babies' names (influenced by the name of Theresa's baby brother). The teacher asks the girls what they bought at the shops and they reply baby food. Theresa gives the teacher her coffee. Lisa and Theresa make mashed potato with yellow dough (the baby food) and pretend to add milk to it. The teacher chats to them about their babies ('Your baby is being very good Lisa'; 'Yum, look the baby likes that.' 'Do you think I could have another one?' ' Lisa, she is enjoying that, you got mashed potatoes.') Lisa says 'You have to mash them so it's nice.'

This episode shows that Lisa and Theresa had found a common language and a shared focus of interest, which facilitated an easy dialogue. The contrasting lack of reciprocity in kindergarten highlights the importance of shared interest and a relationship in encouraging and supporting dialogue. Lisa and Theresa chatted about interests, ideas, shared goals and meanings, and co-ordinated their activities. Theresa was a well known play partner and she and Lisa were 'on the same wavelength' during the ongoing collaborative planning, checking and affirmation. They improvised the stories and collaboratively devised their goals, plans, and activities. The teacher was also involved in building this pretend play and they enthusiastically included her. She was sensitive to their ideas and helped them elaborate on them.

The children were clearly the main authors of the script here and were aware that it was pretend: Theresa told the teacher when they were pretending that the dough was mashed potato, that "It's not real food." Lisa's first comment to Theresa that they should show the teacher what they were playing, suggests that she perceived the teacher as interested and supportive. The teacher also introduced ideas like asking if she could come for a cup of tea. The engagement was mainly between Lisa and Theresa (with occasional participation by the teacher), but other children were peripherally involved. A photograph during this episode shows the teacher sitting surrounded by four children but face to face with Lisa and Theresa. In some other episodes Theresa was the dominant partner, but the partnership was quite equal in this episode. Lisa did not engage with other social partners besides Theresa except very briefly during phase one. She was comfortable and at ease with Theresa and with the teacher. Nevertheless interviews with the teacher suggest that Lisa did not readily interact with other children in the group.

Beginning to establish dialogue at kindergarten

When the researcher talked to the teachers at kindergarten at phase two of the study, when Lisa was nearly five, they had an interesting new perspective on Lisa. They now described her as much more confident and selective about interacting with peers or engaging in dialogue. They still did not see her as at ease in large, or noisy, boisterous groups, but they said she would talk if she felt comfortable. They commented that Lisa felt more comfortable and willing to engage in dialogue if an adult was nearby.

As long as there was an adult there … it's like that sometimes she's really unsure of what the reactions of the other children are going to be, but as long as there's other adults there, probably she feels more comfortable. (Kindergarten teacher interview, phase two)

Lisa had stopped attending childcare by phase two when she was nearly five and attending kindergarten five mornings a week[8]. Theresa had gone on to school from the childcare centre. Lisa was now more directly involved in centre activities than she had been at phase one. In only one of the ten episodes did she simply watch and listen on the edge of an activity. She was still quiet and rarely engaged in pretend play (she did so in only one episode). She did, however, make an effort to engage with peers and even persisted after rejection in one episode of outside play. (She wanted to join in a group of peers playing and was at first not allowed, but after suggesting a role for herself as a little sister she was accepted.) In nine out of the ten episodes Lisa talked with either peers or teachers (or both). Five of the episodes involved talking with teachers, and in eight of the ten episodes Lisa was talking and/or playing with other children. Her engagement with other children was not always smooth but she was initiating much more than she had in this centre in phase one. She used more productive language – making suggestions and volunteering information as well as answering questions – in interaction with the teacher. Teachers chatted with her regularly – often making suggestions for activities for her to participate in. She usually accepted their suggestions and support, and did engage in conversation with them, though she rarely initiated conversation. She sometimes appeared isolated, but was more assertive in gaining entry into play.

In an initial interview at phase one, Lisa had said very little, but by phase two she had got to know and feel comfortable with the researcher, and chatted amicably about the places she liked best on her trip to Europe (the boats and pigeons in Venice), and who her friends were (she named five children who were her friends). In the following episode Lisa is engaged in shared activity (painting) with three other children.

Painting (phase two, kindergarten)

Lisa watches three other girls painting. They mix the paint and are intent on painting their carpentry creation. Then Lisa starts her own painting on the other side of the easel. She does a painting (totally purple) while chatting with the other children about their paintings.

Lisa:	I've got lots of purple.
Another Child:	It is red, put some on here, beautiful colours.
Lisa:	Oh yeah that's beautiful colours. Now we need some red so let's do red, some gold on there.
Another Child:	I need some gold because I have not used gold. Up and down here please, I want it up and down here.
Lisa:	Who's wood is that?
Sally:	Mine.
Lisa:	I just painted the wood. Oh it looks nice and dashing. It looks nice eh. Very nice
Sally:	And I will put some, just a wee dot.
Lisa:	Yeah.
Sally:	But we need some dots don't we?
Lisa:	Oh yeah.
Sally:	I think we need some dots on here to.
Another child:	I will do some dots.
Lisa:	Just need to do some green so it is nice and [inaudible].
Another Child:	Shall I make her one?
Lisa:	What is that?
Another child:	Just powder.
Lisa:	Ethan just told me about it.
Another child:	Can I have some gold?

Lisa tells the other child to wait until she has mixed the gold. There is an ongoing discussion between Lisa and other children over adding gold dots to the painting, whether the painting is finished or whether it needs more colour. After adding some more gold dots the children agree that it is finished and express their satisfaction ("That looks cool.") Lisa thanks the others for their

---

> help and tells the teacher she has finished. The teacher gives her a crayon to write her name on the painting, which she does and then puts the painting in the basket.

During the observations at phase two, Lisa initially watched the other children, but then got involved herself. She engaged in an ongoing dialogue with the children as she worked. Children worked collaboratively, giving each other feedback, sharing resources and making suggestions (adding gold dots). This episode did not involve a teacher until it was completed. Lisa was much more talkative and willing to affiliate positively with the other children than she was at phase one in this centre. The use of the word "we" as children worked on their projects suggests the togetherness and collaboration involved in this activity. Other children more frequently included Lisa in the activity and conversation .

An episode in phase two involved Lisa being the morning 'mat-time teacher'. During mat time a child (supported by a teacher) leads a routine and daily discussion about the day of the week, the date, the weather conditions, and a collective *mihi*[9]. Lisa was given the responsibility for choosing a child to answer questions and pointing to the appropriate cards for the day. She was thus positioned as an authority in this episode, and she had no problem with leading the group routine, choosing other children to respond, asking and answering questions. One of the teachers commented:

> She knows. She's really very very confident with that [being the mat time teacher]. I was surprised because of the fact that she talks not a lot, that she could do all that. She obviously knew all the words too, or at least, you know, she pointed to the words as she read. ...... She's extremely selective. She'll talk when she wants to talk. She's very much in control of it, you know, and if she does not want to talk... She's an observer. And that's a skill of hers. She is actually an observer. And that's what she tends to do with things, wait until she's very, very clear about what it is that is going to happen. (Kindergarten teacher interview, phase two)

The teachers now positioned her as 'selective' rather than 'shy'. One of the teachers commented that "If she's got an interest and everybody is listening she can certainly hold the group's attention." Lisa was now comfortable with reciprocal activity in kindergarten at phase two, where initially in this centre she had been withdrawn and on the margins of activities. Although she did not have one strong friendship, the teachers (and our observations) indicated that she played regularly with some children, engaged regularly in conversation and took responsibility within the group. She regularly asked for help from teachers, and gave much longer answers when the teachers talked to her than she had previously. She deliberately made efforts to break into the play of others (not always successfully). She could communicate with peers, share meaning and contribute to group goals without the intervention of an adult.

An authoritative participant in the classroom

Lisa went to school when she was aged five, and her teacher described progress at school at phase three to the researcher in glowing terms. She said that Lisa was very independent, fast and accurate in her work and did not require much teacher attention. She commented that Lisa was sometimes reluctant to participate in classroom discussions, and had to be encouraged to make a contribution. Interestingly the school teacher characterised Lisa in a similar way to the early childhood teachers at phase two. "I don't think it's a capability thing. I think she chooses to sit back a bit." The following quote shows the different style and rules of teacher-child engagement in the school classroom. This was in the context of a discussion about whether Lisa was shy, and how Lisa had enthusiastically initiated talk with the teacher on occasions, despite the teacher's "first impression .. that she was a very shy child."

> At times she's coming running up to me and just – I've been in the middle of teaching, and I really always emphasise: 'Please don't interrupt me when I'm teaching, unless you say 'excuse me', and it's really important – especially at reading time.' So I really emphasised that. And she would have seen the same reactions that some of the other children would have got, but she still came rushing up to me and I haven't actually reacted in the same way because I have been so surprised. She'll just jump straight in there and go: 'Miss Wilson blah-blah-blah-blah.' (Teacher interview, phase three)

The teacher acknowledged that:

> If it's me who's initiating the conversation with her or trying to get something out of her she doesn't give as much as when she's really got something to say – when she's got something to communicate. (Teacher interview, phase three)

During phase three there was less opportunity to see Lisa interacting freely with peers, but she fitted in well with the ordered and structured routines of classroom interactions. During six of the ten episodes Lisa was interacting with peers in achieving classroom goals, during maths, reading, or art. She was equally at ease with being the initiator and respondent in News Time and Small Group Math Time, and made useful contributions to classroom discussion. She received a lot of positive attention and praise from the teacher (in five episodes). Only one of the ten episodes allowed time for a lengthy period of engagement with peers, over a lunch period, in the absence of the teacher.

Wet Lunchtime (phase three)

This episode occurred when Lisa was playing inside the classroom with her friend, Jennifer, during a wet lunchtime. (Other children are watching in the background). Lisa and Jennifer are playing being teacher and writing on the white board. They argue over who will be the teacher. In the absence of agreement they both amicably decide to be teachers. They chat with each other about the printing they are doing on the white board – providing feedback (Jennifer: 'The lines a wee bit squiggly, this line.' Lisa: 'Right these are a wee bit long but that one's good.. We need to do them a bit thinner okay?') They give each other prizes (stickers) for good behaviour. Another two children join the game. The children chat with the observer about the stickers and tell her that they are friends, and that they are "getting a prize". Lisa says that the prize is "for ten stickers on our sticker chart. We've gone past it, we need a prize." They then play with a box of plastic animals, and pretend that they have a zoo. Lisa puts a cover on the zoo to prevent the animals getting cold. They play collaboratively moving animals and building the zoo.

The affiliative language of togetherness was evident in this episode as children played school and later zoos, and talked with each other and the observer. The children's joint pride in being eligible for rewards for good behaviour in the classroom, was evident in their discussion.

In the following episode Lisa was deeply individually engaged in the task of making a sunflower collage in school art, but there was an interesting brief interaction between peers at the end (while she was washing her hands) which illustrates the powerful position Lisa now occupied within her peer group.

Making a Sunflower (phase three)

The teacher explains to children how to draw and make sunflowers. They sit in a circle on the floor around her as the teacher makes her own sunflower. Lisa is called on first to start work and keenly follows directions. She sketches an outline of her sunflower and is the first to finish it. The teacher tells Lisa it is beautiful. The teacher brings glue and paper and Lisa starts glueing. She is deeply engaged in the task, asks for (and gets) more paper, and talks with the teacher about her picture. She finishes the picture and asks if she can wash her hands. The following exchange between peers occurs while she is washing her hands.

Lisa (to other children): I got to help you cos I'm going to your house. And you got to help me cos you're coming, cos um, I come to your house. So you guys have to help each other.

Child: Yeah.

Lisa: I'll put these back up.

Lisa: [inaudible] nearly to the ending of the story, that was cool wasn't it Kim?

Kim: Hey you chose mine. You changed yours, yours used to be here.

Lisa: But Tania _____ "

Lisa: Just go Kim, you're just wasting our time.

Kim: Ouch, ouch.

Lisa was singled out and received individual attention – praise, feedback and instructions from the teacher – as she carried out this whole class activity. The exchange as she washes her hands (invisible to the observer but recorded on tape) suggests that how children work together in the classroom is affected by their relationships and social activities outside of school. Lisa tells the other girls that they must help each other because they plan to play together outside school. Lisa gets into a dispute with Kim and tells him to go away (Kim was frequently excluded by the girls; while in phase one Lisa was excluded by peers, in this episode she is excluding another). Lisa at school had less opportunity to engage in collaborative and reciprocal activity with others, but within the classroom genre of interaction, she was very competent and authoritative.

JACK

Jack lives with his parents, his older sister and his grandparents; they have all immigrated to New Zealand from China. At the time of the study, his mother worked full-time in accountancy and was also undertaking part-time study in law and business. His father worked as a researcher at the university. Jack's grandparents, who were both doctors in China before they retired, looked after the children during the day. In phases one and two, Jack attended a kindergarten (not the same kindergarten as Lisa); his grandmother stayed with him during phase one, when he attended three afternoons a week. During phase two she and/or the grandfather brought Jack to kindergarten and then picked him up at the end of the morning. Mostly Mandarin was spoken in the home, especially as his grandparents could speak very little English, but Jack's mother read stories to him in English and Mandarin. In the final interview, when he had been at school for several months, his mother commented that "he doesn't really want to speak Chinese, unless I really demand him to do so. But he can understand it." His Dad added that "sometimes the Chinese is used [by Jack] very well. Sometimes he surprises us". During phase two of the study Jack's older sister was learning to write Mandarin in special classes after school and when they were asked when Jack would start to learn to do this, his parents replied that it would not be until he was older and had established his writing in English first. By the final phase Jack was attending keyboard classes with his sister. During our visit after he started school his parents talked about their aspirations for the children's education and commented on the difference between the Chinese education system and New Zealand's, describing the very intense pressure on children to achieve educationally in China.

The early childhood centre had emphasised the value of art, and between phases one and two the kindergarten children had visited the local art gallery to see the drawing and paintings by a Samoan artist. Examples of the work by the artist were displayed on the wall in the kindergarten art area and children were encouraged to refer to this to gather ideas for their painting work. One example on the wall had been of three stylised hibiscus flowers, a symbol of the Samoan culture, and Jack had painted three flowers, inspired by the display and the visit to the Art gallery. We were aware that during this period Jack was becoming interested in a number of symbolic representations as well as his growing competence with English. Languages and literacies at kindergarten included art and mathematics, and symbols from television programmes.

Soon after Jack started school the family moved to a different college (high school) zone, and a new house, and after his parents visited the school for a 'parent-teacher' meeting, they asked Jack how he thought he was getting on. "I'm like the smart boy, in maths", he said. The family showed us his drawings of dinosaurs, displayed around the home. The drawings included the evaluation 'Good' on them, written by Jack himself. The following episodes (one from phase one and two from phase two) exemplify Jack's shift in social action from phase one to phase two.

Watching and listening

Five of the seven phase one episodes over two afternoons in phase one are of Jack exploring the outside playground area on his own, with his grandmother close by; typically the episodes lasted about ten to fifteen minutes and he smiles at other children and adults, but does not play with them. The next episode is typical of this play.

> ### Ladders, Planks and Boxes (phase one)
> Jack is climbing on ladders, planks and boxes, occasionally talking, smiling and laughing with his grandmother. He later comments on one of the photos of him climbing into a large box: "This is my secret home. I can do magic in it. No-one should come near my place". He talks briefly with others. He pulls himself across the metal ladder. Grandmother helps him to get off down the other side. He appears to be evaluating the level of challenge and his ability: the researcher takes a photo of him lying across the metal ladder and when he looks at it he comments "This is very difficult". Grandmother watches and helps. Jack watches two children making a swing bridge wobbly; he waits until they have left and then he goes across. He later tells his mother, when he looks at a photo of two stacked reels, that he cannot jump from that height.

Jack's grandmother had been made welcome at the early childhood centre, and a number of the children's family members stay for the entire session, watching the children, helping them, making tea and coffee, and assisting with tidying up. They recognise that resources are readily available to the children, and they can access them too. In one episode, Jack's grandmother went inside and brought out a piece of chalk to Jack who was outside. Jack drew a cross on the concrete and said to the researcher: "X. X Files.... Not on the TV, on the video". His grandmother watches from a distance, then takes his hat off, and pours him a drink. She holds his hand to write the first two letters in his name, but he protests.

Finding a community language

Ten months later, in phase two, Jack is typically engaged in dramatic play with one or two other children, taking and sharing a leadership role in directing the story-lines. Eight episodes over three half-day observations were of more than ten minutes duration, and four of these were over forty minutes. As in Lisa's Shopping and Feeding Baby episode, these episodes illustrate the overlap between reciprocity and imagination. The kindergarten documents the children's learning in portfolios of 'Learning Stories' (Carr, 2001b), a narrative mode of describing and analysing key episodes. On the day that Jack shifted to 'Morning Kindergarten' one of the teachers wrote:

First Time at Morning Kindergarten: Extract from a Learning Story

Today was the first time that Jack had been left at kindergarten. Jack really enjoys playing with Sally and John. They have been good friends since they attended the afternoon session. Today they played in the dramatic play area together, pretending to be asleep. [Photo] They arranged beds on the floor, the cot (for the baby) and the big bed.

Jack was very comfortable being left in the company of his friends. He engaged in sustained dramatic play, taking on different roles, discussing and collaborating with his group of friends. Jack is actively establishing relationships with his peers and developing strategies for collaborating, problem solving and taking other children's points of view into account. We will ensure that Jack has an opportunity to explore the environment extensively. (Learning Story in Jack's portfolio)

This described a domestic script being played out. By the time we visited, sustained play with two other boys, Tom and Ossie, was a feature of phase two, associated with a mutual recognition of key characters and general intentions in common storylines from popular culture (television and video). There is a sense in which Jack's play was 'multilingual'; he had added to English, Mandarin and painting a shared community language, especially with Tom, that featured common characters and storylines and words (hotshot, power, transformers, missiles, cancelling the project, Optima and Cybertron).

Optima and Cypbertron (phase two)

Tom's Mum arrives. Jack: "Is that your Mum, Tom?" Tom goes over to talk to his mother. He and Jack walk alongside her as she goes across the playground towards the centre building.

Tom: But now I'm going to play transformers. Now Mum you can be Optima.
Jack: But Optima's a boy! Cybertron's a girl.

In the first of these long episodes (forty-five minutes) Jack and Tom run around the playground: to the swings, behind the shed, to the bars and boxes, and sit on the swing bridge... They play-fight and talk together to accompany a game about shooting the baddies and firing missiles. Jack: "Fire the brain control, the brainwash. Kill him....I will give you more fire...I'll give you 100 fires – here. OK. Now fire your missiles, all your missiles." Tom: "I can't fire my missiles." Jack: "Why?" Tom: "Cos I knocked myself out". In an imaginative turn, Jack says: "If you don't fire now, I'll turn you into a brown school jacket".

Taking leadership roles

By phase two, four episodes of play involved a teacher directing the play in some way: three of them were initiated by a teacher: a game in the sandpit (hiding a 'bone' and guessing who has it: "Can we play again tomorrow? Can we always play this game? I love playing this game" says Jack), a rhyming group number game in which Jack counts carefully and accurately, and a skipping game. A 'Going on the Bus' pretend episode with chairs outside was developing alongside some skipping: Jack initiates and directs the play, and a teacher joins in.

Going on the Bus (phase two)

Jack: Have you a steering wheel? Have you a steering wheel, Joseph? He gets a steering wheel from the shed, and an adult assists by bringing some chairs. He alternates between skipping and nearby bus play.

Jack: I'm the bus driver....OK Ofeina, where do you want to go? Ofeina: I go in the shop.

Jack: Okay, the shop. Brrm Brrm.

The following comments occur throughout the play: "Here's your ticket and here's your money". "Are you coming in my bus or not?" "OK It's time for you to get off" "Where do you want to go? "Do you want to go to Pak'n Save? [a supermarket]".

Rosie and Joseph: Can we come?

Jack: Sorry, there's no more seats. Yes there is some seats over there.

There is a discussion about running out of petrol. Joseph puts petrol in.

Joseph: Go go go go go.

There is also some discussion about being the driver. Jack gives Joseph a turn.

Jack: for a little while but not too long, okay?
    Okay Rosie you can be the bus driver for a little while but don't be the bus driver for too long. Okay Rosie? Got it?
    It's my turn, because I made the bus and you guys didn't.

Ofeina (distributing popsicle sticks): A dollar.

A teacher is sitting on the back of the bus; she asks how much (for the ticket).

Jack: Three hundred and twenty three hundred double eight.

Teacher: Wow! Big numbers. There you go (gives him pretend money).

There is a long interchange with the teacher who comes and goes as she assists another group of children who are playing hopscotch; the conversation ranges over missing the bus, discussing where the teacher wants to go, running out of petrol (again), and the steering wheel breaking.

The authorship of the play script remained mainly the children's, but the teacher took on a role (sitting at the back of the bus and asking the price of the ticket) and joined in on a reciprocal conversation.

Mathematical language

Jack's growing interest and competence in mathematical language, later a feature of his experience at school as well, was apparent in phase two. In a brief episode where Jack is watching a game in which Tom is fishing with a magnet for 'fish' that have a number of dots on them, an adult asks Tom how many dots. He gives

47

an incorrect answer, and Jack says, helpfully, "It's something that comes after six". In the following episode, where he is playing a 'transformers' game with Tom, Sally joins in and it becomes a discussion about age and height.

Transformers (phase two)

Playing with Lego. Jack has created several different items, which he has identified as a series of 'transformers'. There is some discussion about whether the figures are evil and 'baddies' or friends. He is playing with Jack, and Sally joins the group.

Jack: I'm four and a half. ...
Sally: Stand up and I'll measure you (to Tom). You're going to be the youngest I know. Jack and me are the same height.
Jack: Yeah.
Tom: I'm the youngest.
Sally: The youngest don't have birthdays so quickly.
Jack: Because I'm higher than you.
Tom: Come on Jack, let's get on with the game. [Sally leaves]
Jack: OK let's see if we're the same. Oh, we're not the same – you're the lowest and I'm the highest. ... You're too low.
Tom: Well, if you say yes then we'll be your friend all right, if you're the lowest and you say no, well, we'll not be your friend okay? [He starts to leave].
Jack: Wait, Tom, come back. I'm the youngest as well.

Other episodes continue to show Jack's enthusiasm in dialogue with teachers and with other children.

Taking Turns (phase two)

Jack queues up to have a turn at skipping rope, with a teacher holding one end of the rope, and a child holding the other. He jumps five times as the teacher counts. He then tries to 'jump' the queue. There is much discussion about turn taking. When it is Jack's second turn he says "I'm going to count in Chinese this time. I'm going to count in Chinese". He counts in Mandarin. Teacher: "How many was that, Jack?" Jack: "Six". Teacher: "Six. Well done."

Guns (phase two)

Jack and Ossie spend some time searching for a storyline, They have constructed 'guns' from the Duplo, and are firing on the trains and trucks; they spend some time looking for desirable pieces of Duplo.

Jack: I'm not your friend Ossie.
Ossie: Why are you not my friend?
Jack: Because...because it's not fair – you got two (guns) and I've only got one... Peeow...yah! Stop shooting my train Ossie! (They are joined by Sally with puppets).
Sally: This is my puppet walking down the street (laughs) Hello Jack.

Jack shows Sally how to shoot ("Just press this button and it will change fire"). Another girl arrives. Jack pretends to shoot the girls.

Sally: We won't die, we're strong girls…. (Introducing her interest in being 'four and a half' again.) Hey Ossie, remember when we first met?…at morning tea time? Remember? When I said four and a half and you said you're four and a half too. (Ossie doesn't reply).

Jack: I'm four and a half. (The boys make a lot of firing noises, and the girls leave.)

Later, Jack and Ossie go off to have a drink and when they return, Jack shifts the topic from shooting to driving: "Okay, oh do you need some more petrol? Do you need petrol Ossie?. … Give me three hundred and forty three, and double eight." He holds his hand out and Ossie pretends to give him money. Jack: "Okay I'll give you fifty five dollars." Ossie: "Thankyou".

Becoming a school pupil

At school the schedule is different. The day is tightly timetabled with news time, letter of the day, story writing, reading in groups, whole class reading, worksheets (on the two days we visited this was a cutting and pasting activity to sort pictures of 'present' day and 'olden day' artefacts), a library visit, preparation for the end-of-the-year production (the singing of a song and the class recitation of a poem). There was frequent chanting of numbers; counting forward to two hundred and backward from fifty. On two days a week, Jack spent half an hour in a group with the English as an Additional Language (EAL) teacher, where, on the days we were visiting, the children answered questions and listened to stories. Here is an episode while Jack participates in a group reading and writing activity.

Reading and writing (phase three)

Jack is chosen to write "I like to read" on the whiteboard. Jack was delighted to be asked to participate in that session, and to be asked by (the teacher) to write "I like to read" on the board. The first time he wrote it he wrote 'R e A b'. He was pleased with this, smiled, and sat back down on the mat. And then the class discussed whether or not it was correct. He did his own assessment … arms waving in the air, wanting to correct it himself.

Teacher: *Read.* What are the letters you have written?
(Children call out the four letters in the word)

Teacher: OK. Well done Jack. Let's look at the word. *Read.* Is it correct?

Children (chorus): No.

Teacher: It's not correct. What's wrong? …. It's become a 'b'. We write 'd' this way. But there's something wrong too. I keep telling you children you have to remember.

Jack: Small writing.

Teacher: Good boy. You don't use capitals when you're writing a word in the middle of a sentence. Okay. Don't use capitals. So can you come and change it please?
(Jack comes up and changes it. A bell goes)

> Teacher: All right. Just wait. Before you go, you're forgetting that I haven't finished my story. Full stop! All of you have to remember to put a full stop.

There was no opportunity here for Jack to develop sustained negotiations, but when we asked Jack for his viewpoint he was pretty content with the state of affairs. Although he had joined in on the number chants with great expression, he later told the researchers "I don't like counting the numbers". "Why don't you like counting the numbers?" "I already know how to count to two hundred". At the home visit after school had begun however, it was clear that Jack's interest in negotiation, reciprocity and numbers had shifted to the telephone. He had memorised a number of the phone numbers of children in his class, and he had at the time we visited planned a Halloween trip around the neighbourhood, negotiating the distribution of the prospective lollies. His father explained that he went with the children, but Jack did all the organising.

Mother: So he said to his friends…. "You will sing a song, and the lollies will belong to me".

Father: Yes, "because I recruit you".

Researcher: Did he get all the lollies?

Father: No, no, no. (Parent interview, phase three)

LEARNING IN THE MAKING

Disposition-in action: work in progress

This section looks at the three dispositional components, introduced in chapter two, to structure our interpretations of work in progress on establishing dialogue. Authoring, recognising opportunity and connected knowing as descriptors for being ready, willing and able emerged from the triadic definition of a disposition, the data in this study, and the literature on learning continuity. Lisa and Jack, each as a person-participating-in-a-practice (Miller & Goodnow, 1995 p. 8), were beginning to take some authority, recognise and construct opportunity, and strengthen their 'connected knowing'.

Authoring. Lisa and Jack both faced challenges in developing their disposition towards reciprocity, and over the course of the study their journeys were very different. When just four, Lisa appeared reluctant to participate in conversations, especially at the centre where she did not have an established friend; and Jack was in an unfamiliar cultural and language context, enjoying the company of his grandmother. By phase two, Lisa was positioned by the teachers as competent, rather than shy, and she became more inclined to establish a dialogue. She moved from being a peripheral participant towards being a more inclined and willing participant. In phase three, in a classroom where she was achieving well, her teacher was encouraging her to participate in classroom discussions, and she was initiating interactions with the teacher. By phase two Jack enjoyed inserting numbers like 'three hundred and forty three, and double eight' and 'three hundred and twenty three hundred double eight' into the conversation, probably because he liked the sound of them – and perhaps because they did some of the authoritative positioning work that he enjoyed as well. Words may acquire a particular sensory quality for a young second language learner; we struggled to recognise the meaning in "If you don't fire now, I'll turn you into a brown school jacket", but acknowledge that it has a certain evocative and persuasive quality. In phase one, when his grandmother stayed with him, Jack and his grandmother talked together frequently in Chinese; their laughing and smiling reflected a warm and close relationship. In phase two, without that scaffolding, he began to author his own curriculum, engaging in dialogue with a range of children. By the time he had spent three months at school, Jack was describing himself as "I'm like the smart boy, in maths".

Recognising opportunity. By phase two Lisa was more likely to recognise an opportunity to engage in dialogue after watching: she watched the three girls painting, and then joined them, talking together with them about the painting as they worked. At school, Lisa's teacher commented that "I don't think it's a capability thing. I think she chooses to sit back a bit". Lisa appeared to interpret the school classroom as one in which she could initiate a conversation with the teacher; the teacher commented that "she'll just jump straight in there" and she was tolerant of being interrupted because she wanted to encourage her to make a contribution. Like Lauren, in chapter six, Lisa was just beginning to 'read' the classroom for the right time to dialogue with the teacher. By phase two, Jack was recognising and constructing opportunities in a programme that was flexible and well resourced. As a school pupil, he was constructing opportunities for dialogue outside the school programme: orchestrating a group of children to participate in a Halloween trip.

Connected knowing. By phase two Lisa was making suggestions and volunteering information as well as answering questions when she interacted with adults; she was also developing strategies for gaining entry into play. She had extended her repertoire of dialogue. Jack's interest in number was valued at the early childhood centre, and shared with his parents. During a visit to his home soon after he had started school, Jack's father demonstrated Jack's competence to us: "Four plus four equal to?" Jack: "Eight. Easy. Give me a hard one!" Dad: "Forty plus forty." Jack: "Eighty!" Dad: "Forty minus twenty." Jack (after a pause) "Twenty". Perhaps assisted by the protocols in adult-initiated games with rules, Jack was learning to modify his demands to be the leader if the play was to continue, and to negotiate with other people's views in mind.

The design

A number of features of the educational design in these case studies appeared to afford, invite, engage and provoke this facet of reciprocity.

Teacher expectation. Lisa's early childhood teachers worked hard to develop a warm and responsive relationship with her through engaging in family talk about recent experiences, and this helped to give her courage to engage in dialogue. Inviting Lisa to take on a responsible role, for example being the 'teacher' at mat time at kindergarten, was another way that Lisa's agency was supported, and this helped her to move away from her role as a passive observer. As teachers got to know her they came to see her less as 'shy' and more as 'selective' about her conversations with others. The teachers' change in view about the reasons for Lisa's reticence was an important affordance in this learning context. Teachers came to position Lisa as smart and capable, exercising agency in selecting when she wanted to engage in reciprocal activity, rather than lacking in the skills for engagement or labelled as being 'shy'. She was seen as someone who participated when there was something which interested her, or when she needed help. "She is actually an observer. And that's what she tends to do with things, wait until she's very, very clear about what it is that is going to happen". Teachers played a very important role in supporting the children's disposition to reciprocity by building a trusting relationship with them, and participating, monitoring and mediating in their interactions with peers. The familiarity, warmth and special attention provided by Lisa's teacher at the childcare centre helped her to feel safe and secure and have a sense of belonging. Her increasing ease with this relationship seemed to be in part a reciprocal response to the deliberate and intentional work by that teacher; this ease was later observed at her other centre, where she had been much less inclined to reciprocate. Teachers in Lisa's kindergarten in phase one had encouraged Lisa to get involved in social interaction, but the kindergarten had a less favourable staff/child ratio and a larger group size, which made it more difficult for them to do this. When they recognised that she was capable, and selective, they were less likely to ask her closed questions and they became comfortable with her entering the dialogue in her own time. This shift in the dispositional milieu for Lisa may have contributed to a favourable adjustment at school, both within formal classroom routines and informal play settings.

Spaces available for dialogue. Both Lisa and Jack's early childhood programmes allowed the children long spells of uninterrupted play, enabling extended interactive play sequences. This encouraged children to get to know each other well and to develop negotiating experience and skill. At school, it was only during a long wet lunchtime that Lisa was observed in animated peer play, and Jack's extended dialogues moved to the telephone after school.

A familiar peer. During phase one, the presence of a familiar peer, Theresa, clearly helped Lisa to establish reciprocity in one centre. Lisa also knew Theresa from neighbourhood and church contexts, and they were familiar play partners. Lisa was much less inclined to engage reciprocally and stayed in the background as an observer during phase one at her kindergarten. The larger group may have made it harder for the teachers to get to know Lisa, and for Lisa to make a friend, at kindergarten. Lisa and Theresa's joint repertoire of meanings and enjoyment of family play provided a good starting point for lengthy episodes of reciprocal play and talk. But in phase two and three, without Teresa, the teachers' expectations and understandings became a salient aspect of the curriculum design. Lisa demonstrated her authoritative grasp of the routines of the kindergarten in phase two, when she led mat-time discussion, and engaged in talk about joint activity (painting).

Home-centre links. Family members played a role in helping children engage reciprocally. Lisa's mother and Jack's grandmother spent time at the early childhood centres helping them to adjust and become familiar with the novel environment. At the same time, this enabled links to be made between the family and the teachers. Family members created subject positions for the children because of how they constructed them and what they expected for them. Lisa's parents were very worried at her 'shyness' and refusal to talk, but believed that she was bright and would do well at school. Jack's parents had confident expectations of his educational success, and these were reflected in his confidence and competence.

Joint attention with objects. Shared pretend play was one useful source of communication and interactions with peers. It illustrated the overlap between reciprocity and imagination. Lisa's episodes of joint attention included family play with props, painting on one side of an easel and chatting to children on the other side and at another easel, playing 'school' at school using a whiteboard. Jack's episodes of joint attention included arranging the furniture in the 'family' area, playing on the playground equipment, making a bus from inside furniture that was allowed to go outside, and making 'transformers' from Lego blocks. Like a common language, these materials and equipment were material affordances for shared meanings and common interests. Having similar interests and a repertoire of shared meanings (as in knowledge of transformers, television characters and narratives about babies) and common goals (as in measuring who is the tallest) provided the glue to build a collective intentionality and enabled reciprocity. These shared meanings encouraged the children to become tuned in to and prepared to incorporate the viewpoint of others.

Multiple languages available. Jack was also, like Lisa, an observer much of the time during phase one and rarely played with other children (in contrast to his later engagement). His story is, in part, a story about languages. In phase two, his interchanges with other children were often accompanied by strong feelings as the children negotiated the distribution of resources and Jack tried to manoeuvre himself into leading roles. A willing collective desire for reciprocity was mediated for Jack and Tom in part by their mutual recognition of the language and themes of storylines from popular television programmes and videos. Jack enjoyed playing at the early childhood centre with the language of mathematics as well, a language that was valued at the kindergarten. In phase two, Sally introduced 'being four and a half' as an indication of being 'higher', and Jack picked this up with interest. In the early childhood centre Jack was recognising some of the functions of number: using numbers as part of the play (one hundred fires), and counting carefully and accurately in group number games. This valuing of mathematics was a feature of the dispositions at home as well. The design here was providing children with common words, phrases, languages, stories and characters, from different cultural sources, so that this joint knowledge could mediate episodes of reciprocity – the negotiated bridging and structuring that Barbara Rogoff (2003) has researched and written about. For most children in these centres it was a hit and miss affair: in the episodes in which Jack and Lisa were involved, common stories depended for this mediation on play about driving cars or buses and running out of petrol, caring for babies or on shared knowledge of television programmes or videos. A prior common understanding assists with successful bridging and structuring, and this in turn enhances the complexity of and interest in negotiating story-lines. Of course, having a common language does not mean that the learner will be disposed to engage with dialogue: in these case studies authoring and recognising opportunity played a large part as well.

ENGAGING RECIPROCALLY

Being and Becoming a Group Member

> Relational agency is not simply a matter of collaborative action on an object. Rather it is a capacity to recognize and use the support of others in order to transform the object. It is an ability to seek out others and use others as resources for action and equally to be able to respond to the need for support from others. (Edwards & D'Arcy, 2004, pp. 149–150)

The possibilities for learning across a range of domains are widened if, beyond the opportunity for collaborative action, children can begin to notice and recognise the value of other people as resources for action and become ready willing and able to respond to the needs of others for support. The disposition to engage in such relationships (Edwards and D'Arcy's 'relational agency') extends children's capacity for learning. Hence being and becoming a group member is included here as a critical facet of developing a disposition towards reciprocity.

This chapter explores how three children were learning to become group members: gaining entry to play, engaging in sustained ongoing interactions, and negotiating their way around conflicts or exclusion. We explore the way that the children learned to negotiate reciprocal engagement, finding their way around obstacles. There were many features of the educational designs in these case studies that maintained or held back the momentum of this ongoing learning and sustained play. Interaction between peers was often fragile, and gaining entry to a group frequently difficult. Children strive to maintain stable relationships and sometimes reject or exclude others in the process (Corsaro, 1997; 2003). Paley (1992) has suggested that the voices of exclusion can be pervasive in early childhood and school classrooms:

> By kindergarten … a structure begins to be revealed and will soon be carved in stone. Certain children will have the right to limit the social experiences of their classmates. Henceforth a ruling class will notify others of their acceptability, and the outsiders learn the sting of rejection. Long after hitting and name-calling have been outlawed by the teachers, a more damaging phenomenon is allowed to take root, spreading like a weed from grade to grade. Must it be so? (Paley, 1992, p. 3)

Paley's book *You can't say you can't play* suggests that it is possible for children to understand and put into a practice a regime of inclusion, and a more equal distribution of power and control in peer relationships and interactions, with skilful teacher guidance. The children's own skills, understanding and agency have to be supported, however, to enable this change in classroom climate to take place. Being allowed to play, however, is only one step in facilitating a disposition towards reciprocity.

Children who have friends are at an advantage when it comes to the opportunity to develop their disposition towards reciprocity, as Lisa's experience in chapter three illustrated. Friendships are relationships that are perceived to be relatively stable and trustworthy which both construct and are constructed by dispositions towards reciprocity. They often develop on the basis of shared interests, as we saw in the last chapter. They provide a context for intimacy and acceptance while at the same time they often involve conflicts that need to be resolved if the group play or activity is to continue (Handel, Cahill & Elkin, 2007).

In this chapter, we describe the pathways towards being and becoming group members and the progress towards reciprocity for three children – Buzz, Ofeina and Samuel. We look at how these children developed relationships with other children in early childhood and school classrooms, what success they had in joining in, how they dealt with exclusion or conflict, and how their contexts helped or hindered their reciprocal engagement.

BUZZ

Buzz was an only child. His mother was a part-time primary teacher and his father was studying at a tertiary institution. Buzz had attended a parent co-operative childcare centre since he was about two years of age, and his mother had been a parent helper from time to time in the centre. He had a particular talent and passion for art and making things, which seemed linked to his father's work (which was art-related). Buzz also had a strong interest in vehicles – both representing them (drawing or modelling them), driving them (a pedal car and vehicles at his grandparents' farm) and playing pretend games driving vehicles. His father told the researcher that the art work which Buzz did at home was superior to the work he did at the early childhood centre. His talent was greatly valued by his parents: his father gave the researcher a CD containing a lot of Buzz's art work.

Buzz's mother said that it had taken him a whole term (three months) to settle at the centre, and that before that he had often been upset and uncomfortable with her leaving. In the phase one interview, Buzz's teacher described how Buzz acted when he first started at his early childhood centre, and his recent friendship with an older girl, Clara, who was soon to start school:

> Now he's a very shy wee man, when he first came in and he still clings to mum every morning. He's actually...building up quite a lot of friendships, which has helped quite a lot. These two [Buzz and Clara] at the moment are: 'We're playing together, you other children can't play with us.' (Teacher interview, phase one)

She thought, however, that Buzz was very empathetic towards other children though.

A lot of empathy for children. He's very, very caring and very upset if children get hurt... You know he's always looking after them and keeping an eye on them, yeah, which is really good. (Teacher interview, phase one)

During the phase one observations Buzz at first did seem shy, staying close to his mother who was often at his early childhood centre acting as a parent helper. Buzz's mother said in her interview that Buzz was very reluctant in new situations, and that it took him a long time to feel comfortable. She thought that this might be because he was an only child. She said that he found it hard to initiate friendships, although there was no evidence of this when he was observed. He always seemed busy and involved, either on individual projects or on play themes with a group of peers. His particular friend during phase one was Clara, but she was a year older and would leave for school between our phase one and phase two visits (their parents were also friends).

Taking Care of an In-Group Member

In phase one, Buzz and Clara frequently acted as protectors and supporters for a two year-old, Sylvia. They helped her by providing her with resources (e.g. paints), writing her name on paintings and collages, and protecting her from children who appeared to be annoying her. The mixed age setting in this centre encouraged this mentoring of a younger child by older children, and helped Buzz and Clara to develop a feeling of responsibility and control as they looked after Sylvia. They were able to act like grown ups in their separate world. In the following episode, there is play fighting and a battle for domination between two groups of children, pretend (being monsters), examples of inclusion and exclusion, while at the same time Buzz and Clara are 'looking after' Sylvia.

> *Playing in Tents (phase one)*
>
> Buzz has been outside on the pedal car. He goes inside the centre, and approaches his friend, Clara, to suggest that they play in a toy tent, which the teacher has set up in the front playroom. Clara is holding Sylvia's hand. Buzz says "We are going to hide in the tent" and Clara concurs "We're hiding from adults."
> Clara, Sylvia and Buzz go into the coloured play module (which is like a little tent). Buzz is whispering to them (possibly keen to hide from the observer as she has been watching them all morning.) There is giggling and the teacher, asks who is hiding in there. They say they don't want anyone else to come in. They are making whoofing noises. There is lots of screaming and shouting. Clara says 'out' to her younger brother, Fred. He cries. Clara explains that Fred has been bothering Sylvia. "He did put his hand over Sylvia's neck." And Buzz says "No kids allowed". Clara excludes another child trying to get in, saying "You can make a tent for yourself". The teacher sets up another play module for the excluded children. Clara and Buzz hug Sylvia and tell the other children to go into the other tent. Fred and Dennis go into the other tent. There is more yelling and whoofing from Buzz's group at Fred and Dennis in the other tent. Fred climbs on top of Dennis. Shelley (Fred and Clara's

mother, a parent helper today) removes Fred from the tent and takes him outside. Dennis (from inside his tent) hits the walls of the next tent. There is a lot of yelling. Clara says (to Dennis): "We're not going to play with you. Sylvia is not going to be your friend".
Buzz gets out of the tent and is pretending to be a monster, and a lot of roaring is coming from him and Clara. Buzz says: "This is our house not your house!" Play fighting continues between Dennis and the occupants of the other tent – Buzz and Clara's monster noises continue. Buzz waves a red blanket about. Colin joins Dennis in the second tent and defends it against the others. Colin says: "Stay out from here."
Play fighting continues – it is a bit wild and Clara and Buzz are still protecting Sylvia.
Clara: It's alright Sylvia. We'll look after you.
Buzz: She is sick of hearing noise.
Barbara: (another child): Do it together.
Shelley, hearing the noise from the other room comes in and intervenes. She is followed by the head teacher who tries to calm the children down, and says that it is getting scary. She tells them they should sit in the tents quietly. Buzz reinforces the teacher's message: "Calm down. You might scare Sylvia. And then I'll go and get Shelley and all the teachers." Dennis calms down.

When Buzz talked to the researcher about photographs of the tent episode, he told her that his "secret group" (of four children) was hiding in the tent. He said that they did not want Dennis in the tent because there would have been too many children "and then he would hit me and Colin and Clara and take Sylvia away from us. She was scared of Dennis."

The children were bound together in a pretend theme, but much of the episode involved annoying, teasing and play fights. The children hid away from adults, had a dispute over space, pretended to be monsters (scaring each other), and included and excluded others. The older children enjoyed their mentoring and nurturing role with the younger Sylvia. Buzz and Clara were particularly empathetic with Sylvia; Clara even spoke on her behalf when she tells Dennis that Sylvia is not going to be their friend and that they won't play with him; a denial of friendship that was a common strategy for trying to gain the upper hand in a dispute. It also illustrates the use of a danger-rescue theme, common in children's play (see also Henry in chapter seven), constructing an implicitly shared knowledge of danger or threats to safety, and enabling the leader or leaders to gain control over it (Corsaro, 2003). During this episode the play became rather wild, and led to some adult behaviour management. Marjatta Kalliala (2006, p. 94) describes this type of play as "dizzy play", where children do not actually hurt each other but are freeing themselves from the rules of the 'real' world for a time: "Yes, we kind of kick almost for real, but we know how to budge in a way" (Pia, cited by Kalliala, 2006, p. 96). A range of adult strategies were in evidence here, some of which provided short-term solutions to exclusion and disruption. The introduction of a second tent by the teacher helped de-escalate the conflict and gave all the children a space of their own. When the play seemed to get 'too noisy' the parent helper intervened, temporarily removing a disruptive child and suggesting that the children be gentle to each other. The shared play theme did not appear to be robust or engaging enough for the children to sustain the group on their own, although Buzz was disposed to recognise (or construct) another's perspective ("she is sick of hearing noise").

Developing an ongoing shared theme

In the following episode during phase two, Buzz was involved in ongoing play on the theme of Harry Potter. When the researcher asked Buzz's parents about whether Buzz had seen the Harry Potter film, they said they took him to the film when he was quite young, over a year previously. His grandparents had the video of this film and for a while he had watched it repeatedly. He had not seen it for months, though, they said. The Harry Potter theme, combined with car and train play, had occupied a group of two or three boys for many days – and for six of the ten episodes in phase two. Buzz was now engaged as part of a group in a shared theme and shared scripts which engaged him for long periods of time. During this play they negotiated their way through minor conflicts and formed a common purpose. The overlap between reciprocity and imagination is illustrated well in this episode.

Is it a flying car or a flying train? (phase two)

The children are talking about a train and a flying car/train as they wait for mat time. There is a dispute over whether they are in a car or a train and whether Buzz should have thrown a cardboard wand (a light sabre – a prop for the Harry Potter game) away. They are seated in chairs lined up behind each other. Buzz is squashed in between Jeff and Charles. (The functional group is three although other children are nearby forming a group, ready for mat time.)

Buzz: Hey, it's already mat time. Silly old me.
Charles: Come and get on the train.
Buzz: No, it's not a train.
Charles: Yes it is.
Buzz: How do you know?
Charles: Cos. Cos you said it's a train.
Buzz: I was pretending it was a flying train. Hey, it could be a flying train and a flying car.
Charles: Yes.
Buzz: It could be both. It could turn into a flying car.
Charles: Yeah.
Buzz: It could turn into a flying car.
Charles: Yeah.
Buzz: This is a flying train and it could turn into a flying car.
Charles: There's no such thing as a flying car. And I'm Hermione.
Teacher: Can you help me get the seats around so we can all see? Come and get the seats around.
Charles: I need my wand back too.
Buzz: Well I just threw it in the rubbish because you said you didn't want it.

> Charles: [Protesting noise].
> Buzz: Well I didn't want it so I threw it in the rubbish.
> Charles: I didn't want you to.
> Buzz: Well I did.
> Teacher: .... Can everyone come around? Good one. Thanks Buzz. We
>   want to get that big circle going.
> Buzz: And we've got to go outside after morning tea. And I'm pretending I
>   have a wand.
> Charles: Why did you put my wand in the rubbish? Why?
> Buzz: Because you didn't want it.
> Teacher: Lucky you are so good at making them though. You will have to
>   make another one.

This episode included several short-lived disputes, about for example whether they were in a car or a train, and whether Buzz should have thrown away the cardboard wands. This sort of dispute was very common in Buzz's extended play with Charles and others within the Harry Potter theme. It never stopped the play and such conflicts were usually resolved by negotiation and argument. In this episode the children are filling in time until they have a mat-time story, by discussing and shaping the theme of their ongoing play, which they will return to after mat-time and morning tea. Charles is annoyed with Buzz for throwing away the wand, which is one of the props for the game, and the teacher's response is to defuse any conflict by suggesting that they can easily make another one. The children are sharpening their skills of argument and negotiation with each other. Buzz justifies his actions of throwing away the wand, but Charles continues to question his motives, and adds his own perspective. Buzz changes the story line, suggesting that they could be in a flying car *and* a flying train – instead of one or the other, but Charles retains his critical stance ("There's no such thing..." and stakes a claim to a valued problem-solver role (Hermione). No-one is really upset and the ongoing momentum of the game will continue. Buzz and Charles (and often Charles' older brother, Jeff) are part of a stable and ongoing group in which the power play is always in question, always open to compromise and negotiation.

The pretend theme of Harry Potter was a persistent one, which had lasted over many weeks at the centre and continued over the three days of observations. Buzz plays largely with Charles (and occasionally with Jeff) but other children come and go from the game. Buzz and Charles had developed a reciprocal relationship where they ask for (and occasionally give) reasons for their actions and (usually) listen to each other's point of view, incorporating it into the play. Buzz was one of the key initiators and leaders who sustained the ongoing game with suggestions, ideas and negotiations. He played the role of Harry Potter's lieutenant, Ron, the driver of the flying car, an important role in the drama. When the researcher asked him why he nearly always played the part of Ron in the Harry Potter stories, Buzz told her that the other children always wanted to be Harry so he was being accommodating! He said that his favourite thing to do at preschool was playing Harry Potter stories. Driving the flying car helped Buzz to connect with his interest in vehicles. The children's deep involvement in the theme can be seen by their continuing play while the teacher is trying to organise them for mat time.

During phase two Buzz spent the majority of his time involved in elaborate pretend play with a group of other children. His initial reserve had totally disappeared by phase two, and he had a wide range of friends and playmates. He was very popular amongst the other children at the centre. This was illustrated when the children all wanted to sit next to him at mat time. When the researcher asked him who his friends were, he listed six children (including both boys and girls) – more than at the first interview when he and Clara spent most of their time together. Buzz and Clara were still friends even though she had now gone to school. In phase two Buzz still enjoyed playing with younger children: in phase one he had been a minder for Sylvia, and in phase two he had a close and more reciprocal relationship with Charles, who was at least a year younger than him. His parents described him as gentle.

A kind and helpful all-rounder

Phase three took Buzz away from the familiar environment of the early childhood centre to a school on the other side of town, near his home. (The early childhood centre had been near to his mother's work). Buzz had an easy transition into his new entrant classroom, despite his mother's worry about how he would cope. She had feared that the social aspect would be hard for him. His teacher believed that he had been a bit 'clingy' at first but had settled very quickly, commenting that he was a very good listener and that she never had to tell him anything twice. This fits well with all the observations, which showed him to be a very busy, on-task, and involved participant in classroom life. His teacher also described Buzz as 'an all-rounder', who is good at everything and entered school with a lot of knowledge. Like Lisa in Chapter four, Buzz fits the stereotype of the 'ideal' pupil, from the teacher's perspective (Stephen & Cope, 2003). He followed instructions, concentrated well and knew what was expected of him.

Buzz was a fast and accurate worker in all of the academic tasks in the primary classroom. He worked well with others when he had an opportunity. In the episode below he enjoyed chatting with his partner at News Time, both listening and contributing to the conversation, as well as later doing an articulate presentation to the whole class. Buzz was still a very well-liked child, despite the fact that initially he had no familiar peers at school, having moved across town. The teacher spoke very highly of his social skills and how kind and helpful he was to other children. She said:

> His relationship with other children is quite special. I personally always promote that we look after one another and we're kind and we're helpful to one another. I would say he is one of the best children at modelling the things that I really want to encourage. (Teacher Interview, phase three).

The teacher said that he has lots of friends, and listed seven of them. Buzz in phase three gave the researcher the names of eight children who were his special friends, including two girls. Most of his interactions with children in the classroom and playground were very harmonious. A minor conflict occurred when he got annoyed with a boy during a shared reading task (the other boy was turning the pages too quickly). His mother said that he really loved lunchtime, and he told the researcher when she asked him if he still played Harry Potter, that he plays Batman, Superman and the Lord of the Rings with his friends at school. Buzz came to the researcher once in the playground telling her that another child had hit him. His mother also said that when his father was at school, Buzz had come to him crying at being hit. These seem to be minor incidents typical of the school environment, because generally Buzz is happy at school and has a harmonious relationship with his peer group.

News Time (phase three)

Buzz is paired with Leo at news time. The teacher gives instructions about how to proceed. The whole class sits cross legged on the floor in pairs facing each other. Buzz and Leo have an animated discussion though it is very difficult at times to know what they are talking about. They go from one topic to another – colouring books, their painting, their fathers. The teacher starts them off by saying: "We're going to have a little bit of talking time with a friend now." Buzz starts by telling Leo that he has a colouring book, and Leo says he has one too with sharks and a Nemo colouring book. Leo asks Buzz whether he knows what his dad did. Buzz says no and Leo explains something (hard to decipher) about a van. They talk about their paintings and point out where they are hanging on the wall. Buzz asks Leo where his is, and he points it out. Buzz says he has an orange painting, and Leo asks him which one. Then he points out that Buzz has green in the top of his painting. They then joke with each other about their dads.

Leo: Do you know what Buzz?
Buzz: What.
Leo: Um, my dad, he, um, he has a runny nose, but it dropped in the water, in the Nemo pond, …. ate it. And then he burped.
Buzz: [laughs].
Leo: And then he was dead. A dead Nemo and then I hit him and then he came back alive and then he hit him again and then he got back dead.
Buzz: Do you know what my dad says?
Leo: No.
Buzz: …. my darling.
Leo: And then [both trying to talk at same time and then start whispering].
Teacher: Class, I see that you're not quite sure whether you're finished yet. Are you still going to do some talking, or have you finished?

Buzz and Leo share a conversation and happily fill up the time given for this activity by the teacher. They cover several topics of conversation, have fun and a laugh together, and talk about real dads and fantasy (Nemo is a film fish) characters. The reciprocal format is "Do you know what…. ?" Even within regular classroom routines the children enjoyed a bit of playful silliness.

Although Buzz's mother had been very concerned about his shyness and difficulty making friends during phase one, he quickly became one of the key players in the early childhood classroom. This disposition towards reciprocity carried over into his school transition where he engaged in strong relationships with others both within and outside the classroom. Buzz was seen as a child who cares for others and understands how to behave as a member of the classroom community.

OFEINA

Ofeina lived with her mother, father and older brother. During the course of the project, just before Ofeina started school, a younger brother was born. They were all very close to their extended Tongan family. Ofeina, her older brother and her cousin were looked after by their grandmother during the day, and after school, while their parents worked. Ofeina's grandmother spoke mostly in Tongan to the children, but both Tongan and English are spoken in Ofeina's home. At times during the project Ofeina's mother said that the children went through temporary phases of being reluctant to converse in Tongan at home. Close links were maintained with other members of their family in Tonga and around the world. The wider Tongan community and church was also an important feature in their lives with a lot of time spent both at church and on church business where Tongan is mostly spoken.

Ofeina's parents came to New Zealand as teenagers with their respective families and undertook the final part of their secondary schooling there. During the project Ofeina's mother worked in a bank and her father had his own lawn-mowing business. During the course of the project he went to work with family members in America for a few months before returning to New Zealand and taking up a position in a factory.

Ofeina's mother was the fifth of seven children and when she left school she held down two jobs at the same time for a number of years, even after Ofeina and her older brother were born. She talked about her ambitions for Ofeina and her brother: "I told them, you go to University 'cos I didn't, I know I should have, but I didn't". The mother had noticed a difference in the way Ofeina and her brother approached their studies and was very proud of Ofeina's obvious interest in writing and drawing, and later her success at school. She also identified Ofeina's growing confidence over the course of the project. At the time of the second family visit, just before Ofeina started school, she described how Ofeina was participating in church activities such as getting up on stage and announcing the performances, and joining in with them. Observations at both the kindergarten and school also reflected this growing confidence and ability.

Watching and listening in

Ofeina spent a lot of time during phase one, like Lisa, observing and listening in: described by Barbara Rogoff (2003, p. 299) as "intent participation in ongoing shared endeavours". The research record on Ofeina in phase one highlights this process. Six episodes of ten minutes or longer were identified from observations on two days, and two further episodes were fifteen minute 'mat times' at the end of the day when the children listened to a story, sang songs and participated in action songs. During these mat-time episodes, Ofeina watched, listened and sometimes carried out the actions. In four of the six other episodes Ofeina watched the other children before she tried out the activity. She then interacted with the physical resources alongside of, and only briefly with, other children playing in the same area. On one occasion she offered to assist another child (the offer was refused), and on two other occasions she offered children a pretend cup of tea: one of these was accepted and a short period of collaborative group play followed. The other was ignored. Two further episodes were group activities initiated and supervised by adults.

The first episode on day one was sited on a matted area where Ofeina was completing jigsaws. It lasted for about an hour, although for seven minutes in the middle she turned a nearby plastic building block activity into a 'form board' (filling the spaces on a base board) activity, before returning to the jigsaws. This matted area was just inside the front door, where parents often stayed and chatted. There were two sofas to sit on, shelves with jigsaws displayed, and a variety of wooden blocks and plastic building bricks. Several of the parents who sat and talked in this area during the first phase of the project spoke English as an additional language. Tongan was spoken by some parents and by another child who played in this area during the time Ofeina was playing there.

The jigsaw area was popular with the children, especially early in the session, because so many mothers, aunties and grandmothers stayed there to watch their children and to chat. On the second day of our observations we counted seventeen family members early in the afternoon session: five chatting together on couches, four on the floor helping children to do jigsaws, one at the playdough, one standing watching, one with her child at the painting easel, one with her child at the collage area, one in the children's family/office corner, two sitting outside talking, and one talking to a child outside. Half an hour later there were still fourteen there; by then two were in the kitchen, making cups of tea and cutting up fruit for the children.

> ### Puzzles (phase one)
>
> Ofeina completed two puzzles on her own, sitting close to, but not interacting with the other children. She worked alone on two puzzles, and then attempted a third difficult puzzle, and became distracted by the other children building with the blocks nearby. She watched them, then spent some time building with the plastic building blocks. She was very meticulous and concentrated on her task until she apparently deemed it completed and wandered back to the jigsaws. There were no interactions with other children during this time. After wandering around for a short while, Ofeina returned to the matted area and this time a nearby adult talked to her and encouraged her to try another puzzle. When a parent said "Well done. What is it?" Ofeina just shrugged her shoulders and didn't respond. When the adult left, Ofeina completed a number

of other easy puzzles very quickly. During this episode, Ofeina sat at times just watching the other children – the activities they were doing and the interactions between them - also with the adults close by. She did not attempt to join any of the children but did return to work at jigsaws.

Offering a role in pretend play

In two phase one episodes, Ofeina was involved in pretend play, and invited others to join in.

The Sandpit (phase one)

After wandering around for a while, inside and out, watching the other children, Ofeina walks over to the sandpit where a boy (who spoke Tongan) was playing. She picks up a cup and filled it with sand. He wanders off and she was left alone in the sandpit. She continues to fill up the cup and called after him "Cup of tea?", but there was no response. She continues then to fill up jugs and cups, smoothing off the tops with intense concentration. There are children playing nearby on trolleys and on the climbing frame and she sits and watches them for a while before, after twenty minutes in the sandpit, she suddenly jumps up and runs off.

Ofeina's attempt to entice other children to join her were not successful at first, but she persisted. In the following episode she succeeded in involving other children in her pretend play.

Family Pretend (phase one)

Ofeina wanders over to the family/office corner where some other children were playing. She sits down at the table and picked up the toy phone, pressing buttons while watching the other children. Shortly afterwards the other children leave, leaving Ofeina to play at the office table on her own. She pretends to have a conversation on the phone and then moves on to take a jug to the sink, pretending to fill it with water A teacher comes past and briefly speaks in English and Tongan with her ("What are you making? Cup of tea?"). Another child arrives in the area and pretends to eat 'fruit' with a spoon. She smiles at Ofeina, who pours her a pretend cup of tea from the tea pot, hands it to her, and then asks if she is "Finished?". The child nods, and Ofeina pours tea for another girl who has joined them. All three play briefly together. She picks up the phone and talks into it. She pretends to eat some fruit. The first child asks Ofeina: "Can I have dinner?" and the second child replies: "No. You come and get fish and chips. Here's some dollar to pay fish and chips". Ofeina leaves for the jigsaw area.

Offering help

Five minutes after this Family Pretend play episode, Ofeina offers assistance to another child, and again the offer is refused.

> ### *Don't Help Me (phase one)*
>
> Ofeina is in the jigsaw area and completes two jigsaws very quickly. She watches Sally working on a large floor puzzle for a while and then hands a piece of the jigsaw to her. Another child also joins them and tries to help, at which point Sally, who had started the puzzle, states forcefully and clearly:
>
> Sally: Can you please? .... I don't want you to help me. I don't want you to help me. I've got my own friend to help me. I don't want these two kids to help me. Teacher! I don't want these two kids to help me. I want to do it all by myself. I want to do this puzzle all by myself. Teacher!

The message that Ofeina's help was not wanted was clearly stated. No teacher arrived, and Ofeina and the other child wandered off. However, Ofeina continues to offer assistance and, in an episode four days later, she was more successful. She confidently used her expertise to help others with puzzles with verbal direction and encouragement: accompanying her assistance with words in English: "No, no, the other one. In there. There. No. There. There! There..... No way. No. Yay!"

Group activities, initiated or supervised by adults

On two occasions during our observations in phase one Ofeina participated in group activities with other children, led by teachers and parents. The following episode was a combination of dough play and pretence as the children made 'food' out of the dough and 'sold' it to grown ups.

> ### *Making Rice Cakes and Dumplings (phase one)*
>
> Ofeina is sitting at a table with dough and various utensils set out – there is a toy kitchen set up around it. The teacher and a parent are at the table with a number of children; one of the children speaks Tongan, as does the teacher. The occasional comments are in Tongan and in English. Ofeina sits down and begins playing with the dough. The teacher talks to Ofeina about what she is doing with the dough. The parent makes a 'dumpling' with the dough, Ofeina gives her a small ball of dough and the parent says "One dollar?" The children make rice cakes and dumplings out of the dough and 'sell' them to the adults at the table. The teacher and the parent alternate between talking to the children and talking to each other. The children say very little, but there is much laughter.

This joint involvement with peers and adults was a secure and safe place for the children to collaborate over the shared goal of making rice cakes and dumplings with dough. This is yet another example of the overlap between reciprocity and imagination; the shared imaginative theme allowing children to pick up and support each other's play. The adults played an important role in this episode by suggesting ideas for the play, and attending to and supporting the children's contributions. In contrast the following episode is a different kind of reciprocity, where children competed for turns on an obstacle course.

> ### The Obstacle Course (phase one)
>
> The children have constructed an obstacle course where they have to jump off some reels and climb along some ropes. Ofeina follows another child and jumps onto a mattress from a high reel, while a teacher checks that the children take turns and jump safely. However, some children push in out of turn. At first when children move into the queue in front of her Ofeina makes no objection, but later, after hearing the other children saying "My turn" she also takes up the cry "My turn" and moves fast to establish her position. She completes the obstacle course a few times successfully before running off for afternoon tea where she sat at the table and spoke in Tongan to some of the adults there.

In that episode Ofeina watched and learned an important lesson from her peers about reciprocity, and discovered how to successfully claim a turn at jumping and climbing.

An expert helper

By phase two of the research, ten months later, eleven episodes of ten minutes or more were observed on three different days. Ofeina now appeared to be deliberately choosing sometimes to engage with others in play, or with teachers in small group lessons and games. She was almost always actively engaged, and appeared to be seizing opportunities to learn something new. These latter occasions included making a puppet, screen printing, and combining recognition of shapes and actions with Māori language in a 'bingo' game. A combination of competence and helping was a key feature of reciprocity for Ofeina; often the 'reciprocity' was in one direction, with Ofeina taking the initiative to teach or help others in a number of contexts.

By now she had developed a close friendship with Kyung-Ja and Leah (who had recently gone to school). The teacher told us that Leah used to choose their activities and games, but now Ofeina had taken up the leadership role in group play. In the following episode Ofeina and Kyung-Ja were painting together, and Ofeina was providing skilled help and support. The two children were engaged in a common goal, and Ofeina enjoyed taking the role of expert and helper.

> ### Painting a House (phase two)
>
> Ofeina carefully paints a picture of a house with Kyung-Ja watching beside her. They are talking to each other as Ofeina paints. She pretends she is going to paint Kyung-Ja and playfully daubs the paint at her. Kyung-Ja ducks away laughing. A teacher joins them and talks to Ofeina about her picture. Ofeina tries to write her name and writes four of the letters. She runs off to get her name card, comes back, and attempts to write her name, copying the card. She writes two more letters. The teacher mounts her picture onto black paper for her and hangs it up. Now Kyung-Ja sits down to paint, with Ofeina standing beside her 'helping'. Ofeina is holding the paintbrush and Kyung-Ja

is telling her where to put the paint. Kyung-Ja takes over the paintbrush briefly before Ofeina takes the painting and puts it on a piece of black paper. They use the stapler together with Ofeina lining it up and Kyung-Ja helping to push it down. "I'm helping Kyung-Ja" Ofeina tells the researcher.

There are several other examples during phase two of Ofeina engaging with a difficult task and helping others to complete these tasks.

Magnetic Fish (phase two)

The children are making fish to attach to metal bottletops for a magnetic fishing game in the water trough. Ofeina is very focused on cutting out what she has drawn, although the task is quite difficult: the card is thick and cutting with scissors is challenging. She shows another child how to draw around a small wooden fish and says to the teacher, "She can't do it". She explains to the other child what to do and then carries on with her own work.

Later on, in another episode, Ofeina shares the swing with Masika and Kyung-Ja. At one point Ofeina hops off the swing, gives Masika a push and returns to her swing. At another point, Ofeina holds Masika's swing for her as Masika goes to the sandpit to pick something up.

Conversations about friendship

By phase two, friendship had become an implicit topic of discussion for Ofeina. It appeared in conversation in a number of episodes, with several different children. Such conversations did not occur during phase one, except where the topic was introduced by Sally when she was rejecting help from Ofeina. On the whole, Ofeina's conversational turns were brief, but the following two turns were the longest recorded on these three days. In the first part of the conversation she refers to Leah, who has now left for school.

Swinging (phase two)

Ofeina was talking to Masika and Kyung-Ja while she was swinging alongside them. They communicate in a combination of speaking and singing.

Ofeina: ... I do it (laughs) go on. Ah la la la (giggles) I .... Do it again. (sings again loudly) It's Leah. Come I missed you Leah. Come, go, Leah's gone and left me. ... Leah. No you're not having a go Leah. No Leah my friend and you my friend. Yes. What? 'Cos I'm going to ... can you ... my friend?

Although the next conversation with Masika sounds like exclusion, the children were playing collaboratively and cheerfully together.

Ofeina: I'm not your friend, Kyung-Ja's my friend okay? No I'm not your friend. Kyung-Ja I'm your friend ok? You're my friend. No, better say you're my friend ... you're my friend. (laughs)

Collaborative play

Three other episodes were of collaborative play with peers: two ten minute episodes (a telephone conversation in the family corner, and peripheral participation in play about going on a bus trip with chairs outside), and a 26 minute episode of playing with large trucks. In all of these episodes Kyung-Ja was an important play partner. In the telephone conversation, Ofeina pretended to phone up Leah at school. She and Kyung-Ja shared the telephone, and Ofeina wrote notes as she talked. In the truck episode Ofeina was sitting on a truck, using her feet as locomotion and pulling Kyung-Ja in a trailer at the back. They ran the truck down a sloping pathway, with Ofeina using her feet as a break. Kyung-Ja and Ofeina pushed the truck and trailer back up the top and they mastered the slope again, five more times, shrieking with excitement as they went, with Ofeina steering onto the grass by the side of the pathway so that they managed not to career into the gate. Kyung-Ja drove the truck only once.

Public affirmation of knowledge and skill

> "Legitimate peripheral participation" provides a way to speak about the relations between newcomers and old-timers, and about activities, identities, artefacts and communities of knowledge and practice. It concerns the process by which newcomers become part of a community of practice. A person's intentions to learn are engaged and the meaning of learning is configured through the process of becoming a full participant in a sociocultural practice. This social practice includes, indeed it subsumes, the learning of knowledgeable skills. (Lave & Wenger, 1991, p. 29)

During phases one and two, Ofeina's intentions to learn were engaged on four aspects of the process of becoming a full participant in this early childhood community: developing reciprocal relationships with teachers and peers, figuring out the rules and the intentions here, developing new knowledgeable skills, and being recognised as competent in at least some areas. All four of these intents were, for Ofeina, closely entangled together. She began with 'intent participation' – watching and listening – and on the last day of our observations in phase two she was deeply engaged in learning a new process, a 'knowledgable skill', for a screen-printing task: overprinting on a screen print that she has completed earlier in the week. This episode lasted nearly an hour, and Ofeina was publicly acknowledged for her competence at screen printing and at helping others. The teacher reminded Ofeina to remember how she cut out windows last time, and commented: "That's very intricate, what you're cutting out Ofeina".... And "amazing, careful cutting out, Ofeina" ...[to the other children also working on their screen prints] "She's being very careful not to cut the leg off". The teacher says to another child in the small group "Ofeina can show you how to screen print", and Ofeina affirms "I (can) tell her". Ofeina later assisted Kyung-Ja with the screen printing process.

On another occasion, the children were making a cardboard puppet figure, attached to a stick. They frequently participated in puppet shows with silhouettes behind a back-lit screen or used a puppet theatre. Ofeina was again positioned as an expert when the teacher asks other children in the group to have a look at her design.

> ### Making Puppets (phase two)
>
> Teacher: Are you going to make something Ofeina? Do you want to have a look and see what you'd like to make? We could give you some of those special sticks.... would you like to do that? I'll come and show you.
>
> Ofeina sits down and begins to draw. Other children are working at the same table, and the teacher (Zoe) is giving advice and assistance.
>
> Ofeina: Zoe, look.
>
> Teacher (to the other children in the group): Wow look at Ofeina's excellent design. Have you seen Ofeina's design? ... Look, have a look see. You made that design there like that. Oh what's this person doing?
>
> Ofeina: Um the boy.
>
> Teacher: The boy, oh what's the boy doing?
>
> Ofeina: Cleaning.
>
> Teacher: Cleaning. The boy's cleaning. Gosh look at the way the arms are out like this. See the arms are extended out like that. Did you want to cut that out with the scissors? Cut around the outside with the scissors. Want to cut it?

Teacher-initiated games

A game of skipping was initiated by the teacher during phase two, following on from the same game the day before. At first the teacher reminded the children when it was each of their turns to jump. Ofeina was quick to say when it was her turn and she was also very keen to have a turn at holding the rope. The teacher held the rope with the other end tied to a fence, but occasionally she invited the children to turn the rope. Skipping and turning the long rope were difficult tasks for many of the children. Ofeina however was an expert at skipping, and on one occasion completed thirty-three jumps. She also turned the rope, but admitted that she found this too difficult. Recognition of competence was an intrinsic quality for this activity: during this ten minute episode Ofeina commented, mostly quietly to herself: "I can do it", "I can jump", "I can go like that" "I can jump the best" seven times. By now she knew that turn-taking was taken seriously at the centre, although three times she called out to remind the teacher: "It's my turn".

School: a different community of practice

When Ofeina went to school the community of practice became very different, with limited opportunity for choosing to become a group member in the classroom. In the playground, however, Ofeina frequently played and laughed and talked with two other children. They were both boys, members of the group of eight children who attended the half-hour English as an Additional Language (EAL) class two days a week. They were not from Tonga, nor were they peers from her early childhood centre. The EAL class, designed to facilitate English language, was apparently also facilitating a friendship group.

The opportunity to spend a long time on learning a difficult new skill, building on the personalised work that had established her as a member of the 'guild' of screen-printers (or skippers) was now not available. The new entrant class was around twenty-five children, and on the days that we visited Ofeina was required to spend two relatively long spells of time at an assembly (forty-five minutes), and on practising for an assembly presentation with another class (thirty-five minutes). Other episodes were very short, and Ofeina, who was a quiet student for whom writing and reading were not strong points, received very little feedback about whether she was on the right track. The school structure had set up rules and practices for art classes that were different from the screen printing, making puppets, and painting that had engaged Ofeina at the early childhood centre. Her classroom teacher explained how her art syndicate developed art topics which afforded little room for incorporating the children's ideas.

> Teacher: The art people get together and decide according to our levels. Okay this is the topic. This time it's wearable art. We finished it. In fact I'll show you what we made. We had to make one thing that the children can wear and we had a fashion parade. ... I think my class, everyone liked what my children did. They made these glasses.
>
> Researcher: So you sort of... Did you cut out the shape for them?
>
> Teacher: No I asked my teacher aide to do it. I've got a teacher aide time in the holidays. (Teacher interview, phase three)

The class was divided into five groups, depending on their ability, for reading and writing or mathematics, and these rotated through activities. It meant that the children often worked on their own on prescribed tasks like buddy reading, worksheets, puzzles and games. Ofeina spent some time on a matching worksheet, cutting out and colouring in, even when the time for this task had elapsed and she was required to move on to reading a poem book to herself. Field notes record "This is the first time this morning that she has kept focus (apart from the ears and eyes test) for a period of time". Perhaps she recognised the task from the 'Making Fish' task in phase two, a task which at the early childhood centre was physically challenging, clearly linked to the game that was being prepared, and one in which she was able to assist another child. Ofeina's experiences in the early childhood programme had ensured that one of her particular identities on entry to school was as someone who recognised and called on her competence to help others to jointly solve problems. She was inclined to spontaneously offer to do so, sensitive to the appropriate occasion, and by the time she went to school she also had the knowledge and the ability. At school on three occasions she offered to assist another child to complete a puzzle; on two occasions the two children completed it together; on the third occasion the help was resisted (as she, too, had resisted an offer of help with a puzzle and completed it on her own). On another occasion she 'read' to another child, being the teacher. And on a fifth occasion, during tidying up, she and another child saw that a puzzle was incomplete and completed it together, with Ofeina taking the lead. She was confident in the big group, shooting her hand up when the class was invited to ask questions, for example at news time, and made an appropriate contribution. At school, Ofeina had to adjust to a setting where the goals were very different, but her identity as a competent and confident helper appeared to remain viable. When we later visited Ofeina's family in her second year at school she was doing well: her mother reported that her assessments were all As and Bs, with a C for physical education.

SAMUEL

Samuel arrived at his early childhood centre with almost no English. By phase two, despite some setbacks, he had developed a sense of belonging and a learner-identity that included recognised expertise and an understanding of the culture of the centre – understanding what was valued, how one might enter into a peer relationship, and how the activities 'worked'. Teachers, activities, and trial and error strategies appeared to mediate his resourcefulness and strengthened a disposition towards reciprocity.

Samuel's family came to New Zealand from Kerala in India, a year before the study started, in order for Samuel to have more opportunities for education. His father read an article about New Zealand in a newspaper, and they decided to come. They did not have any other family here but had become part of a strong Indian Christian community from the same region. Malayalam was the main language spoken at home, but both parents also spoke English, and they had learned Hindi, the national language, at school. They were very keen to have Samuel speak Malayalam fluently in order to enable him to maintain close relationships with his extended family in India. During the course of the project, Samuel and his family travelled back to Kerala for six weeks to see family: all his grandparents and most of his relatives were there. Both of Samuel's parents had university degrees, and before coming to New Zealand Samuel's father had worked in the Gulf. He now worked in a semi-skilled job in a warehouse, and Samuel's mother worked part time in a laboratory. Samuel came home from school in the afternoons and had a sleep so that he could stay up later to eat with his parents when his father came home. On Saturdays they went to the library, shopping, and the park. On Sunday it was Sunday School. Samuel's father was a keen amateur cricketer (Mother: "His first love is cricket!") and in the summer he and Samuel often played cricket at the park on a Saturday.

Samuel's mother referred to a saying they have in India, which says that "parents should try to maximise the learning experiences a young child has before they are five, because this is when a child's mind is fresh". They commented that in Kerala children start formal instruction in reading from the age of three and a half, but they were happy with Samuel's kindergarten programme.

Mother: At first we were a bit worried he was just playing... [But] While playing they are learning things, you know?

Father: They learn from experience. (Interview with Samuel's parents, phase one)

While they were very happy with the broader view of education in New Zealand, they still wanted him to be able to perform well when they returned to India to visit. Samuel and his mother spent time together with the educational materials they brought from India, which were in both English and Malayalam, doing spelling, reading and dictation. His parents read to him in English, but the language at home is Malayalam. His mother commented "We don't use English. When we go home it would be very difficult for him". However, they were keen for Samuel to mix with other children at kindergarten and school, and to learn English. Following their trip back to India they said that they were even more convinced that the New Zealand system is what they want for Samuel. His father commented: "It's good in the sense that he's treading at his own pace, rather than – [as] in India – they are failing too much in childhood" referring to a large amount of pressure on children at a very young age.

An early sense of belonging: interactions in the home language

At the start of the study Samuel had a friend at kindergarten, who also spoke Malayalam and was known to Samuel from the church community. Samuel and Simon frequently speak Malayalam together. Seven episodes of involvement, over two days, all centrally included Simon and in only two episodes were other children participating. The two boys appeared to take turns in choosing what activity they were going to do next, and how long they stayed there. Often the actual time spent on any one activity was reasonably short (four episodes are twenty minutes or less, the other three range from twenty-three to thirty-five minutes) with lots of running around in between, but the focus appeared to be on doing whatever it is together.

Learning the rules of competence in English

Samuel's ability with English language was developing, assisted by the adults at the early childhood centre. Here are some examples of episodes, and of his conversations with the teacher as they review photographs of activities together. These photographs were provided by the researchers, but conversations about them were typical of the routine of revisiting Learning Stories in the children's portfolios at this kindergarten. They illustrate the teachers' ability to assist children to communicate a shared meaning. On one occasion, for example, as the teacher and Samuel were revisiting a photograph of a construction, Samuel labels one section of the building as a 'slider' and points outside to the playground: "Over there, the slider". The teacher responds: "Oh, like the blue slides out there...so you've put slides like the kindergarten in". A later building of the 'school', and the conversation in response to photographs, is described below.

Building a School (phase one)

Samuel and Simon and are now building together with Lego blocks. There are five children on the mat, building, with a parent (not Samuel or Simon's) sitting on the floor watching.

Samuel: Look!
Parent: What are you building?
Samuel: A school.
Parent: A school.
Samuel: A chimney tall.
Parent: A chimney – did you say a chimney? What comes out of a chimney?
Samuel: A fire.
Parent: I see – the smoke, the smoke from a fire.
Samuel: A big tower. A big school....Look at that! I build tall.
(It is knocked over accidentally by another child).
Samuel: Simon!
Simon: It's not me. It's not me. Okay. (The children re-build it together, and later knock it over several times, laugh, and re-build it)

The following day Samuel reviewed photographs of this building with the teacher:

Teacher: Who was that by you?
Samuel: Simon
Teacher: Oh, that's Simon by you. And what were you doing with Simon?
Samuel: Building big tower.
Teacher: Oh, you were building the big tower. Oh. Look, yes, look I can see you working together there … What were you talking about?
Samuel: Blue, yellow, yellow and blue.
Teacher: (points to the structure) What structure have you made here?
Samuel: A big tower. Ahh … broken
Teacher: Ah. The big tower and it's broken.
Samuel: Yeah
Teacher: Oh. How did the tower get broken?
Samuel: The tower, uh, broken
Teacher: The tower broken Mmm.
Samuel: Ah … a train is did … a … well … a lorry come get it.
Teacher: A lorry?
Samuel: Yeah a lorry come hit it.
Teacher: And hit it.
Samuel: Yeah. And b … and the building 'bomp'.
Teacher: And the building went bomp down.
Samuel: Yeah.
Teacher: Ooh. And look. Here's a photo of you Samuel.
Samuel: And that's Simon.

In art activities, the teachers do not always invite children to verbalise about the creative process, but here is an example where the teacher has done so, and enabled sharing of meaning about one of Samuel's interests: the bible story of Noah's Ark.

> ### Painting (phase one)
>
> At the beginning of the afternoon session, Samuel is in the block corner, not very engaged until Simon arrives. They play briefly with the toy animals, speaking Malayalam together. Samuel leaves the area and goes to the painting easels. Simon follows. They paint on easels alongside each other. A teacher comes over.
>
> Samuel: I'm going to paint...Look at that!
>
> Teacher: Oh wow! It's a big circle isn't it? A circle – it's great. The pink and the blue all mixed together....
>
> Samuel: I've finished. Look at the finished.
>
> Teacher: Finished? What is that?
>
> Samuel labels three places on the painting: rain, flood and sea. The teacher writes the words, and his name, on the painting. [At home his mother says he is very interested in the story of Noah's Ark]

By phase two, Samuel's friend Simon had left for school and Samuel had mixed success at finding another friend. He was frequently rebuffed. During phase one there were several observations in field notes of Simon and Samuel taking each other's hand when they went from one activity to another. In one episode in phase two, while he was playing with several children on the climbing equipment and the slide, Samuel tried to take one of the girl's hands, but she removed it and moved away. However, he remained cheerful and appeared to be optimistic, and he developed a number of strategies for interacting with other children. For Samuel, whose competence in English was still developing, these attempts to join or construct a social group often included non-verbal and embodied communication: smiling, making engine noises to assist the communicating of purpose in play, holding hands (a failed strategy), growling to stop other children disrupting his play, gesturing and whooping with mutual enjoyment, and physically coordinating trolley and tractor play.

Learning the rules of the game in phase two

Initiation by teachers continued to be central in phase two. Of the ten episodes over three half-days in phase two that were ten minutes or longer, five were ten to fifteen minutes long, three lasted twenty minutes, one was thirty-five minutes long and one was fifty-nine minutes. Six episodes were initiated by a teacher: a game of throwing bean bags, a small group story episode where Samuel holds the book and turns the pages, two group games, a police visit, and a group activity with clay. In the following adult-organised activity Samuel is learning some of the rules associated with group games.

> ### Bean Bag Game (phase two)
>
> In a back room at the kindergarten a group of children are playing with small, hand-held bean bags and walking along a small beam that has been set up. There is a teacher supervising the activity and organizing the children. At first Samuel tries to join the activity by taking the bowl of bean bags when the teacher left the room but the other children object. The teacher returns and helps Samuel to join the group by explaining what he needs to do. He tries to throw the bean bag unsuccessfully at first and then is successful and is delighted, as is the other child he is throwing towards. He continues to participate in the activities with balls and hoops and bats and they all get very excited. Eventually the teacher calls a halt to the activity for story-time.
>
> Field notes. This is the first time we have observed Samuel as part of a larger group activity. He appears a little unsure of how to participate in these kinds of activities but the teacher encourages and explains to him what he has to do. When the teacher is elsewhere he loses focus a bit and runs out of the room, returning again shortly afterwards and continuing to participate. Although rebuffed at first, because he tried to take all the bean bags, Samuel does persist in trying to join the group and is successful in the end.

One episode of twenty-two minutes occurred when a police officer came to visit, talked to the children and then allowed each of them to sit in the car. Samuel, who is interested in machinery and cars, and at home with his father takes books out of the library on these topics, was totally engaged during this episode.

Successful strategies for self-initiated group, caring or 'togetherness' play

Samuel is also developing some successful strategies in self-initiated group or 'togetherness' play where there are no obvious rules. Here are two examples from our observations (*Caring for Another* and *Protecting a Play Partnership*) and two examples from the teachers' recorded observations during this time (*Taking the Initiative in Pretend Play* and *Participating in a Joint Construction Task*).

> ### Caring for Another (phase two)
>
> Samuel participates enthusiastically in a group game of racing to the centre of a circle in the sandpit to pick up an object (organised by the teacher). When there is a collision, Laurie gets hurt. The teacher takes Laurie inside, with a large group of children following. Samuel remains with Laurie after the other children have returned to play, looking after him and showing concern. He and Laurie then play (run around) together.

> ### Protecting a Play Partnership (phase two)
>
> Samuel and Ossie are playing in the sandpit where they have one digger each.

Samuel: (makes digger sounds) Mine wants to go rocking I think. Oooh –ow! (the diggers crash).
Ossie: Sorry!
Samuel: D-d-d-d. (makes digger noises). Stop in a minute.
Ossie: Shall we go next, like soon?
Samuel: Yeah. (makes engine noises) You can never crash me. You can never crash me.
Ossie: Yes I can.
Samuel: Move out of the way! (laughs) Sorry! Sorry! I said sorry! I've found something. I've got something ….
They begin by digging holes side by side, and then they develop a collaborative game together, with both of them defending their play against others who want to dig in 'their' space and use their diggers. They each dig their holes side by side. They jump off together and collect buckets and spades and start making castles – talking to each other. They mix the sand in the buckets, carry them into the gazebo (a nearby open-sided shelter) and start eating 'muffins' that they have made in the sandpit.
Ossie: This is our house.
Another child comes along and starts filling in their hole and Samuel follows Ossie's lead;
Ossie: Don't put sand in my hole.
Samuel: Yeah. Don't! (child leaves).
Ossie brings a big yellow box over.
Ossie: Here is the oven.
They hop back on their diggers and then go back inside their 'house' to 'eat'.

Samuel is confident in cooking-and-eating pretend play. In phase one Samuel enjoyed playing at the dough table with Simon, where they played cooking and eating games, facilitated by a toy oven and cooking utensils nearby. This game has now been transferred to the sandpit, without Simon and without the realistic props. Six weeks later, not observed by the researchers, the teachers wrote up a Learning Story for his portfolio in which Samuel, Sally, Jack and Tom are playing 'restaurant' in the sandpit together. Samuel tells the teacher, who role plays as a customer, that he is cooking "chicken on rice, nachos and macaroni".

The following pretend play initiative was recorded by the teachers just before we visited, and this story was also included in his portfolio for the family to read. The common symbolic language includes making the noises of engines and mechanical tools.

Taking the Initiative in Pretend Play
(Excerpt from a Learning Story, written by a teacher just before phase two)

Samuel was playing outside in the carpentry area where he found a piece of wood and pretended it was a saw. He went to the playground and pretended to cut the big tree. He made a cutting noise – then he walked to the sandpit and showed his saw to Alan and pretended to cut the bucket with his saw and made noises. Alan said "Can you make a big spade for me?" Samuel said "OK. I will cut some wood with my saw and will make you a wooden spade".

> Then he waved goodbye and said "I am going to the shop to buy some more
> things for the spade"... *Teacher's analysis (abridged):* Samuel shows an
> interest in pretend play, was involved for a sustained period of time, interacted
> with other children and expressed his ideas.

A month after our phase two visit to the centre, the following observation was also
recorded by the teachers as a learning story for Samuel's portfolio. Sally had taken
the initiative to make a kite. Samuel, who has had mixed success in being accepted
by Sally as a playmate, has copied her. The story records his comment: "We tried it
and it worked, me and her". The joint activity ("me and her") has been
documented, made public, available for revisiting at the kindergarten or at home.
Here is the story, also slightly abridged.

> *Participating in a Joint Construction task*
> *(Excerpt from a Learning Story, written by a teacher, between phase two and
> phase three)*
>
> Inside at the collage, Sally and Samuel came and showed me their kites.
> Then Sally explained how she made her kite. She said she first drew a picture
> on her paper, cut it out, then got this blue string and stapled one end to the
> pointed end of her picture and tied the other end to a straw. Samuel then said
> "Yes, I did the same too. I drew a happy face picture and she drew a diamond
> shape one." Sally smiled, then explained why she tied the other end of the
> string to the straw. "It is because if I want my kite to fly up high I will untie the
> string to let go of the kite and if I want it to come down low I can wind it around
> a straw like that" (she demonstrated). "That is right" replied Samuel, "We tried
> it out and it worked, me and her". *Teacher analysis (excerpt):* Sally and
> Samuel worked out strategies cooperatively, planning to complete their task.

Samuel's mother reported that he was keen on kite-flying, and that they often fly
kites at the park on a Saturday.

A fourth story in Samuel's portfolio at around this time tells the story of Samuel
being read a story about a dinosaur. When the reading was finished he sought out
Jacob and gave him the book. The teacher said she was surprised by this, because
she had had the same idea: Jacob was fascinated with books about dinosaurs. She
added "Samuel must have been observing Jacob as we, the staff, had".

Tasks and artefacts mediating group play

Frequently opportunities for group or peer play were mediated by a teacher.
Equally frequently they were mediated by the tasks and artefacts: a bean bag
activity in which one child throws to another, a sandpit in which there are two
diggers, trolleys that need one person to push and one to steer and a teacher to
make the activity purposeful and challenging, tractors and trailers where Samuel
can drive and invite children to ride. Earlier on the day when the police officer
came to visit, one long episode of play occurred when Billy arrived new to the
morning session from the afternoon (younger children) session: Samuel recognised

him and they participated in an extended reciprocal interaction around trolley play. Each boy mimicked the other throughout the episode, repeating each other's comments and actions. Samuel then appeared to focus on mastering the activity of driving the trolley, and the teacher gave him some instructions, which he followed. Both the children did some of the driving although Samuel was the more skilled and it seemed that by mutual consent he did most of the driving. A number of trolleys, a child with a Stop sign, and a teacher all contribute to mediating the play.

Trolleys (phase two)

Samuel starts to play with Billy who has a soccer ball. They are playing at one end of the playground, where a soccer net is set up. The ball keeps rolling down to the gate and Samuel runs after it – he is goal keeper, standing in the net and running after the ball when it goes past. ...

They run off and get a trolley and Billy pushes Samuel in it. They have a few crashes as they get steering and speed sorted out.

Samuel:	Oh! I'm going very fast ... ha ha ... faster! Go Billy, go. Oh no! Ok man. Go faster Go, go. Very fast! Push. Faster... Slow.
Teacher:	No, you need to turn your steering wheel. Don't push him so he crashes. And you need to turn your wheel like that. You don't just let it crash into a building. You need to drive carefully. Careful driving Samuel.
Samuel:	Whoa. ... Watch out.
Teacher:	When you drive, remember Samuel, turn your wheel. You don't just collide with someone, you need to turn your wheel. Looking! Looking! Like that! Turn it.
Samuel:	Go go go.
Billy:	We're going faster now.
Samuel:	Yeah ... Why are we going slow?
Billy:	We're not crashing. We're not crashing. ...
Samuel:	Zoe! (teacher) We're not crashing.
Teacher:	No, you're not. You're driving very (well?)
Samuel:	We're not crashing any more, isn't it?

The teacher puts a rubbish bin in the middle of the path for them to drive around. They understand the meaning of the move, and drive around it. The teacher puts some cones out – "It's a race. It's a race. It's a race', says Billy. A bit more traffic (other trolleys) is encountered and they negotiate their way around it, avoiding crashes. After 8 – 10 minutes they swap places, and Billy has to learn how to steer. The teacher positions Samuel as the tutor.

Samuel:	Hey! You're going the wrong way! Wait!
Teacher:	You can turn your wheel and come around that side, by the deck. You show him Samuel. ...
Samuel:	You have to stay like that. You not turn this way, that way. See, do you know? ... Come on, go, go!

They crash through the cones and then have to stop to straighten them up again. Gradually Billy becomes more skilled but they still get stuck in a pile of leaves. Another child joins in by putting a stop sign in front of them; they wait and then he waves them on. After six minutes Samuel is back driving with Billy pushing. They spend some time lining up cones in exactly the right way.

In the previous episode, it was the teacher plus the equipment that mediated the expertise. In a final phase two episode it is artefacts or resources that mediated the social play. For thirty-five minutes Samuel drives a tractor-trailer, picking up and dropping off children as he completes a circuit around the playground. (Joseph hops off and on: "Pick up me in eighteen minutes – okay?" Samuel: "Good"). He invites children (and teachers) by name to take a ride in the trailer; some said yes and some said no, and occasionally he relinquishes the driver role and rides in the trailer himself. When the trailer is full (two passengers) another child has to push as well as the tractor driver scooting with his or her feet. For all the players, and of special interest to Samuel perhaps, it is okay to say yes or no to participation; the choice is built into the affordance of the game, and saying no does not imply exclusion or rejection.

Doing school

There was little opportunity in the classroom for Samuel to develop his interest in interacting with other children informally and on topics of interest, except at lunchtime and morning tea break. And Samuel appeared to want a nearby adult to mediate group activities. He seemed to be constructing opportunities for social play in the classroom by writing very short stories ('the mouse waitd and waitd and waited' and 'I like to play', for instance) because the reward for finishing the writing task quickly is to play – and sometimes to lead – games like 'I Spy', or to generally play around at the group-time mat until the others are finished.

In a way, the pattern of short adult-organised tasks in phase two has continued at school, although in phase three there is no choice about the matter, and the extended *Trolleys* interaction with Billy in phase two, for instance, mediated by an adult, would not be possible. The activities in phase three are shorter as well: on the second day of observation (from nine a.m. to three p. m.) there were seventeen curriculum events or activities, with a few moments of roll-taking, informal group and tidying up in between. Ten of these activities took ten minutes or less; four took eleven to twenty minutes, and three were twenty-one to thirty minutes in length. The three long episodes were when he was taken out of class to join the EAL group, provided with books for independent reading, and listened to poetry reading when another class joined his classroom. Except for the EAL episode, informal play on the mat, a ten minute exercise session outside, all these activities were linked to reading, writing and arithmetic. Samuel has some literacy skills and he enjoys knowing what to do, but he is also interested in activities like kite-making and joint problem-solving with tracks and wheeled toys. His hand is often the first up in the large class group and he usually has the right answers (and so is frequently called on to answer) – for instance, a word beginning with s (seed), and a maths addition (5 + 4, which he successfully answers using his fingers). His teacher tells us that Samuel enjoys maths, and is always keen to participate in mathematical tasks.

LEARNING IN THE MAKING

Disposition-in action: work in progress

This section looks at the three dispositional components (authoring, recognising opportunity and connected knowing) introduced in chapter two, to structure our interpretations of work in progress on being and becoming a group member. Authoring, recognising opportunity and connected knowing as descriptors for being ready, willing and able emerged from the triadic definition of a disposition, the data in this study, and the literature on learning continuity; although they are separated here, all three worked together, building diverse learning dispositional journeys towards being and becoming a group member.

Authoring.   There were two aspects of authoring in this facet of reciprocity: *becoming a group member* (entering a group) and *being a group member* (taking on a role or an identity associated with the purpose of the group, and assisting to sustain togetherness by negotiating, improvising, and assisting others). Authoring as a collective disposition to look after the younger children had been established as a dispositional milieu at Buzz's childcare centre, and this was taken up by Buzz and Clara as they took responsibility to look after Sylvia, taking on identities as 'grown-ups'. Ofeina and Samuel were, by phase two, both positioned by teachers as experts and as teachers.

Indications of authoring while *being a group member* included the children taking on or constructing recognised roles: as Ron (in Harry Potter), a cook, an expert driver, a screen printer, a person who cares about and for others, someone who knows what to do. It included making meaning together, taking on and letting go leadership roles, teaching, helping and protecting others. Ofeina being playful with Kyung-Ja when they were painting, and seeing herself as a competent teacher and helper, would sustain group play for her. In all the early childhood centres, by phase two, the children had come to enjoy working and playing in pairs and small groups. There was an affective and desirable factor to group work, one that made it worthwhile to manage conflicts, persevere after rejection, and seek opportunities to interact with others. These case studies suggest that while young people may have the inclination to interact in groups, to belong, to be an author and an actor in group enterprises, they are often yet to develop the capacity for recognising opportunity or a wide-ranging repertoire of connected knowing. Early years programmes and practices play a significant role in connecting these three components of a disposition together.

Recognising opportunity.   Children recognised and constructed spaces for social play, and this became especially noticeable at school, where they had to be imaginative in order to do this. Samuel relished those times of 'free play' between set activities, doing set tasks as rapidly as possible to maximise the times for free play and interaction with peers. Ofeina formed a relationship with the other children that she had not met before in her small EAL group. Buzz seized the opportunity to chat about a diverse range of topics and to start a joking relationship with his partner at News time at school, managing to listen and contribute, and then to later construct a plausible presentation to the class. All three children became attuned to diverse partners, and had to improvise from what they already knew in order to recontextualise their social capacities. Ofeina spent time in phase one observing and listening in, and then tried a number of strategies: offering a cup of tea (as her mother would have done) was one, and offering help was another. It was trial and error, and was sometimes successful. Samuel, who had been rebuffed a number of times by Sally, successfully worked with her on a kite-making project, and his comment that "We tried it out and it worked, me and her" was written down by a teacher and could be revisited in a portfolio as an affirmation of his success and a reminder of a good strategy. He soon learned, at the early childhood centre and at school, not to take children he didn't know very well by the hand. For all three of these children, the loss of a constant play partner when a close friend turned five and went to school afforded the opportunity – usually supported by teachers, group activities and objects or equipment – for them to learn how to play with diverse others.

Connected knowing. The children brought knowing from home experiences, and incorporated them into their play. Samuel called on his repertoire of 'funds of knowledge' (González, et al., 2005) from prior experiences at home and the library of cooking, diggers and kites in order to join or form purposeful groups. Buzz's talent and passion for art at home also appeared during phase one and three, and the Harry Potter theme had been learned by him when he had watched the video many times at his grandparents' house. Samuel brought his interest in vehicles to the trolley play and made connections with prior events: on one occasion, when he was in a group working with clay and confused by the instructions, he remembered earlier work with play dough and ran inside and brought out a pattern-making resource (a carved-face rolling pin) from the dough table, rolled out the clay and made a patterned tile that interested the rest of the group. The children were building up 'subject-based' expertise that would later be useful for becoming a legitimate group member later (Ofeina found her skills at solving jigsaws came in handy at school). But they were building up 'disposition-based' social knowing as well: learning to notice, recognise and respond to the viewpoints and interests of others, and recognising their own strengths and abilities in this area. They were developing complex skills in language, in order to co-construct meaning with others, and they were able to recognise and use common languages, as Jack had done in chapter three. They were becoming very attuned to the different protocols in different activities (group games with rules were different from open-ended pretend play, for instance), and this knowing would serve them in good stead when they met the protocols of schooling.

The design

A number of features of the educational design in these case studies appeared to afford, invite, engage, provoke – and hinder or ignore – this facet of reciprocity.

Some of these are discussed here: affective engagement and relationships, multiple languages and common plot-lines, and resources and tasks.

Affective engagement and relationships.   A powerful factor supporting children's acceptance of each other and their ongoing harmonious play was their degree of familiarity with each other and the group. Settings where peers are very familiar through attendance at the same centre from an early age (for example Buzz's centre) seem to support complex play. Such familiarity allows children to take up where they left off and continue with shared activities or pretend play, continually challenging each other to produce more complex and elaborate ideas and activities. Familiarity seems to also help children to adjust quickly and deal with difficulty. Ofeina's Tongan background was recognised and supported in her kindergarten, and she was comfortable in the presence of the many familiar adults (parents and relatives) from the community, who were welcomed into the kindergarten. That her home language was part of her early childhood setting, was also important in helping her to develop a feeling of belonging in the group. All the children were content at the beginning to be peripheral participants who watched and listened, but the environment invited them to gradually move towards being more active participants. The presence of a friend, Simon, who spoke Malayalam helped Samuel to settle in to his early childhood centre, and the supportive scaffolding for his developing English provided by his teachers was also crucial. The demography was relevant here. In early children centres in New Zealand, children lose friends when they go to school at age five. In our case studies this loss was keenly felt by the children, but it appeared to us that it also created opportunities for them to transfer this love of social play to perseverance in new social contexts. This recontextualisation required improvisation and the development of new strategies. Buzz missed his friend Clara when she went to school, but he then established close relationships and sustained play that developed a 'Harry Potter' theme in complex ways, as the children negotiated their way through minor conflicts for the common purpose of a shared story-line. Ofeina in phase two missed Leah when she left to go to school, but this enabled her to make more of her own choices and to appropriate Leah's leadership role. Samuel missed Simon – who could speak Malayalam with him – when he went to school, but the teachers assisted him when they introduced games with rules and included themselves in pretend play; he had learned some strategies from his previous experiences, and he called on his developing ability in English and his interest in 'cooking' and 'restaurant' play to establish new play partners. The mixed age setting at Buzz's centre was relevant to his journey. It afforded the opportunity for the older children to exercise responsibility and take a nurturing protective role with younger children, as when Buzz and Clara looked after Sylvia. Charles was a year younger than Buzz and Jeff, but seemed to have no difficulty co-ordinating his play and sharing themes with the two older children. On the other hand the smaller children, like Sylvia, were vulnerable to both the boisterousness of the bigger children and the perhaps overwhelming nature of the older children's protection and care. A mixed age setting has the advantage of providing older children a role as expert peer support and guide in a collective ethic of care. But even in the kindergarten setting, where the children came from a narrower age band, with support from the teachers and the tasks, Ofeina strengthened her enthusiasm for acting as a helper and resource for other children; and Samuel cared for Laurie when she was hurt, demonstrated concern by staying with her when other people had left, and was a teacher for Billy.

The teachers were central to these children's capacity to enter and sustain groups: setting up groups for art activities and for games with rules, allocating roles (as experts and teachers) inside the groups, providing resources and artefacts, suggesting activities, and allocating time and space. They also talked to the children, illustrating for Samuel, for instance, the processes of sharing meaning with others – bridging and structuring, as Rogoff would describe it. Teachers played a role in helping children maintain reciprocity but they did not always seem to find it easy to directly influence peer acceptance or friendship. They stepped in to supply extra resources (providing another tent in Buzz's story) and suggested alternatives (making another wand) but being and becoming a group member appeared to be most likely to develop in a combination of relationships and resources or tasks that afforded, invited or provoked group membership. The teachers and the parents took roles in pretend play with Samuel, as they had done in the childcare centre with Lisa, in chapter three. There is a difference of opinion amongst early childhood researchers and teachers on what the role of the teacher should be in children's peer play. Corsaro (2003) argued that teachers should not be involved in encouraging children to accept others into their play, but Paley (1992) was convinced that teachers could help children to learn the rules of social justice and help them understand how it feels to be left out. Katz & McClellan (1991) argue strongly that a curriculum which focuses on ideas, activities and other intellectual concerns, rather than who gets the upper hand, is important in encouraging harmonious social interactions. Smith & Barraclough (1995) found that early childhood teachers wanted to prevent children feeling upset or hurt and believed that they had an important part to play in supporting children's developing social skills. They recognised that conflicts had a valuable role in helping children understand others' perspectives and reach solutions through problem solving, but they were wary of leaping in unnecessarily so that children did not learn to manage their own conflicts. There is, therefore, a delicate balance between sensitive intervention and standing back, and this is a matter of careful professional judgement. Of course, a 'conflict' to be resolved, from a teacher's perspective, may for the children be an enjoyable tension or trouble that keeps the affect at an optimum level.

Resources and tasks. Artefacts and equipment were mediating group activities and reciprocity: for example, a 'family corner' with telephones, an outdoor play area where inside furniture (chairs) are allowed, and trucks and trailers, together with permission for mildly dangerous play. The physical affordances of these artefacts are mediated by teachers' monitoring and guidance; and the history of their use. When Ofeina and Kyung-Ja careered down the sloping pathway they were continuing a game that had been invented by Joseph (in chapter nine). The tent provided a space for Buzz's 'secret group' where he felt empowered to protect Sylvia from the onslaught of other children, who were banished to another tent. In Samuel's trolley episode the teacher adapts the 'going fast and crashing' game that Samuel and Simon are playing, by teaching the two children how to steer the trolley and adding some obstacles for them to steer around. Other children start to become involved – other trolley teams and a boy with a Stop sign. Trolleys on flat land are classic artefacts that afford dyadic play: one child has to push, and one to steer. So are tractors and trailers: a driver and a passenger. The existence of many possible activities and artefacts (the tractor-trailer, the trolley, the carpentry and collage activity) for joint activity, encouraged Samuel to become mutually engaged with others, and to be resilient about being rejected. For Samuel, these activities and artefacts are a good match with his interest in engines and vehicles, together with his disposition towards social play with one or two peers and an adult nearby. Objects provided a common focus of attention for children which could encourage reciprocity in small groups, but children were not always skilled at co-ordinating their activity, and compromise and negotiation was necessary. Since many conflicts are around objects, scarcity may lead to difficulties between peers as in the case of the argument over access to the tent. Addition of extra resources can defuse conflict and allow play to continue, as for example when an extra tent was put up in Buzz's centre. Having to share resources did, however, encourage children to see the point of view of the other person, find ways to collaborate, resolve differences - and perhaps add an interesting note of tension and trouble. Ofeina's role as helper was often in the context of acquiring a knowledgeable skill, for example doing puzzles and screen printing, alongside other children, and she was keen to pass on her expertise to others. Although she initially experienced rejection of her offers to help, she persisted with using her expertise to assist other children, often very successfully. Ofeina and Samuel learned about 'turns', and how to be strategically flexible about them. Group games with rules, and small group art activities, assisted Samuel and Ofeina to become part of adult-initiated and scaffolded small groups, and at school the routine of joining the EAL group of eight children appeared to establish, temporarily at least, a group for Ofeina to play with during the morning break and lunch-time. A skipping game revealed Ofeina's competence, and provided her with another leadership role, and the puppet-making and screen-printing activities also enhanced her public identity as a competent learner.

Multiple languages and common plotlines. Having similar or complementary knowledge was another factor which helped support reciprocity, as we have discussed in the previous chapter. Buzz, Jeff and Charles were immersed in the Harry Potter story and played with flying cars and wands for many hours. Ongoing conflicts and minor disputes were resolved in the interest of the bigger story: Buzz illustrated a skill at compromising, for example, when he said that the vehicle he and his friends were travelling could be *both* a flying car and a train, when there was a disagreement. It seemed that these early friendships, when common meaning is created in mutual activity, could readily survive occasional rejections. Sustained groups tended to be all girls, or all boys, but this was not always the case (as with the strong friendship between Buzz and Clara). Ofeina's interest and skill in establishing friendship also became increasingly evident in phase two: family pretend involving offering cups of tea and making rice cakes and dumplings was a productive ways of engaging with others. Samuel's initial shared knowledge with Simon of a language which others did not know drew them together in phase one, and his shared interest in cooking and restaurants enabled new play partners in phase two. His interest in and knowledge about machinery and technology (enhanced at home by the books he took out of the library) enabled a shared interest in diggers with Ossie, with Alan in pretending to cut down trees in carpentry, with Sally in making kites in the collage area, and with Billy in driving trolleys. Teachers assisted with the language development that would contribute so centrally to group play partners' communication with each other. An emphasis on art in Samuel and Ofeina's kindergarten provided another group language for the children, taking some of the pressure off being verbal in English for these young English learners. Recording episodes of successful social play in documents like Learning Stories made them public, accessible in portfolios for revisiting by families, children and teachers, and providing a documented 'dictionary of experiences' (Rinaldi, 2006) that afforded and invited review and reflection.

BUILDING RESILIENCE

Initiating and Orchestrating Projects

> Being able to form projects is not a minor competency. It is essentially a linkage with life and the world that presupposes a sense of identity, will, energy, and self-esteem, poles apart from shame and depression. (Perrenoud, 2001, p. 135)

The case studies in this chapter illustrate the initiating and orchestrating of projects by three children. We have described this as a facet of resilience, one of the "plurality of meanings individuals negotiate in their self-constructions as resilient" (Ungar, 2004a, p. 354; see the discussion on resilience in chapter two). In this chapter we explore the ways in which learners were orchestrating (or attempting to orchestrate) people and resources (often in cross-disciplinary ways) in order to pursue projects that mattered to them. The projects that we observed during this research study frequently made connections beyond the world of the early childhood centre and the school classroom, so the learning in them was seen by learners and teachers and families as learning that matters. They also called on funds of knowledge (Gonzales et al., 2005) or 'virtual school bags' (Thomson & Hall, 2008) that children take to the early childhood centre or school from other communities, especially home. Etienne Wenger makes this point:

> [T]eachers, parents, and other educators constitute learning resources, not only through their pedagogical or institutional roles, but also (and perhaps primarily) through their own membership in relevant communities of practice. ... What students need in developing their own identities is contact with a variety of adults who are willing to invite them into their adulthood. (Wenger, 1998, pp. 276 & 277)

Guy Claxton, in his book about Learning Power describes being resilient as being "ready willing and able to lock onto learning" (Claxton, 2002, p. 21), to stay focused in spite of (or because of) interruptions, setbacks and errors. He maintains that there are four aspects to this resilience: absorption (being rapt in the flow of learning), managing distractions (recognising and reducing interruptions), noticing (seeing and sensing what's out there), and perseverance (stickability). He notes that we attend to what we find interesting.

> We attend to what our brains find novel, interesting, important, enjoyable, perplexing, disturbing or threatening. To get someone to lock on to learning, the object or activity has somehow to matter to them. (Claxton, 2002, pp. 20–21)

Taking an interest and locking on to something that matters can be perceived as a first step in the deep engagement and task involvement which is part of resilience (Csikzentmihalyi, 1996; Dweck, 2006; Goodenow, 1992). This chapter discusses three children, David, Leona and Jeff, all of whom illustrated what we saw as two of the 'verbs' of resilience that might include this absorption, self-management, resourcefulness, and perseverance: initiating and orchestrating projects.

DAVID

David's activities at the early childhood centre and school reflected a capacity for focused engagement on projects that connected with experiences from other times and other places. All of these projects have strong connections with places and people other than the here and now, and appeared to be interesting to David because of those connections. He makes 'concrete' and 'muffins' in the sandpit, making connections to his experience of making concrete and cooking at home as well as to the making of concrete in a building site a few doors down from the childcare centre, a site that all the interested children have been visiting regularly. He practises being a cricketer and a cyclist, referring to his knowledge of cricket at the local cricket ground and to cyclists at the local 'speedway' race track. Associated with these projects there are examples throughout our observations of David caring about others who were different from him: younger, newer to the classroom, or less skilled.

David lives with his parents, older sister and younger brother. His father is a marine mechanic and his mother works in the office, looking after the books for their business. One of the children's grandmothers lives close by, as does one of their cousins. When we visited the family during phase three, he was enjoying going to music classes once a week, and said he would like to start playing rugby. His older sister is a tap dancer, and his mother commented that he followed his sister around as she practised, and she has considered enrolling him in tap classes as well. One of his early childhood teachers commented that David liked to dance with a group of children when they had music playing, and would pretend (using blocks) to strum a guitar. David's parents told us that David had an inclination to sit back and watch before becoming involved in something new.

David was observed at a childcare centre's 'over-twos' programme. He had begun attending the under-twos programme (down the road) at twenty months, and attended for three days a week until he started attending the morning programme at the local kindergarten (a sessional programme for three- and four-year-olds) just before he turned four. Although by the time we met him he was attending only one full day a week, he was in a sense an 'old hand' at the childcare centre and his mother now felt very comfortable with the staff there too. She said that leaving children there was like leaving them with the family. At phase three, David went to the same school as his older sister.

Constructing projects

David was an enthusiastic participant in carpentry activities; he both persisted with difficult tasks, and sought help from others when he needed it. When the researchers observed him at carpentry with another younger child, Jason, using a screwdriver to screw a piece of wood back onto a wooden box that was part of the carpentry equipment, the researcher commented to the teachers that "He follows up. When you couldn't find the screwdriver and three screws he didn't let you stop looking". A teacher replied: "That's typical David. The Friday before, they (the same two children) spent forty minutes to an hour *unscrewing*" this same piece of wood (setting up the project for the following Friday!). The transcript of this episode also illustrates his assistance to the other child, Jason, and the teacher's adding complexity by introducing the words 'anti-clockwise' and 'clockwise' (after her good-humoured reaction to this task of undoing the previous week's work: "oh David").

Using the Screwdriver at Carpentry (phase one, extract from transcript)	
David:	These are pretty hard to screw, have you ever tried screwing one in – you try and screw it in Jason, you try and screw it in.
Jason:	Hard.
David:	Good, Jason. If you turn it that way, that means open. Shall I do it? ..... Watch out Jason because it might fall on your toes .....
Teacher:	Did you take the screws out again – oh David.
David:	Good that's better, I took them all out again.
Teacher:	You did too. So you figured out which way to go to take them out and which way to turn to put them in.
David:	This way – that way's out.
Teacher:	That's right, that's anti-clockwise and clockwise to put them in. Have you finished using the screwdriver or are you going to do some more work?
David:	No.
Teacher:	You're not going to do anymore? Shall I put it away somewhere safe?
David:	Can I have a turn on the motorbike?

In phase one, we observed seven episodes of joint attention for David: playing cricket, riding a bike (and watching the lawn mowing next door), swimming (splashing and kicking and jumping), sandpit with trucks, mat time listening to a story, digging in the sand pit and making a road, and the screwdriving task at the carpentry table. Each of these episodes were sustained for between twenty and thirty-one minutes. And each of them made connections to activities that were familiar to David outside the centre, and roles that interested him: cricketer, bike rider (later at mat time he announced "We're going to the speedway next week"), swimmer, concrete-maker, reader, and someone who uses technology to fix things.

> ### *Playing Cricket (phase one)*
>
> It is a warm summer's day, and David suddenly decides that he wants to play cricket. He seeks out the equipment, persuades a teacher to assist him to search for a ball, and then gathers a 'team' together. He has a turn at batting, and then becomes the wicket keeper, fields the ball and throws it back to the bowler. The game stops when he and Harry both dive for a ball and bang their heads together.

> ### *Riding Bikes (phase one)*
>
> He rides for half an hour on a (three-wheeler) cycle around a track designed in a loop around sandpit and climbing equipment, with a slope at one point and a number of corners. There are not enough cycles to go around; when one child calls out: "Five minutes is up now; your turn is up now David" he hops off and waits until another child relinquishes his cycle.

During this phase, one of the teachers expressed some anxiety about his counting and his reading skills ("Recognition of name, when we're doing name games – who starts with 'D'? – he hasn't got (the) concept...."). One of the teachers commented: "Counting one to one is quite difficult for him" and another teacher said "The counting thing I've been trying to follow that on and he'll just change the subject". They nevertheless provided a programme in which he was given permission to stay with focused tasks for as long as they last, and they recognised his interest in problem-solving, especially if he could orchestrate a group of others to work with him.

Extended projects

Six episodes of focused engagement were observed in phase two, and all of them also connected with projects of interest to David outside the centre. The episodes include extended play in the sandpit: making muffins (thirty-five minutes), watching concrete-making near the centre and then 'making concrete' in the sandpit (one hour), building a construction from pipes and wet sand (a version of the concrete-making earlier in the day: fifty-eight minutes), and setting up an elaborate game with tractors. He also has a conversation about cooking with one of the teachers.

> ### *Making Muffins (phase two)*
>
> David is in the sandpit with two younger children. He has taken on the role of the Dad. He fills the muffin trays and puts the muffins in the stove. Another boy has joined the game and announces he is the 'five year old brother', and during the episode David refers to him all the time as 'brother'. He pats sand down on top of the stove then adds water and slurps it all around. "I've got tired of cooking" he announces to no one in particular. 'Brother' has made him a coffee. "No, I really don't need a coffee brother" David says and scrubs the stove, then a cooking pan, with a brush. A number of children join him by taking the cooking equipment to the water trough for scrubbing and cleaning.

David later has a lengthy conversation with the teacher about making biscuits. He tells her that he made afghans (a type of biscuit) and ate them at home with Dad. Together he and the teacher reconstruct the recipe. The following is an extract from the transcript.

Teacher: And what sorts of ingredients do you need to make afghans. Do you remember?
David: Sugar.
Teacher: Yeah. Sugar will help make them sweet, won't it. What else do you need?
David: Um. Butter.
Teacher: Yes, lots of butter in afghans. Yeah.
David: And flour.
Teacher: Flour. Yes. You definitely need flour when we make, when we are cooking afghans.
David: And water.
Teacher: There might be a bit of water in it, I'm not sure.
David: Jug water.
Teacher: I think maybe some milk. I'm not sure.
David: No. Just the water.
Teacher: Just the water you think?
David: Just jug water.
Teacher: Jug water. You have water in the jug in the fridge do you?
David: No, we've got a real jug with a switch.....
Teacher: Do you remember what it is that makes that chocolate taste? (David: Yum) Do you know what you need to put into afghans to make them all chocolaty, do you remember what that ingredient is called? That one would be the cocoa.
David: Cocoa.

Another episode provides an insight into the curriculum at this centre. A house is being built two doors away from the centre, and the children regularly visited the site and commented on the processes and progress. The teachers took photographs and videos, and re-visited the building with the children on a number of occasions. Some of the children contributed drawings for the teachers to construct a video story that will be revisited with the children.

> ### Making Concrete (phase two)
>
> The children all go for a walk to see the concrete mixer pouring the concrete. David watches with great interest. He talks about using 'cement' to make the concrete. He goes back to the centre and digs a hole in the sandpit with great enthusiasm. He asks for some water, so the teacher finds the water trough and they fills it with water. They make holes in the sandpit and pour in water and flour to make concrete. Other children are involved in the activity alongside David. It looks as if he has done this before. He is totally focused on the task in hand, determined to get the concrete just right. He gets a [toy]

> tractor and drives it all around. He keeps going back to his original concrete
> and smoothing it out. He runs inside to get one of the teachers to come and
> see. More children join in, including the younger ones, and he shows them
> what to do. He fetches a number of pipes and manoeuvres the pipes into
> place – setting them deep into the 'concrete'. (Field notes)

Later during a home interview he and his mother talk about how he had helped his
father to concrete a wall at home.

Mum:	It might have been the weekend we took the garden out.
David:	And we knocked a wall down.
Mum:	We did, remember there was a big concrete wall. We thought we'd make a new wall.
David:	That's what we decided, we'd make a new wall eh mum?
Researcher:	You did a pretty good job, didn't you, getting those stones.
David:	And the last one was the tricky one.
Researcher:	Why was it tricky?
David:	Because. (pause)
Researcher:	What was the trickiest thing about it?
David:	The concrete.
Mum:	Keeping it up on the wall, because we had limited stones. (Parent interview, phase two)

Engagement in projects at school

We observed eight episodes of joint attention over three days in phase three, after
David had been at school for several months. David's mother commented on how
well he had settled into school, and engaged with school activities. Although she
had described him as a sandpit boy, she said that she didn't think that he played in
the sandpit at school. David had not been interested in writing or drawing before he
went to school, so, although she commented that she thought David would
concentrate at group time (see her comment in chapter one) David's mother's was
surprised to learn from the researchers about his engagement in writing at school.

> And I suppose he's learnt that there are certain times and places for
> things... He went to school a lot easier than I thought he was going to. Out of
> all of them, I thought he'd be the one who would not cope and not settle into
> it, but he just has.... When he started they started a new class, and he was,
> like, one of five in the class, which was just fantastic. It makes a huge
> difference, doesn't it? (Parent interview, phase three)

Although most of the tasks are now initiated by the teacher, David manages to
author some projects 'his way' (a colouring-in activity and 'writing' a story), and
there are two episodes where he does take the initiative: an episode of play on the
senior play equipment, and building a complex aeroplane with stikkle bricks during
a period of free play. Except for the ten minute play on the senior play equipment,
the three episodes described below were focused activities of about half an hour.

When David began school he joined a class of five; by the time we visited, five months later, the number was still small (fifteen), and the teacher was assisted by a teacher aide. The pace was relaxed and half-hour enterprises, with some opportunity for agency, were possible.

Colouring in – David's Way (phase three)

The class has been outside looking at the sun, and talking about the sun in a group and what they might write about the sun. They are now colouring in a picture of the sun, having talked about what colours they might use. The teacher aide asks David about the sun colours – he is colouring in blue and green.

Mrs M (teacher aide): You can do the eyes blue, but mostly orange, red and yellow. (David picks up an orange crayon, and does some colouring). Good boy, David, good listening.

When she has left the table David says "I'm making mine a rainbow colour". He colours in diligently, very focused on what he is doing, ignoring the instruction and using all the colours. He is then invited by Miss J. (the teacher) to dictate a story about the sun. They sit together at the computer and she reads what she has written:

Teacher: The sun is very hot'. Is that all, or do we need a full stop?
David: Full stop.

She asks him to type his name, and she watches while he searches for and types the letters in his name. She prints the story for him and he retrieves it from the printer. She says that she will put it together with his cut-out sun. Miss J. gives instructions about cutting out the sun – cutting around the rays. David starts to do this. He constantly checks what the other children are doing to make sure that he is doing it correctly. Mrs M is helping some of the children cut it out. "Can you help me?" he asks her, She does so, and David continues to cut his sun out in the way shown. He concentrates on what he is doing. Again he says: "Can you help me Mrs M?" "Yes of course – it doesn't look like you need much help, you are doing a good job. It's just these bits around here". He continues to cut out, occasionally waiting for Mrs M to come and help him. Suddenly he realizes that he has successfully finished cutting it out. He gives it to Miss J who reminds him to write his name on the back. He has worked away at this task for twenty-seven minutes.

The Big Kids' Play Equipment (phase three)

The children and teacher then all go outside to look at the sun, to see if its position has changed from earlier in the day. David takes the opportunity to ask the teacher if they can play on the big kids' play equipment. The teacher tells him that this is a very good idea and lets the children run over to the senior playground and play there for ten minutes.

> ### Being a 'Clever Writer' (phase three)
>
> It is mid-morning at school, and the children are sitting on the mat discussing what they are going to write for the scheduled story-writing session. The theme is the sun. David says "I won't need help today; if I need a little bit of help I'll put my hand up. " The routine is to draw a picture first and then write a story about it. He starts drawing, every now and then looking at the letter chart, as the other children are doing, discussing the letters. He leans over to watch Mrs J who is writing for one of the children. The teacher asks him what he is drawing. He replies: "A motor boat". He draws himself in it, and a propeller at the back. He holds his book up to show the people near by: "Look at all my work, look at mine". The teacher says she will come to help him. "I've got my own writing" he says, then asks the teacher aide "Do I start here?". He 'writes'. David says: "I spelt some, look at my story. I went on a boat". The teacher writes on it: "You are a very clever writer. Did you enjoy the boat ride?". He shows it to the researcher. The teacher suggests that he show Mr R. the caretaker, who is working outside the classroom. David presses the book up against the window to show him, and the field notes read "Mr R gives him a big grin and the thumbs up. David marches off with a HUGE grin."

His mother commented that the teacher had also said to her " 'You must come and see David's story that he's written'. So I was expecting really good writing (like) 'Today I went to ... .' No, no, it was nothing like that. And she said "I didn't have the heart to write what it was actually meant to say" so she's just written this nice comment ... It was one of those moments – apparently he went to the window and showed everyone." She added, "It's as if that day, something clicked about writing a story. Up until now, he hadn't attempted to have a go, and that day ...". The teacher later commented that this was the first time he had 'written' something by himself, and that usually he just waits for the teacher to help him. She did not comment on the fact that David had ignored the instruction to write about the sun. She had described him as a 'very clever writer', recognising perhaps, like his mother, that 'something clicked' that day.

Some days later, the class sat in a circle and discussed the theme for story-writing that day: stars and words that might be used to describe them. The teacher demonstrated to them how she would like them to paint a star shape she has cut out ready for them, and to write a story about a star or stars. As Miss J (teacher) sends them off to start their stories she says "And I had some very clever writers last week: have those clever writers come back to school today? I'm hoping they came to school. David, did you come to school today?" David replied "Yeah" and Miss J asks if he is ready to write another story for her. They are then sent to their tables to do the activity and David is one of the first ones to finish his picture and he then 'writes his story', writing a series of letters without asking for help. He 'reads' the story to Miss J and then runs off to get an art shirt to do his painting. He finishes painting his star before anyone else has even started and so he is allowed to choose an activity. He chooses his favourite stickle bricks. The following lengthy (twenty-four minute) episode constructing with stickle bricks is unusual for the school episodes in our study. David had an extended period of time to play a co-

constructed script and author his own project. It is reminiscent of his earlier early childhood centre episodes of sandpit play in phases one and two.

> ### A Construction Project (phase three)
>
> David constructs with stickle-bricks after the writing activity. He is joined by other children as they finish their writing and painting. He selects the stikkle bricks and talks quietly to himself as he plays "I'm going to build a house". He calls out to anyone who might listen: "Look what I've made, I've made a house". He also builds an aeroplane, and, as they complete their writing and their painting, he is joined by six other boys and one girl to play a game about fighting and bombing: "You'll never hurt me – I'm too powerful", "Bang, bang, bang – now I've got big wings that will bang". They talk about 'lasers' and David uses an unusually deep voice as he scripts the story with the others: "We can shoot everyone in town, can't we?".

Caring for and about others

Two episodes observed in phase three illustrate traces of the disposition to include and support younger children in projects that we had observed in phase two. Neither of them are 'projects' of David's choosing, but the disposition to help younger children appeared to have its genesis in projects that mattered to him in phase one and two (and it may be relevant that he has a younger brother at home). The first is during one of the regular morning small group reading activities: 'Alphabet Bingo', where he manages to watch his own card as well as the other children's and offers assistance when they don't see a letter on their card that has been called. The second, an excerpt of which is included here, was while colouring in a worksheet.

> ### Colouring Shapes (phase three)
>
> The children are given a mathematics worksheet, where they have to colour in each shape a particular colour. At David's table two children tell Kenny that he is 'naughty' because he has coloured in with all the wrong colours. David says to them "He's only new, you know". He takes on the role of teacher, and when Kenny asks him if a shape on his paper is a square he responds: "Yes. Orange".

LEONA

Leona too was developing her capacity to author projects in a number of different contexts. At the start of this research project Leona was living with her mother. Later, near the end of the project, Leona's mother re-married and her new partner came to live with them both. Leona's extended family included three sets of grandparents to whom she was close: her mother's, her father's and her step-father's parents. Leona's mother had completed early childhood teacher education qualifications when Leona was very young and she had a very clear idea of what she wanted in terms of early childhood education for Leona:

[I wanted the] holistic learning, and I wanted to send her to a daycare that did not have educational programmes. It was the Learning Stories and the value put on play, and what they can learn that way. ... Because I went to so many around the city, looking, and everyone showed me all these wonderful education programmes in these great books, and showed me these worksheets they were doing, and I'm on another planet. ... Then I rang (the early childhood centre) and I said 'Do you have any educational programme?' and they said 'No, we have a holistic approach to early childhood' and I thought 'thank goodness for that.' And I said 'What about morning tea, do they have to eat morning tea when you tell them to?' and they said ' No, they can eat morning tea when they're ready to eat morning tea, and that way we're not interfering with their play' and I said 'oh, can I book my child in?' (Parent interview, phase one)

When asked in the final interview what she thought Leona had received from her early childhood experience which helped with what she was now doing at school, Leona's mother replied that the early childhood staff put a high value on children's interests (in Leona's case, writing) and taught Leona that she could do things and learn new things. One of Leona's interests, at both the childcare centre and at home, was writing and drawing and making things with paper, pens and sticky tape. In phase one she and two other girls were very involved in an activity of wrapping up presents for each other, and a multitude of things (drawings, collage, small boxes) would be created to then be wrapped up. Her mother commented that Leona and her step-father would often 'hatch schemes' to surprise her mother. She described an incident in the final phase of the project where Leona and her step-father had eaten all the passionfruit and there was none left for Leona's mother, so Leona had shut herself in her bedroom, asked her step-father for help, and created a passionfruit – seeds and all – out of paper, for her mother.

Ten episodes of more than ten minutes' duration were observed on three different days for Leona in phase one. In fact only one of these episodes of play lasted less than twenty minutes and six of them lasted from thirty-one minutes to forty-nine minutes. Leona was often deeply focused in play with two frequent companions, Olivia and Lizzie: working at craft activities (five episodes) and developing pretend play (four episodes). It is folk wisdom to say that "three's a crowd", but Leona's story is, in part (like Jeff's) about the way she came to be ready willing and able to include others in her projects, recognising and enjoying the value of collaborative storylines and problem-solving, and managing the complexity of working with two other children with minds of their own. Leona told the researcher (in a conversation with her, Lizzie, and Olivia) that there was nothing that was difficult for her at the early childhood centre (Olivia said that she found it difficult to draw a proper picture of a fish, and Lizzie said that she found it hard to catch flies – for the frog). She did describe some difficulties that she was having getting on to a swing at home, because it was too high, but her mother commented that she was becoming much more 'adventuresome' on the trampoline. Our observations suggested, however, that during phase one Leona found it difficult to cope with exclusion games played by Olivia and Lizzie. One of the values of participating in the community of an early childhood centre is that the hurly burly of everyday relationships gives children the opportunity to explore the shifting balances between competence and fragility, between being knowledgeable and being confused, between authority and powerlessness. An aspect of resilience is to be able to more confidently bounce back from fragility, confusion and powerlessness, and to recognise where to go for support. We observed Leona's increasing confidence in early childhood centre and school, to take up and construct opportunities to develop projects in complex environments that provide both affordances and constraints. She began to be recognised, and enjoyed this recognition, as an expert and as an authority in some areas.

Confidence mediated by focus on a project

Leona particularly enjoyed making things in several craft episodes. In the first one she drew on the teacher's help, and in the second one she resisted being interrupted by her friends, and stayed focused on the project in hand.

> ### Constructing a Book (phase one)
>
> This is a long episode (thirty-five minutes) involving the teacher and a changing group of five to ten children. Leona is constructing a book. The observation notes comment that Leona is 'involved and interested', 'carefully cellotapes'. The teacher contributes some suggestions to her book construction, and comments on her solution to a problem.
>
> Teacher: (to Leona) Turn all the pages until we can find a space to fit your new picture in.
> Leona: That's too big to fit in there.
> Teacher: It does look a bit big, doesn't it – what could we do to make it fit?
> Leona: Fold it.
> Teacher: We could fold it. Good thinking Leona.

In another craft episode, Olivia calls Leona to go outside but she is focused on what she is doing, and ignores the invitation. A third craft episode a week later, *Working on a Collage*, involves Olivia attempting to exclude her but Leona is able to cope with this, perhaps because of her expertise and intense interest in collage.

> ### Working on a Collage (phase one)
>
> Lizzie and Olivia exclude Leona from looking at the pictures they have cut out and pasted. Leona responds: "Look I can see it. Yes, it's people" while at the same time looking at her own picture carefully. She sticks on another picture with cellotape, cuts and focuses (tongue out). Olivia: "This is SO beautiful". But she won't show it to Leona when she tries to look at it. Leona stays busily cutting out and cellotaping on. This is one of her domains of expertise, and

she has learned to handle (ignore) exclusion inside it with a certain amount of equanimity.

Projects mediated – and interrupted – by others' ideas

Leona spent a lot of time with Olivia and Lizzie but they sometimes had trouble in smoothly orchestrating their interests, as the following episode illustrates.

Searching for a Script (phase one)

Three children – Leona, Olivia and Lizzie – are outside at their childcare centre, searching for a common script. Olivia has the final say, and Leona leaves.

Olivia: Pretend you're stuck on the bars and I saved you.
Leona: Can we go to the park?...can we have a picnic there...I have my hat on and I'll take my togs (and) Lizzie (and) I can go for a swim.
Lizzie: I've got my togs on – I've got my bikinis on.
Olivia: You're walking in the swimming pool and there's whales in there and sharks.
Leona: I know, pretend I got lost.
Olivia: No, you didn't get lost.
Leona: I know, pretend I got lost...

She joins a small group nearby where the teacher is reading a story.

Although the competitive nature of the relationship between Olivia and the others in the project-making threesome often interrupts Leona's focus, in the following episode she draws on the other children's ideas to experiment in her major interest: drawing, decorating and collage.

Drawing with Crayons (phase one)

Leona starts drawing on a card with crayons, copying the coloured stripes Olivia had been working on and shown her earlier. She carefully lines the crayons up in the basket and puts them back after using each one. She has the following forceful and confident exchange with another child, holding her own in the face of an equally confident alternative view (the lead-in to this conversation was not recorded):

Leona: Cos we can't breathe under water.
Child: I can.
Leona: No you can't.
Child: Yes I can.
Leona: No you can't (more forcefully).

This exchange (Yes I can; No, you can't) is repeated several times. On this occasion there is no recall to a higher authority, the exchange is abandoned, and Leona continues with her Olivia-inspired creation.

Positioned as powerless

In one long episode in phase one, Olivia literally holds the power (in a stick that she has designated as the magic wand) and Leona's confidence and resilience fails her. Olivia imaginatively positions Leona as powerless with her 'magic wand', and although Leona appears to want to play (she doesn't leave and retreat to the craft table), any alternative storylines or discourses are made unavailable by the magic wand in Olivia's hands. Olivia uses magic to disempower Leona, then offers to share the wand with Leona and then withholds the promise, randomly changing the rules. Finally, Leona appeals to social justice when Olivia creates another game with secret rules.

> ### The Magic Wand (phase one)
>
> Leona is outside playing with a doll, and arguing with another child about who will have the big box for their 'baby' and who will have the little box. Although Leona had six days earlier been adamant in her disbelief that anyone can breathe under water, she becomes anxious that Olivia's magic wand will indeed make her doll disappear. The children are outside, near a climbing frame that includes a cargo net, steps, a platform, and a slide. Oliva asks: "Would you like me to get my magic wand out and just disappear your baby so there's no problem? Want me to do that or not? You'll never see her again." Leona (sounds anxious): "I don't – I want to have her." Olivia: "I now present to disappear Eeyore and the purple earring – he's gone."

Olivia has promised Leona that she can borrow the magic wand. She (Olivia) has climbed to the top of the cargo net and calls to Leona and invites her to do some magic. However, she sets up some challenging tasks for Leona to complete before she can have the wand, and then keeps changing the rules.

Leona: Can I do some magic now – give it to me – can you give it to me – when are you going to give it to me? Give it to me. Give it to me – Olivia when are you going to give it to me?
Olivia: I'm just seeing if it works.
Leona: Okay.
Olivia: Could you go and get my shoes?
Leona: Yep (she climbs down, gets Olivia's shoes, takes them inside, returns).
Olivia: Leona, just in time, quickly up here – not a minute to lose. Not a minute to lose. Whoever wins this game gets to do the magic and the other two people who miss out do it. Okay you've got to walk down here [the slide] without putting your hands on the side, without falling over. (Leona walks down the slide)
Oliva: I did it, so I get – I did it.
Olivia: No you didn't. Sorry you lost. ....

Olivia says she is making another game, and Leona resourcefully calls on social justice.

Leona: What will we do in this game?
Olivia: I can't tell you because it's a secret. I'll see who wins, if I win or you win.
Leona: No you can't win because it's your game.
Olivia: I know, but I'm.
Olivia doesn't finish the sentence. She then suggests a game of jumping and a small group of children, including Leona, jump about enthusiastically.

Olivia's strategies for positioning Leona as powerless and fragile appear to have been incomprehensible to Leona. However, they play together frequently, so she is presumably accustomed to such a mercurial relationship, even although she could not (yet) bring herself to walk away until she finally called on a principle of fair play ("You can't win because it's your game"). It appeared to be Olivia's employment of *magic* that disabled Leona's authority and – initially at least – her sense of fair play.

Positioning herself as a knowledgeable expert

Finally, however, on the same day and with Olivia as a key player, there is a twenty-eight minute episode in which Leona is calling the tune, as teacher, doctor and vet. Although it is not a well-rehearsed activity, it is one that is particularly interesting to Leona. She is an expert in the roles and routines of teacher, doctor and vet: making connections with what she knows from home experiences (her dog had recently been to the vet to have minor surgery). This interest – and the physical plant here (dolls, high chair, computer) – set up an activity in which she is engaged and positioned by her peers as authoritative.

Taking Dog to Vet (phase one)

Olivia and Leona adapt the typewriter as a dispenser of medicine, using a straw and a paper cup. Leona is the vet and field notes record that she is 'really in role'.
Olivia: Lizzie come up, Lizzie and doggie (play voice).
Lizzie: Doggie has got a broken eye and it suddenly has gone.
Leona: (in an authoritative voice) He has to have an operation – he's going to stay here the night and then it will be all shaved off – the eye will be back on and that fur will be all shaved off because look there's a lump there cos I got to shave that off – zoom, shave and then I'm going to put a new eye in, okay?
Olivia: Okay.
Leona: I'll pick you up today – I'll go to the hairdresser and I'll pick him [the baby?] up at 5 o'clock.
They discuss Lizzie's plans to take Leona's baby (which she is allowing Lizzie to play with) to McDonalds and Leona says she will write it down.
Lizzie: This is my car here.
Leona: Yep – pick him up later.
Olivia: I'm set up now.

> Leona: Shall we get some pens down here and write all about it what happened. Please can I get a pen – two pens, one for you and one for me so we can write down OK?
> Leona changes role and becomes a mother with a sick baby. She puts a doll into a high chair and 'feeds' her with a straw. She adopts a 'special' voice and then appears to go back into role as the doctor or the vet. Olivia is the nurse and asks Leona "What much [medicine] do you want?" Leona holds up some fingers. Olivia dispenses some medicine by putting the paper cup over the lever of the typewriter. She presses some of the typewriter keys, then hands the cup to Leona "There you are". Lizzie comes over and says to Leona: "And you are my teacher and then you turn into my Mum, Okay?" She also uses a special voice when she says to Leona: "Mum, I just came to show you the book I made at my work". They continue a 'sick babies' game for some time, with Leona taking the lead although the script is jointly constructed.

Discussing resilience-related dilemmas with a peer

By phase two, Olivia has gone to school, and of ten episodes, over two days, eight are shared activities and discussions with Lizzie. In two of these episodes Leona and Lizzie discuss their relationship with their mothers. In the first of these, Leona gives information about why she cries when her mother leaves, and Lizzie offers a solution. In the second of these Lizzie appears to rehearse what she would like to have said to her mother about not being allowed to bring her doll to childcare, and Leona offers a solution. The children are now articulating resilience-related dilemmas, and competition and power play in the triad has been replaced by trust and mutual interest in the more easily managed dyad.

> *A Conversation about Crying (phase two)*
>
> The children are reading their portfolios with a teacher.
> Lizzie: (to Leona) How come sometimes you cry [when your mother leaves]?
> Leona: Because.
> Lizzie: But how come?
> Leona: Because I do, because I miss my Mum. I cry because I don't want Mummy to go.
> Lizzie suggests a solution: Well, she can be a teacher here.
> Leona: Because I miss my Mum. Look (changes the subject by referring back to the portfolio) rugby, double rugby. The All Blacks.

Later in this episode, inspired by a mention of her family in the portfolio, Leona, who spends every second weekend with her father, talks to the teacher about going to stay with her father and going to the ballet with him. In another episode in phase two Leona and Lizzie are at the dough table and they begin by negotiating dramatic play roles and co-constructing a storyline about running a café (Lizzie: "Want to be the server and I will be the cooker?" Leona: "No, we will both be the cooker....". Lizzie: "You make some sandwiches too. Put them in the fridge.") The conversation then turns to the topic of managing Lizzie's mother.

Leona: Lizzie, why doesn't your mum let you take [bring] your baby [doll]?
[Lizzie's mother doesn't allow Lizzie to bring her doll to childcare].

Lizzie: Cos my mum thinks it will get lost but I know it won't because I will put it in my bag whenever I don't want to play with it. And she just don't understand me because she thinks I am really going to lose it, but I really aren't.

Leona gives advice: Tell her you're really not going to.

Lizzie: But she still won't let me. (Then she shifts back into role) There we go, a sandwich … .

Sustained projects

The café episode continued as the two main actors continued to develop the script together. Leona says that she is making some food for her baby at their café. Lizzie appears to misunderstand and says that she (Leona) can't do this. Leona threatens to tell a teacher, but then she shifts to a reasonable argument ("Lizzie, when we play this game we've got to give my baby some food otherwise she'll go starving") and this argument is successful. Lizzie then gives in very cheerfully ("Silly me. Eggs and ham"). A teacher arrives and they offer her some food ($10 for a sandwich and $2 for the bacon and eggs). They have a sustained interchange with the teacher over what is for sale and at what prices. During phase two, the partnership with Lizzie appears to be a good context for sustained projects. The project with Lizzie in which Leona made a necklace was described in chapter one; it involved her in using the glue gun and finding out how it worked, with the teacher's help, to make a necklace with a shell and string, and 'sizing' it to make it just the right length.

In the following episode Leona was writing a book, a more complex task than the preparation of a book in phase one, because it includes writing. A teacher took on the role of the teacher of writing, assisting Leona to get it right. Lizzie was making a book at the same time, and the episode is characterised by sustained concentration from Leona (the episode lasts for forty-six minutes), who doesn't stop for morning tea, or when Lizzie has finished her book.

Making a Book (phase two)

Leona has joined pages together to make a book, and she discusses with the teacher what words she should write. The teacher writes words for her on a piece of paper, and Leona copies them into the book. The paper reads: "Leona. Author: Leona. Illustrator: Leona. Once upon a time there was Buddy and George. They were cats".

Leona has drawn a picture of two cats and a person with a smiley face. Lizzie is also writing a book, and Leona watches Lizzie and the teacher as they write together too. The teacher shows Leona how to start a new line on the left hand side of the page. She (the teacher) covers the 'c' in 'cat' and asks Leona what it says. "It" says Leona and quickly changes it to the 'at' in Cat. Another

teacher comes over to remind Leona that she hasn't had her morning tea, but Leona keeps on writing.
[Later in the day they will laminate the pages, and Leona will staple them into a book].

By phase two Leona had been courageous enough to participate in large group activities (although at a 'circle time' at school that we observed, she declined to contribute news when it came around to her turn). When children played a Punchinello game in phase one, Leona watched closely, joining in when there was a group response, but – although she was chosen – didn't want to take centre stage. She and other children expressed great delight when one of the teachers was chosen to go into the middle. By phase two, however, when one of the children was the 'mat time leader' and invited children to come up to 'spot the difference' in two pictures, Leona put her hand up and was chosen. She came up to the front and pointed out the difference.

Challenges and opportunities at school

Despite a relatively problem-free adjustment to school, Leona was still reluctant to part with her mother when she started school. Saying goodbye to her mother at early childhood, and at school, was difficult for her, although her mother thought that the teacher had been very supportive and sensitive.

Leona still finds it hard to say goodbye in the morning, and the teacher says "My son is like that too" and just takes Leona by the hand and says "Come on Leona", and she's quite happy. It's just that she needs that hand to be held. (Teacher interview, phase three)

Leona was now involved in a number of activities such as dancing classes after school. Her dance teacher commented to her mother that although Leona was the youngest in the group, she let her take the exam because "she listens so well and follows instructions". Leona also enjoyed different activities on the computer: writing her own stories, printing them out and then drawing pictures; creating her own Barbie characters on a Barbie website; and playing a Lego game. Other activities she enjoyed were building constructions outside with wood and nails and jumping on her trampoline.

Leona took her expertise at reading and writing to school. At school, seven of the eleven observed episodes of more than ten minutes, over two and a half days, were about reading, writing, colouring in, or collage. In two free time spaces, Leona chose drawing and colouring in, and collage. The other four episodes were: playing with dough, a circle time when everyone is invited, in turn, to contribute some news (Leona declines), an episode on exploring symmetry using shapes, and a science lesson on shadows and light. In the latter lesson, the teacher reads a story to the class and asks "How many light sources are there in your home?" Leona puts her hand up and is chosen: "A light spinning around and it's got dolphins on it and they shine on the roof". The children go outside to look at their shadows. Other events included Assembly and 'Jump Jam' sessions. Although Lizzie from her early childhood centre is in her class, they seldom work or play together; at lunch and play time Lizzie plays with her older sister.

One aspect of what might be described as her being attuned to opportunity at school is the way in which Leona could use her writing skills to keep connected to her family. Martin Packer and colleagues refer here to the role of the children's families in the school classroom in research on 'School as a site for the production of persons':

> Packer and Greco-Brooks (1999) analysed interactions on the first day of first grade, as the teacher worked to establish an impersonal "you" – a person who must raise a hand to be recognized as a speaker, who must follow the classroom rules, pay attention, put their "thinking cap" on – where the students are indexed as a class instead of as individuals. The teacher worked, too, to shift the topic from the family – where the children had taken it, bragging about what made them special – to the way first graders talk about family in the classroom. Discourses moved from the family dog to animals – academic subject matter. Changes were made, then, in context, in topic, and in turn-taking devices. (Packer and Goicoechea, 2000 p. 10)

There was not as much opportunity in Leona's school classroom to talk about her family, as she had done at childcare, where her family appeared regularly in the children's portfolios and were often the topic of conversation. However, Leona's teacher talked about her own family in the first group time of the day, and it seemed clear to the observers that the children were familiar with the teacher's family and interested in her recent trip to visit them. There were thirty stories in Leona's writing book, and sixteen of them were about her family (including her dog): eleven stories were about Mum, Dad (both the mother's husband and her father), Grandma, or Grandpa, and five were about her dog. There is a sense in which she is managing her resilience – if your family is with you, you can cope with the uncertainty of a new context – and although Packer had noted that once one gets to school the family are usually left behind, Leona had found a way to take her family members to school with her as a counterpart to their regular appearance in portfolios and conversations at the early childhood centre.

Leona now teaches others. In one episode a child asked her: "How do you write 'going'?" Leona found the word in the book of common words. The child then said: "I can't draw a bed" so Leona found one in her book and showed her. Other children asked her to help them with their reading; she read 'well-fed bear' for one child, and 'ice-cream' for another. She worked independently in reading and writing, using the resources in the classroom and seldom asking for help. Leona appeared to enjoy the routine and rituals of the classroom.

Playing School at School (phase three)

In one period of free time, after she had completed a collage (helping another child to make a card by folding the cardboard for her), she and two other children play school. Leona and Rosie fold their arms and then follow instructions (The 'teacher' asks them to write their names on a piece of paper). When she completes the task she folds her arms and smiles (a nearby boy, invited to join, says he doesn't want to). The 'teacher' says she will give her drawing to the child who is 'sitting nicely'.

Although Leona had readily chosen and adapted materials at the early childhood centre for her tasks, she seemed hesitant to do so at school. Perhaps still in transition mode after only a few months at school, she is still not confident about what she is 'allowed' to do here.

Seeking Permission (phase three)

Although the craft area includes a box of accessible miscellaneous items, she queues for some time to ask the teacher if she can use the cotton wool, and checks that she can include a feather in one of her constructions. When her group is rolling dough there is only one rolling pin for four children. The researcher suggests using the glue stick. One of the children says "Yes, it works". Leona says "But you're not s'posed to use it for the dough", and she won't use it.

At school, in a new entrant classroom of twenty-four five-year-olds and no teacher aide, the requirement of rules, schedules and set tasks is inevitable. Although Leona was very comfortable with working inside school boundaries, the genre of project-devising (necklace-making, veterinary play, book-making) in early childhood suffered in the more regulated environment of school. She was able and probably ready to construct projects of her own, with others, but she was not yet willing to do so in this place. And indeed there was little space for it. After Leona began school her mother commented on the large size of her class:

> I couldn't stand being the only teacher with 24 four-year-olds [and] there isn't much difference between four- and five-year-olds. (The researchers asked what other aspects would be an ideal classroom for Leona.) Maybe a bit more play.. but I will say that she's just loving the reading and the writing, really. She's just thriving on it. I find it quite interesting: I think it's more important in early childhood for children to be confident and capable, and that confidence thing, rather than reading and writing. And I got the opposite. I've found that Leona's strong point is her reading and writing, and the confidence is not .. But she's got my personality. She's always going to be quiet, and – not the class clown. And never wants to be growled at cos that would be too humiliating. That's me, and I can just see her personality coming through. (Parent interview, phase three)

JEFF

Jeff is a child who carried his expertise intensely into projects, setting very clear personal goals. Jeff lives with his mother (a former hairdresser), his father (a blue collar worker) and his younger brother, Charles. Charles is only fifteen months younger than Jeff, and the brothers play together for lengthy periods, both at home and at the early childhood centre they both attend, which is a mixed age parent co-operative community childcare centre. Their play often turns to conflict and fighting at home, though this does not happen at their early childhood centre. Jeff's mother spoke of having a hard time managing the two boys when they screamed and yelled (which she said occurred frequently). Jeff's father worked for long hours (about sixty hours a week), so the time the children spent with their father was mostly on the weekends: the children were usually asleep in bed by the time he got home from work on weekdays.

Jeff was very much the expert in most of his activities, often preferring to achieve his goals alone or with adult help, but staying deeply engaged in projects for long periods of time. He preferred to do things his way, and at least when observed at just four, was very rarely engaged in joint activities or sharing. He later became more accommodating to peers, but illustrated a disposition to invest intense energy, persistence and concentration in his activities across settings. An early childhood teacher and his mother both described him as a perfectionist. He frequently enlisted an adult to help achieve his goals, and especially during the earlier observations, tended to tell other children what to do, and refused to yield space or objects. His mother described his frequent worries about other children destroying his things (behaviour observed several times at the centre). She ascribed this to having a younger brother who smashed things he had built. She also described Jeff as very emotional, and talked about his crying and saying "I miss you Mum" when she left him at the centre. She said, however, that he really loved going to the early childhood centre, and that this had made her life a lot easier. She commented that Jeff had been upset by changes of staff at the centre: relationships with teachers were particularly important to Jeff, because he perceived them as valued resources. The head teacher at the childcare centre talked about how Jeff created 'things in his mind', and then wanted adults to help him achieve those creations. Teachers tended to find Jeff on the difficult side but to recognise his skill and persistence in initiating creative activities and projects.

> He wants a lot of attention, and if you give it to him he just – wants more of it. You know if you give a little bit you're actually going to be in there for the long haul and I fell into that trap when I first arrived. I gave him that attention, because he gets really busy and involved when you give it to him. …[Intervening discussion about what Jeff likes to do] I think he loves that sort of thing. Like with his farm scene, like he spent ages on it on the first day, but he did have a parent help that was prepared to give that time with him, and then the next day he went straight back into it. So he wanted to see it through, which I thought was a very good thing. (Teacher interview, phase two)

Peers were rather less likely to do what Jeff wanted them to do. But by phase two he had become more skilful in enlisting peers into his projects, and more ready willing and able to join in with other children's projects. Jeff was almost always intensely engaged, and liked to lead and control the flow of play. He was very often the last child to finish an activity and join morning tea, mat time, or other activities organised by the teachers. He talked a great deal when engaged in activities, whether alone or with other children, so his strategies for achieving his goals were often highly visible. His tendency to be emotional (described by his mother) was illustrated when he resorted to yelling and force if he did not get his way with other children. He was very skilful in orchestrating the resources available, and had no problem in asking for help from any adults around (including the observing researcher). In contrast to some of the other children in the study, like Lisa, Samuel and Ofeina, he did not stand back and observe very much, but was usually a key player in activities. Other children were the ones who watched him! He was often intensely proud of his creations, and would show them to other children and even offer to help them with similar projects, but he always had to be the one giving the instructions. (He also enlisted the researcher in documenting his creations, by asking her to come and take a digital photograph of them.) At first he did not seem to want to engage with other children and preferred to engage in solo projects, but this later changed during phase two when he used his expertise in negotiation and bargaining to became a participant in some highly complex imaginative play with a small group of friends.

Creating beautiful things

In phase one Jeff was involved in authoring personal projects and self-initiated activities, in seven of the ten phase one episodes. Two involved making structures (a building and a family group) with blocks (duplo and other connecting blocks); two were water play; two were other imaginative episodes (one talking to an imaginary person on the telephone and one making things in the sandpit), and one working on and completing a very difficult jigsaw puzzle. Most of these activities were carried out alone with Jeff tending to resist other children's attempts to join in. The other three episodes involved Jeff joining an "I'm the King of the Castle" game (mentioned in chapter one) initiated by a group of other children on the climbing equipment, a group game which involved conflict on an outside 'boat', and the final episode was a teacher structured 'school' type activity.

> ### Block Construction (phase one)
>
> Jeff is making a plastic block construction (a building) out of duplo at a table. There is a group of four children watching around the table. A teacher is present for some of the time. He discusses what he is making with her. They have a lengthy conversation. He says that there are lots of bits on his construction and he talks about his activities as he does them – whether the pieces are in the right place, taking bits off the construction, different shapes, colours, and the size of the construction. He says his construction has holes for people to see through, and that the people on the building are going to New Zealand. He seems to know exactly what he is wanting to achieve, and while the teacher makes suggestions ("Can you build some elevators?") he prefers to retain control ("I'm doing that anyway.") He looks at his microphone and says "This is a cool wee microphone". Jeff is very proud of the

construction. When he has finished he says "(Teacher), we made it!" Sam comes and whacks Jeff's construction. Jeff is not happy about this. (He says "Oh No....!"). He carries it over, to give to the teacher and ask her to put it into the office so that the other children can't destroy it. He says "There's no people allowed in here. It's not finished yet. Can you put it in the office?" (to the teacher). He says "I've worked so hard. Can we show my Mum?" He shows it to his mother (who is parent helper for the day) and then describes it to her "Look, that's the bit that people go through, and the other bit's a bus, and these little bits are just the bits to hold it together." She gives him a kiss.

There are several other similar episodes in which Jeff protects his constructions like this in phase one. Other children watched his construction, but he did not like them to touch his work. He integrated imaginative themes into his practical block building activities, as he did in almost any area he played.

Trying to control the group

Jeff's difficulties in accommodating other children into his projects, and his determination to follow through on his own agenda and maintain his territory, is illustrated in an episode on a piece of outdoor play equipment, the boat.

The Boat (phase one)

Jeff is climbing up the rubber tyre steps to top lawn. He gets into the boat and turns the steering wheel. He still has the dinosaur puppet (an object desired by other children and the focus of previous conflict). Charles (his brother) is with him. Someone else tries to get into the boat. Jeff says "This is our ship. This is our boat." Another child, Ray, tries to get into the boat and Jeff yells at him to go away. He goes onto the fort. There is a lot of yelling. He goes down the slide. He gets back into the boat. A lot of shouting to other children about it being his boat. 'This is OUR ship'. Michael gets into the driving seat of the boat. Jeff is running around shouting. A teacher intervenes: 'Jeff, I'm talking to you. You have to let other people play.' Jeff is banging the steering wheel. He gets out. More screaming and running around. Michael again in the driving seat. Lots of running around and aggressive yelling. 'No, No, No, No!' Michael hits Jeff with a stick. Jeff whacks a couple of kids with the dinosaur puppet (still yelling). He is whacking the fence and all sorts of other objects with the glove puppet.

In phase one Jeff was initiating and authoring most of his projects, and he really preferred to engage in tasks of his own choice and design. In one episode that is a teacher-initiated activity entitled 'school group time' for the over-fours, he begins to be involved, then abandons the group. It is a writing activity where the purpose is that the children will write their names and some numerals. He copies the teacher's writing of numerals. Field notes record:

He does a perfect job except for the four. Jeff says 'I can do an H but I can't do a four.' The teacher shows him how to do a four 'properly'. Jeff: 'I can't do a four at all.' Teacher: 'Did you practice up there? (Shows him again). Jeff

Can you do the next number?' Teacher: 'We will do a five tomorrow.' She shows him how to write his name. She writes Jeff in lower case and in capitals. Jeff walks away from the group into the other room. He says 'I'm only four and I can't do any more.' He looks frustrated!

Beginning to orchestrate a team

By phase two Jeff was much more likely to be involved in imaginative dramatic play with other children involved. He was usually very much a leader in setting the rules and boundaries of what was acceptable in the game. He still had difficulties in accommodating to the wishes of other children and engaging in reciprocal play, but he was developing some very effective verbal strategies for orchestrating space and materials. He still tended to maintain his control of the group sometimes through making a lot of noise, but he was beginning to use persuasion and negotiation. Out of the ten episodes, seven involved group sociodramatic play, mainly using family themes with much use of props like blankets, puzzle mats and shopping items (cardboard boxes). Space appeared to be important to Jeff and he often indicated to the teacher (or the researcher) that he wanted more space. Two episodes were teacher-structured activities – a story reading session, and filling in a worksheet about the growth of a hyacinth from the bulb stage. Only one session was a creative personal project: making a necklace. Other people were not always necessary to Jeff in his imaginary enterprises, but he could now include them when they fitted into his script – and he excluded them when they didn't. The following episode shows Jeff's characteristic approach to other members of the group.

> *Shopping (phase two)*
>
> Jeff takes a cardboard box from the shelf, and packs it into his backpack. He has a discussion with Charles and Theresa, both of whom are now participating in the shopping game. Jeff explains to Theresa that some are plastic containers for butter. Jeff says to Charles 'Could I put the mayonnaise in your bag?' Jeff puts the backpack on. He is carrying a plastic container. He goes to the playhouse with Charles and Theresa. Jeff is organising everyone, making suggestions about making the beds. They discuss someone who is coming to stay. Jeff goes back to the shopping shelf. They get eggs and biscuits. Now they are going to get a dog so they need dog food. Jeff is making a little kennel with the plastic puzzle pieces (large flat pieces) for the dog, outside the playhouse.
> Brian arrives and is excluded from the play by all three children; he absconds with all the groceries! and Jeff screams and yells until he gets them back. He returns to making the kennel for the dog. Jeff says to Richard that he can't be the dog because they already have one: 'You be the grandad'. Theresa says she is the grandma. Jeff directs the making a dog kennel. There are now four of them – Charles, Theresa, Jeff and Richard; they need a roof and they pretend to saw and hammer the dog kennel.

Jeff used negotiating skills (and some screaming and yelling) to direct and organise the other children successfully, and they achieve the goal of making a dog kennel.

This episode did not involve any adult intervention, although in other episodes Jeff called on adults for help (such as asking the researcher to make sure no-one went into 'his' playhouse while he was away or when the teacher helped him with making a bead necklace). The following episode illustrates Jeff's negotiations to try to get as many blankets as possible for his play. He uses bargaining skills to suggest that the other children who want some of the blankets could have mats, but the teacher points out that these would not be 'snuggly'. She invites him to experiment: "Snuggle up to them, see what it feels like". He wants to bargain, but is not impressed by the offer.

Blankets (phase two)

Jeff is in the playroom. He is talking to Fergus. Jeff has his arms out blocking Theresa from going into the playroom (which he regards as his territory). She is pointing into the house and saying 'This is where Barbie lives'. Jeff helps Theresa carry the baby's crib upstairs (this is where the girls have been banished to!). Fergus and Jeff come downstairs with the chairs. [This is a segment of the lengthy transcript for this episode relating to negotiation about who is to have the blankets.]

Theresa:	Can I have a blanket from you, Jeff!
Jeff:	No. Because all the blankets... no.
Theresa:	I want one too.
Jeff:	But you don't ___.
Theresa:	Please. Please Jeff.
Jeff:	No, because that blankets are for my babies'.
Theresa:	But, you've got too many.
Jeff:	Yes, but that's because they like being warm in their beds.
[children all talking at once]	
Theresa:	(to teacher) Jeff is not sharing blankets.
Teacher:	Oh, you might need to talk about it. How many blankets are there?
Theresa:	There's lots of blankets.
Teacher:	Well, how about if we count how many blankets and then share?
Jeff:	But I ... I need all of them for the babies because they will be cold in their bed at night.
Teacher:	That's a good point, but what about the other people's babies? Is it alright for them to get freezing cold?
Jeff:	They should use the mats?
Teacher:	Pardon?
Jeff:	They could turn mats into some.
Teacher:	Snuggle up to them, see what it feels like.
Jeff:	They could make it three loads.
Teacher:	Three loads. It's not so snugly, that's my point. Work it out between you. Count them up and then share them out.
Jeff:	But there's no one else allowed in this house.
Teacher:	Well, they can knock at the door. Divide the blankets up please, Jeff.
Jeff:	I need all of them.
Child:	I need just two blankets.

Jeff:	But then give them back!
Child:	Well I need a blanket.
Jeff:	If only you'd give me something for giving it to you. ... Just anything you have. ... [lots of children talking in background].
Child:	Jeff! (offering him a cardboard grocery box).
Jeff:	That's not enough.
[laughter]	

The negotiations continue. Jeff wants something bigger in exchange for the blankets. He suggests again that the other children use mats instead of blankets, and that he will give them a pillow. Finally Jeff comes out with an armful of blankets, donates them to Theresa, and goes to tell the teacher that he has done this. She says 'Good, good sharing.' Later on in the morning he retrieves the donated blankets.

Interest and enthusiasm for learning at school: becoming a mathematician

Jeff's mother told the researcher that Jeff was worried about school and that he did not like change or having a whole day without his mother. She thought that he needed to feel really safe and secure and know what was happening, and was worried that school would not provide this sense of security. His early childhood teacher had thought that he would be fine at school, and commented (in spite of the unsuccessful episode on writing numbers that we observed) that "I think his literacy and numeracy will stand him in good stead [when he goes to school]. I mean he is great with number, and shape and spatial things." It was not just literacy and numeracy which carried over to school, but his intense interest and desire to display and use his expertise. When the researcher asked him what would be hard for him at school he said 'sharing', which was a very accurate and insightful comment! During his early childhood centre experience, he had been very focused on his own projects, and he was obviously going to have less opportunity at school to engage in these. The question was, would the activities on offer at school have the same interest and appeal for him, as those at his early childhood centre. This comment from the primary school teacher in phase three bore out the researcher's observations that he loved the challenge of learning opportunities at school and was highly motivated to participate.

He is just interested in learning full stop. You know, math, writing, he's determined to do it. Reading, he just loves reading and he gets right into the story. Anything you do, absolutely anything in the classroom, he's always tuned in and wants to participate...He just has that expressiveness and eye for detail and just general knowledge and *his interest and enthusiasm for learning*, his language skills. (Teacher interview, phase three; our emphasis)

The interview continued with a discussion of Jeff's ongoing social difficulties in getting on with his peers, and an episode involving Jeff's conflict with another child. Observations of Jeff at school, however, included examples of companionable relationships with other children. The classroom engaged his interest and attention: he was in a small class of eighteen children and there was a teacher aide and a parent helper available in addition to the teacher, so adult attention was readily available. During our observations there was a lot of mathematics activity. Four of the ten episodes were about maths, one was reading, one printing, two writing, one social studies and one science. Throughout the ten episodes, Jeff persevered with the task, even when he was presented with difficult material, not giving up, as he had when trying to write the numeral four in phase one at his early childhood centre. He was still having difficulty getting numerals written the right way around, as can be seen in the following episode, but the teacher was focusing more on meaningful problem-solving and children's thinking, rather than on errors in the writing of the numerals.

Problem-solving Strategies in Maths (phase three)

Jeff goes with five others to work with the teacher (Mrs W.). Each child has a sheet of paper. Mrs W. puts a number of beads on the table. They have to write how many. They work on adding sets like 10 + 10 + 3. Jeff gets it right except he writes the three the wrong way around. (Also the two in another question.) Other examples — three jars of beads with ten in each of them plus four. 30 + 4 = 34. Jeff gets it quickly (except the three is the wrong way). Mrs W praises him. Mrs W gets him to practice writing his threes the right way. They count by tens together. Mrs W tells Jeff he has got his sixes the right way around but his twos the wrong way around. Next they do the same sort of problem with money and he gets three additions correct. Jeff is intently involved. He is writing the formula and answers very carefully. He puts his pencil down when he has finished and waits for the next set of instructions. The next series of problems the teacher uses is the hen sitting on eggs. The hen lays more eggs or some are taken away by the rat. Jeff makes an error but stays focused and quickly gets the answer to the next problem. Mrs W asks him how he knew it was six. He says 'I counted to five and I knew one more made six'. Jeff watches intently as Mrs W does more story problems about hens and eggs. Mrs W asks the children each time how they worked it out and gets them to verbalise the answer. For one problem Jeff explains that he knew that five eggs plus two made seven. Mrs W says 'That was a good way to work it out'. (He had earlier written his three and now his seven the wrong way – but she ignores this.) Mrs W praises all of their different solutions and Jeff is deeply engaged right through.

The maths lesson involved a number of skills and invited the children to become aware of their problem-solving strategies and to find different ways to solve the problems (not emphasising the right answer). All of the children worked hard. The teacher had a calm supportive way of working with the children. During her interview she spoke with great enthusiasm of her school's involvement in the 'numeracy project', a mathematics programme introduced to New Zealand's primary schools.

I've never had children extended as far as this. I love it. Like the [previous scheme] was good, but this numeracy, it's just wonderful. We treat them as individuals like we do at reading time, it's an amazing programme... And the children are always at the end, you know (talking about) what they were learning today. Just for the children to understand what they are learning, so they know what they're trying to learn. (Interview, Mrs W)

After watching his participation in four maths classes and his high level of competence, the researcher was surprised when she interviewed Jeff about school, and he said that maths was "a bit hard like when she (teacher) asks what's a hundred and a million". He said that his favourite activities were reading and writing. Later he referred to another maths problem that he had not been able to solve. "One time I went to school when Mrs W asked me what was two thousand and a hundred. Leo and Frances put their hands up before I did...I didn't know it. I still don't know that." He also said that Leo and Frances were "way ahead of me". Perhaps comparing yourself with others goes with entering the school environment, although it did not seem to be being emphasised by this teacher. Another maths episode was a 'choosing' activity where children were free to make any shape of four or more sides with a construction set involving geometric shapes. Construction activity was familiar to some of the activities with blocks in the childcare centre; Jeff makes a cube, working intently, and was reluctant to leave it for a mat time.

LEARNING IN THE MAKING

Disposition-in action: work in progress

As for the other case study chapters, this section looks at the three dispositional components, introduced in chapter two, translated from the triadic definition of a dispositions, our observations and the literature on the continuity of learning as authoring, recognising opportunity, and connected knowing. All three of these components combined together as a work in progress towards the children being ready willing and able to initiate and orchestrate projects.

Authoring. David's focus and determination persisted through all three phases of the study. His mother, when asked if this was typical said "Yep. It is. Perseverance stuff and nag you about doing stuff!" David's disposition towards taking responsibility for his own learning continued over time and in different settings. He had developed a capacity for 'locking on' and perseverance in tasks of interest and challenge. By phase two there are a number of opportunities for Leona to practise authority, partly because she is mostly working in a dyad with a peer who modelled a strong disposition to cooperate, and because her confidence is boosted by a valued area of expertise: writing. Jeff began to be more actively involved with peers at phase two, especially in the context of pretend play, which seemed to be a good place to resolve differences. Although he was a challenging partner for other children, they were now engaging with him as a member of the peer group. He still liked to be the boss, but he came to accept the norms of the group about fairness and justice (such as that it was important to share and to take into account the views of others). Throughout all ten episodes of joint attention in the school classroom, Jeff was 'locked into' learning, even when the task was challenging (as in the mathematics problem-solving examples). His teacher at school made comments about his interest and enthusiasm for learning: "Jeff is just interested in learning full stop". The only opportunity we observed for him to author his own unique projects at school was when he constructed – on his own – a cube (he called it a 'dice'), reminiscent of the phase one Block Construction episode. The school classroom positioned David as a 'clever writer'. Jeff's capacity for deep engagement and perseverance were very useful when he entered school, even although the projects were very different and (perhaps because) the teacher was usually in control of them. His enjoyment of projects and of opportunities to use his expertise in early childhood could appear again in school projects without the distractions interruptions and conflicts associated, for Jeff, of vying for the leadership role.

Recognising opportunity.   At school, David was attuned to, able to 'read' the classroom (Comber, 2000). As his mother had commented: "I suppose he's learned that there are certain times and places for things". He was orchestrating the resources available, calling on his assumption, developed from his earlier experience in early childhood centres, that teachers are assistants who value his enterprises. At school he was enabled to publicly position himself with agency without disrupting an identity as a 'good pupil': colouring in differently from requirements, seizing an opportunity to spend some 'illegal' time (having initiated the gaining of approval from the teacher) on the play ground equipment, and writing a story with an off-target theme. While the teacher had described him as a 'clever writer', that accolade later appeared to be less motivating than the reward of 'free play' with stickle bricks. While he builds an aeroplane with the stickle bricks he talks to himself and says (about the story he has just written) "Mine's an easy one, it's got easy words". The observing researcher wrote:

> I got the impression that the main motivation to complete the work (quickly) was to then have a chance to play with the toys – especially the stickle-bricks – he has learnt the rules of how the class works? The games he chooses though are always interrupted as there is often limited time to do them, so the faster you get the 'work' done the more time you have to do what you want to do. (Field notes, phase three)

Once 'something clicked' about how to write a story, David decided to hand in a story with 'easy words' to buy himself some time for self-initiated play with others. Samuel, in chapter four, appeared to be playing the same game. Leona's authority with orchestrating projects appeared to depend to a greater extent on the context than David's. She was learning to handle exclusion in peer play and had developed a considerable resilience to the possibility of being positioned as an outsider in those projects where she was knowledgeable and skilled (pretending to be a vet, craft work, writing and reading), and confident about the rules and routines. It was when a peer used a 'magic' wand inconsistently, and unpredictably changed the rules – and no adult was nearby to assist Leona to negotiate for fairness – that a scene was set and a script was constructed that positioned Leona as fragile and confused. But on the same day, with the same peer as a co-player, she was able to co-construct a storyline and develop a play theme that placed her confidently as a person with authority (a vet, a doctor, a mother). At school, unlike David, uncertainty about whether she was allowed to improvise on what she perceived as a set 'school script' led to her cautious attitude to the uncertainties of entitlement (not making a mistake) in a new venue: not sure about whether one was allowed to use a glue stick as a roller or whether she was allowed to choose from the resources at 'free time', she chose the safe and conservative option. Jeff's orchestrating of people and resources depended on adults being available to assist him, and to help him to negotiate with his peers. He never seemed to fail in gaining adult attention from early childhood teachers; they were very responsive to his demands, even though they found him trying at times. By school, these self-initiated projects were not readily available, projects and groups were teacher-initiated, and there was no demand for negotiation and bargaining for resources and scripts. But there were still adults available for attention because of the school policy to keep the new entrant classroom small and to keep the teacher-child ration low. Peers did not play much of a part in his activities in phase one, except as people that Jeff wanted to exclude from interfering with his activities, or as people to instruct or act as followers; by phase two he was learning to orchestrate the other players, by negotiating, but this skill was not in demand in the school classroom, and the teacher commented on his ongoing social difficulties. Jeff's deep engagement with the spatial and material environment in the early childhood centre was encouraged by the almost endless opportunities for him to use his interesting ideas, to create things and play out imaginative scenarios. At school that capacity for improvisation that was evident in the early childhood context with materials and spaces appeared to be called on in the arithmetic episode, where he was asked to explain his strategies, and the class was invited to consider the other children's (also acceptable) strategies for solving number problems.

Connected knowing. Leona's interest in words, the 'code-breaking' of their construction, and her skills at reading and writing was *subject-based knowing* that she relished using at school. Jeff's early childhood teachers maintained that he would do well at school because of his interest in mathematics and literacy. In developing their knowledge and skill in projects that they initiated and orches-trated, all three children called on cross-disciplinary knowing. For instance, David was combining a knowledge of cooking and concrete-making with a know-ledge of what sand can do; Leona was adding writing and drawing to the technology of a book construction, using physical ability as the scene for magic, and impro-vising with the materials at hand to create a text about going to the vet, and Jeff was integrating block construction with imaginative story-telling. This is connected knowing that Gunter Kress (2003) and Carey Jewitt (2008) have argued imperative for the 21st century, but in these new entrant classrooms there was no call for it.

In terms of *disposition-based knowing*, opportunities for David's ongoing interest and helpful stance towards children who were less knowledgeable, younger or in some way 'other', continued into school. This disposition to encourage and orchestrate others, apparent in his kindergarten projects, still had a space in school practice, although we did not observe it as part of the authoring of complex projects, which were not available in the school classroom. Jeff could orchestrate space and materials, and was beginning to negotiate and bargain in phase two, but the teacher at school reported that he still had difficulties in getting on with his peers; in the school classroom, the available tasks of interest to Jeff did not demand the coordination of different perspectives or distributed roles (a topic of interest in Mercer & Littleton, 2007 and Mercer, 2008).

Design

These three stories illustrate the different ways in which children were able to access the affordances of their early childhood and school environments to initiate and orchestrate people, materials and spaces to initiate and orchestrate - and lock onto – learning projects. Some key aspects of the implicit or explicit educational design were: affective engagement and peer group relationships, space and time, and the teacher support and expectations.

Affective engagement and peer group relationships.   For all three children, the early childhood experience provided opportunities to be confronted with a diversity of relationships, and these often presented them with difficulties to resolve – an important aspect of their learning that is closely connected with the issues in chapters three and four. The early childhood centre contexts provided the opportunities for children to learn ways to develop relationships with others in order to orchestrate the smooth running of projects that needed partners. They were finding out that they needed to make some concessions and to listen to other story-lines if they wanted the group to stay on board. These early attempts to recognise, develop and elaborate on interests also provided experiences that confirmed that projects can proceed in a more interesting way if other people are contributing perspectives and roles. Leona played in phase one with two girls who were strong-minded and who sometimes put her in a powerless position, as in the magic wand episodes or when she was excluded her from seeing her picture; at the same time these same partners provided her with ideas which extended the possibilities for joint projects (Lizzie's ideas for a necklace, for instance, were taken on by Leona; and Lizzie and Olivia were imaginative contributors to the pretend play). Jeff began to realise that he needed, and benefited from, the support of peers when he was initiating projects; his abilities in this area were only just catching up to his inclinations. For David, peers were extremely important in sharing his interests and participating with him in carpentry, playing cricket, cooking games and riding bicycles. They were valuable resources for him in authoring and completing projects. The presence of younger or less skilled children, provided contexts for the older children to take on the perspectives of others if they wanted to persuade them to contribute. David (like Aralynn in chapter eight) took on the perspective of children who were 'other' when he was in 'teacher' mode: younger Jason at the carpentry table, newer Kenny as he tried to make sense of a worksheet, and the children who were less knowledgeable at concrete-making in the sandpit. In the early childhood settings, projects that 'mattered' invited Jeff to become more collaborative with others, Leona to resist the power play of her peers, and David to be a collaborative leader in several projects. At school Leona could use her literacy skills to help others, and her help was in demand.

Space and time.   In the early childhood centres the space, time and material props available to develop complex pretend play scripts and other personal or shared projects were important catalysts for the children's projects. Indoor and outdoor spaces were available for children to create imaginary worlds, and to engage in technological projects. Jeff, Leona and David all experienced early childhood environments rich in resources for action and exploration, which made it possible to create projects in which they could invest effort and perseverance. The early childhood centre environments also require them to share the resources, and this lesson was important, but not easy, for Jeff.

Teacher support and expectations.   A major consideration for these young learners as to whether or not to initiate, engage and persist in activities, outside home appeared to be the relationship with their teachers. All three children had some difficulties in leaving their families and adjusting to the early childhood centre and Leona needed teacher support during the transition to school. Leona acknowledged that she was sad when she had to leave her mother, Jeff was similarly very attached to his mother and missed her, while David's mother thought that he was less confident than his siblings at childcare, and that he liked to sit back and observe at first. The sensitive support provided by the teachers helped all of the children to feel more at ease in their centres (or schools), though there were other factors like the presence of Jeff's younger brother, Charles, and his mother being a parent helper, at childcare, which eased the settling in process. David's mother felt that leaving David at his early childhood centre was like leaving him with family, and Leona cheered up about parting with her mother when the teacher held her hand. The teachers' efforts to know all of the children well, and develop relationships with them invited their engagement and interest in activities at the centre. Teachers and their attitudes, and their facilitation of children's projects, were a key aspect of the affordance network. David, for example was able to build on the early childhood teachers' belief that children can take responsibility for their own learning. Jeff's primary school teacher constructed five-year-olds as competent learners. She said that she constantly demanded and expected more from the children, recognised their talents and interest in learning, and gave them complex and challenging tasks. Her attitude and style of teaching demanded a high level of performance from the children.

I have expectations of the children....I, you know, know exactly what the children can do. And I know what I want to teach them. And I just think through that, you know. Quite specifically when they are first starting. I know how far they can count, I know which letters they know, so I know which ones we're gonna work on. I know whether they know any words. I'll notice –suddenly somebody's writing I, or a little shape and I'll go 'Oh, I think you've written 'I' here… look at that, you could write"… You know, all the new entrants. I can tell you quite specifically about each of the children, what it is they can do and what I'm working on next. …I know which letters they know, which words they can sight read, you know, I know whether they've got directionality, all of the different things, and there's quite a wide range. So I'm really watching very very closely to see what they've got to assess readiness for reading and writing and how to move them on to the next step. So it is quite individualized. (Interview with Jeff's teacher, phase three)

Jeff's teacher was in a school with a declining roll, which resulted in a lot of extra space and huge flexibility for the formation of groups and activities in different areas. Not only were there excellent adult/child ratios (three to eighteen – a teacher, teacher-aide and parent helper) in that classroom, but there was room for children to develop projects and for small group work. At the policy level the school put a high priority on the new entrant class and believed that extra people were needed to support the learning. David was in a similarly favourable group size and adult-child ratio (one to five when he started, and two to fifteen with the teacher and one teacher aide five months later). Leona's mother's had commented about the undesirability of working with a group of twenty-four with no other adult.

BUILDING RESILIENCE

Asking Questions

> All depends upon a breaking free, a leap, and then a question. I would like to claim that this is how learning happens and that the educative task is to create situations in which the young are moved to begin to ask, in all the tones of voice there are, "Why?" (Greene, 1995, p. 6)

We ask questions in response to uncertainty and curiosity and indignation. In uncertain and curious conditions, we avoid asking questions if we are convinced that there is a right answer, we ought to know it, and we are anxious to protect our reputations as knowledgeable and competent. These facets of the disposition for resilience were introduced in Chapter two and have been researched by Carol Dweck (2000, 2006). Responding by question-asking (in a range of ways) is associated with learning goals and an incremental belief about intelligence (a growth mindset), while responding by question-avoiding is associated with performance goals and an entity belief about intelligence (a fixed mindset). And we are unlikely to want to ask questions if we don't have enough connected knowing to make us curious.

Responding to indignation with questions may be more of an ethical matter to do with a perception of injustice, a concern for the planet, and a compassionate and caring view of the world. It is also about being critically aware. These are a tall order for four- and five-year olds, but Paley has illustrated their relevance to very young children in her book 'You Can't say You Can't Play'. The quote from her book in chapter four begins with the following:

> Turning sixty, I am more aware of the voices of exclusion in the classroom. "You can't play' suddenly seems too overbearing and harsh, resounding like a slap from wall to wall. How casually one child determines the fate of another. (Paley, 1992, p. 3)

She looks, with Bronwyn Davies and Robyn Hunt, towards a time when 'problem' students are no longer 'other' "in the usual sense of deviating from an ascendant norm, but other in a range of multiple possibilities each of which made sense from the positions they were standing in and the discourses that were available to them for meaning making." (Davies & Hunt, 1994, p. 407). Debbie Meier, the founder of the Central Park East School in East Harlem, and an advocate of small secondary schools has commented:

Learning happens fastest when the novices trust the setting so much that they aren't afraid to take risks, make mistakes, or do something dumb. Learning works best, in fact, when the very idea that it's risky hasn't even occurred to kids. (Meier, 2002, p. 18)

This facet of the disposition towards resilience is built from respectful listening, environments that insist on justice, and adults who are interested in uncertainty and multiple possibilities.

JOSEPH

By the end of this research project, Joseph was the second of four children. He had an older sister at the same school, a younger sister who had just begun attending kindergarten, and a baby brother. Joseph's mother was at home with the children; she had earlier completed a law degree and worked as a lawyer. After attending the afternoon and then the morning programme in a sessional kindergarten, Joseph attended the same school as his sister, some way away from the early childhood centre. His mother was adamant that she wanted the children to be happy and not to be 'pressured'. She commented on how disappointed Joseph was that he could not read during the first few months of school, and that "in the first term, he just wasn't there [into reading]. No matter how he tried, it just didn't somehow click in his memory, but his memory bank improved, and now he's very proud and wants to read". She wondered whether he should have started school at age six, and she added that she wants her children to love books. His father is a sound technician, and Joseph was interested in all things technical. Like Samuel, in chapter four, when they went to the library as a family he always picked up a book on mechanical, technical things. His mother also commented that he made very close friendships "and the other thing about the kindergarten is that you lose a friend a month [when children go to school on their fifth birthday] and he's actually quite sensitive".

One of the themes that characterised our observations and discussions for the case study of Joseph was his exploring of learner self-scripts about rights and entitlement. Perhaps there were three questions that he was asking: when is one entitled to take the lead and make the decisions; what risks are optimal; and what circumstances or rules are fair for all? We might say that in the early childhood centre he was accumulating experiences that would provide him with a repertoire of answers and working theories for these questions. As we will see, he was attempting to explore these ideas in the school classroom as well. And maybe this repertoire will enable him to be more resilient when he is positioned as powerless, when circumstances are unfair, and when events are exciting but may be beyond a dangerous limit. This case study is framed around his apparent exploration of these questions.

When is one entitled to take the lead and make the decisions?[10]

Entitlement to take the lead: being an 'in-charger' in phase one. In phase one, just before Joseph's fourth birthday, we observed seven episodes on three different days, and on each day the interest in 'entitlement' appeared. For Joseph it translated into being 'in charge' or an 'in-charger', and this language reappeared in phases two and three. In phase one, Joseph was interested in establishing who is in charge, although he did not usually want that role for himself. One reason why he did not initiate may be because he had two close companions (Mahesh and Benedict) for most of the activity in phase one, and an order of authority had been established, with Mahesh mostly taking the lead. At the slide, Joseph has a conversation with a fourth child, Craig: "You're not in charge here." Craig: "Why not?" Joseph (gesturing to Mahesh): "Because he is". Craig: "I want to be in charge". Joseph: "Sorry". Craig: "All right".

In an early episode Joseph and three others construct some signifiers of power in the shape of small plastic reels, which they call 'power rings' and wear on their arms.

Power men (phase one)

Mark: Hey guys, don't step in that big part or a net will trap you. A baddie made it and I know who. He made that hole there....
Joseph is about to make a sandcastle (he has filled a bucket with sand).
Mahesh: "Let's go, Joseph. Let's go, Joseph!". Joseph puts down his bucket and goes. They are joined by two other boys, walk along the climbing frame and then run off to collect small reels. They attach them to their arms, two each, and run about. A girl approaches Joseph and he holds his arms and reels out as if to protect himself. One of the children comments: "We are robots".
Mahesh: This is a cool one, with power...Let's go, powermen....
Researcher: What are you?
Mahesh: We are superheroes.
Researcher: Superheroes. Ooh.
Joseph: And we're saving people from dragons.
Joseph picks up a cricket bat.
Mahesh: You don't have to use that. (He puts it down)

In phase one the teachers had made several attempts to engage Joseph in alternative episodes of joint attention, but he was usually called away by Mahesh and then Benedict. However, one of the teachers successfully engages both Joseph and Benedict in an interchange in which the teaching or the responsibility is distributed across the adult and the two children. This is a collaborative episode about sharing the responsibility in a small group learning activity and it builds on a recent trip to an aquarium in the city. All three are 'in charge'.

Distributed leadership: Exploring small animals (phase one)

There is a joint discussion with Benedict and the teacher, Zoe. The artefacts for discussion are small sea animals (plastic, in a water trough), cards that give information about each one, and a poster to assist with identification. The teaching-and-learning is distributed: Joseph contributes to the identification, using the poster; Benedict can read the numbers (the size) on the cards; Zoe can read the cards. The children have recently been on a trip to an aquarium

---

in the city. In this episode they are naming the sea creatures, and talking about them.

Teacher:	Did you find it, the one that matches? (Joseph gives her the card). Oh. (reading from the card) Great White Shark.
Joseph:	See, it has a point up there and a point up there.
Teacher:	So you're looking at the points and they're matching...
Benedict:	Found the leopard shark.
Teacher:	You've found the leopard shark.
Joseph:	Hey look. Hey look, I've found the right one (on the poster).
Teacher:	Oh, do you know what that one's called?
Benedict:	It's called a whale.
Teacher:	Oh. Size. Do you know how big this one is?
Benedict:	(reading) Two.
Teacher:	It's about two metres.
Joseph:	And how big is this one (the whale)?
Teacher:	Let's have a look and see how big this one grows to. It's got all the measurements here. Wow! Up to 31 feet or 9.4 metres. That is so long.
Joseph:	Hey that one's more than that one...... Here comes that stingray, hungry as can be, and snapped one up.
Teacher:	Like [the song about] the monkey swinging in the tree and along came the stingray, hungry as can be.

Joseph sings the song with 'stingray' instead of 'crocodile'.

On the third day of observations in phase one, Mahesh has gone to school but Benedict is quick to establish himself as the 'in-charger'. Joseph comments: "Mahesh doesn't know where we are, won't he. We are the chargers". Benedict: "I'm the in-charger, I'm in charge and you're not". Joseph: "Mahesh's at school now. I miss him". Benedict: "Me too".

Entitlement in phase two. By phase two, Joseph appears to be making a considered judgement about whether to be the 'in-charger' or to follow the leader and follow the rules, set by others: a sensitivity to occasion. Interactions with teachers in this data set were mostly during 'school-like' games with rules, in small groups. The rules are set by the teachers (and often as formats passed on from previous times). He is now observed to be more deeply focussed on tasks, choosing not to be distracted by others (three episodes of the eleven illustrate this: building a sandcastle; making a construction inside with cellophane and boxes; and using Duplo). Although these episodes are short (on average fifteen minutes), this capacity to not be distracted from an interesting task, to be 'in charge' of his own curriculum, did not appear in phase one. A Learning Story in his portfolio near this time describes him authoring the making of peach muffins. The Story is developed as annotations to photographs and was part of a wall display at the kindergarten.

Making Peach Muffins. A Learning Story (excerpt)

Joseph loves cooking. He helps to make peach muffins at home. On Tuesday Joseph's Mum came to kindergarten and made peach muffins.... Here he is

> draining the peaches. Joseph knew the process and what ingredients were required. Joseph is having a turn of gently mixing the muffin mixture. He is careful not to overmix as this makes the muffins 'yucky' (Joseph's words). Joseph is sprinkling the cinnamon and sugar mixture on top of the uncooked muffins. Joseph is placing spoonfuls of mixture into the muffin tin. Look how he is using two spoons. This takes a lot of concentration....

Joseph being in charge of making the muffins, and details of his competence – knowing the recipe and the process – is made public.

Entitlement in phase three. We observed thirteen episodes at school, over three days. On the first day the episodes of more than ten minutes were: a lesson on money and a worksheet (thirty-four minutes), free play time (fifteen minutes), and writing a story (twenty minutes). In the latter Joseph dictates "I went to McDonalds and got a Nemo toy", he says some of the letters and writes underneath. This allows him three minutes for playing 'Spin doctor' on the computer until 'reading time' is announced. Other episodes were: a small group letter Bingo game (ten minutes), story reading (children assist teacher to point to the words: ten minutes), lunchtime (an hour), looking at Dylan's cards and listening to music (fifteen minutes), news time (fifteen minutes), technology lesson on soft toys and battery-operated toys, followed by a worksheet (forty-three minutes), and news time (fifteen minutes). We interviewed Joseph's mother, after she had had a new baby, when Joseph had been at school nearly a year; she reported that during his first year at school Joseph was aware that his older sister was a very good reader, and

> He noticed that he couldn't read in the same way....But he made one of those quantum leaps, probably mid-year, at six, and now he can read.... He's so excited and proud, because it really was frustrating for him. There was no pressure from us, but he was doing a comparison. .... He's enjoying it, so that's good. I did think, in some ways, he has starved at school, because he was unhappy with his progress. (Parent interview, phase three)

Joseph was, however, able to 'read' the classroom; he got on and completed tasks, found resources, seldom asked the teacher for help and contributed ideas at mat time. And he recognised, or constructed, opportunities for his interest in fairness and entitlement to vary the routines: he questioned the validity of a Bingo game in which some of the letters were missing (see page 129); and when the teacher set up a binary between soft toys and mechanical toys in the technology lesson he questioned her framework by pointing out that 'you could put a battery into a soft toy and turn it into a robot'. By now Joseph is not at all dependent on another child to be 'in charge'. In the following episode he interrupts the news time routine, and 'troubles' the discussion format imposed by the teacher. Children are expected to ask questions of the news presenter, but Joseph follows the rules of everyday conversation by making a statement or, in his words, a 'suggestion'.

> ### *News Time (phase three)*
>
> Sara shows a toy to the class:
> Teacher: Did you have a question for Sara?... Joseph, you've got a question, good boy. (to the class). Shhh, show your good manners.
> Joseph: I've had those before.
> Teacher: And have you got a question for Sara?
> Joseph: That was a suggestion.
> Teacher: That was a statement. Thankyou. Good boy. Questions often start like 'What'.

The usual format of the day was instructions and teaching on the mat, and then a worksheet. There was therefore little opportunity for entitlement to be explored. When the children manage to talk together, the children turn the tasks into a race, or chat about topics of interest:

> ### *A Worksheet on Captain Cook (phase three)*
>
> Joseph introduces a topic of conversation into a worksheet activity that involved a lengthy period allocated to colouring in pictures of coins and making rubbings of coins with a pencil in circles of the appropriate size. The topic of interest shifts from Captain Cook's ship (on one of the coins) to pirates and then to burglars. Some of the transcript appears to be about whether burglars will kill you or not, and Joseph positions himself as an authority.
> Joseph: Burglars are very mean.
> Child: They don't shoot you.
> Joseph: But they can take people away.
> Child: And kill you.
> Joseph: But you said they don't kill. A burglar stole once, a burglar came into my house..... They don't show their eyes and their mouth 'cos they've got a beanie.
> Ivan: No, they have a mask, like Spiderman or something else. Spiderman is in the big Yes Yes book, and robbers are in the big No No book.
> Joseph: Burglars don't kill people, they just get you to work with them. But if you say No you'll be in danger, they'll kill you, won't they Ivan?
> Ivan: Yeah.

What risks are optimal?

Testing the limits in phase two. One episode in phase two might be said to be characterised by 'flow': a balance of high challenge and high skill (Csikzentmihalyi, 1997). This was a twenty-two minute episode in which the field notes commented on the 'delight/fear/anticipation' on Joseph's face as he steered a trolley at some speed down the kindergarten driveway.

> *Balancing challenge and ability: driving the trolley down hill (phase two)*
>
> Driving the tractor and the trolley down the driveway. This begins with a small tractor, then with the faster trolley. Field notes comment on the 'delight/fear/ anticipation' on Joseph's face as he goes down the hill at some speed (on one occasion crashing into the gate, on other occasions steering onto the grass towards the end of the run). Joseph works out how to reduce the danger by steering onto the grass near the bottom of the drive. On the second trip one of the children tries to get into the driver's position, but Joseph instructs him to take the passenger seat. They glide down the hill and turn onto the grass at the bottom. (Field notes: 'Joseph steering skilfully'). Joseph pushes the tractor or a trolley back up and then drives down again seven times, five times with another child on the back, once with two children, before mat time looms.

When Joseph and the teacher look at photos of him on the high jumping boxes in the playground, she asks him how he felt when he was up there. "Good". You weren't scared of heights? No? "If it was that high (gestures), it would really hurt somebody" he commented.

Playing sport in phase three. These opportunities to test the limits were not available in phase three in the school classroom, although at lunchtime Joseph played ball games on the field often with older children, and a few days before we visited he had ended up with a grazed knee. Later he would join out-of-school team sports: soccer and touch rugby, and his mother reported that he loved this.

What circumstances or rules are fair for all?

Listening to the rules in phase one. In phase one, Joseph is sharing responsibility for 'the disciplinary order of the classroom' (Packer & Greco-Brooks, 1999) by reminding children of the rules when the play looks, to Joseph, as if it might be dangerous. He does add 'being naughty' to the mix: "No hurting each other and no being naughty" (in the sandpit); "Mahesh, one by one! Hey, watch out! One by one! Come on Mahesh...One by one!" (jumping from a high reel). Joseph appears to be becoming adept at 'reading the environment', recognising that there are different rules in different places, and being prepared to take responsibility for them. He takes responsibility to try to encourage children to keep to the rules: "one by one" when jumping off a high box, "No hurting each other" when a child lifts a spade in a threatening manner, sharing the glue gun to ensure that everyone gets a turn.

Being fair in phase two. Two of the eleven episodes in phase two were games with rules, led by a teacher. Joseph enthusiastically followed the adult rules for group games (taking turns to throw bean bags into a hoop; and a group game called 'Doggie doggie who's got the bone?'). At the same time he develops his own games with rules. The latter are often dangerous, and perhaps they also belong in the 'what risks are optimal?' category. One game involved rolling tyres down the slide, with a child lying in its path and jumping out of its way just in time to avoid being hit. Joseph initiated this game, and added a rule "You have to close your eyes" (fortunately the children ignored this instruction).

The curriculum provided opportunities for small group pretend play, with negotiation of role and story-line. In phase two the play is taken up by Joseph in two episodes. In the first of these two episodes, there is some negotiation of role and the lead girl actor wants to develop an interesting story-line, but Joseph and Carl want to pretend fight. Joseph continues to watch out for safety: admonishing Carl to 'play gently' in the sword game. His awareness of the perspectives of others – also an aspect of reciprocity – may be illustrated by his opting for the king role instead of a prince (but since a king is of higher status in an adult's eyes we cannot be sure). In the second of these pretend play episodes, the children take turns to be in a cupboard (the 'dog house') while one of the children 'locks them in'. Joseph calls on his technical interest to use a wire coat hanger in order to genuinely lock the cupboard, but is unsuccessful.

Super Kings Play Gently (phase two)

Joseph joins with another boy (Carl) and three girls to play a game. Linda wants to develop a story, but Joseph and Carl are more interested in sword fighting. Carl has a toy sword.

Carl:	Joseph, wanna play?…Do you want to be the Prince or the King?
Joseph:	Prince.
Another child:	I want to be a prince too.
Joseph:	I want to be the King.
Carl:	I'm the Superman!
Linda:	We're super.
Carl:	I'm superman with the sword.
Linda:	And I'm superlady, cos I've got the cape.
Joseph:	I'm Superking. (He finds a fly swat).
Linda:	That's your…no, Joseph…Joseph, there's no fly swats in this game.
Joseph:	This could be my sword. (He and Carl fight).
Joseph:	(repeats five times) Let's play a bit more gently before we get hurt.

Joseph and Carl have changed the story-line and are fighting dinosaurs and crocodiles with swords but Linda perseveres as the author.

Linda:	Who wants to be the one who saves me?
Carl:	I'll save you.

Fairness at school.   At school, Joseph continued his concern with the 'whole picture' of fair entitlement that had been evident in phase one and phase two: with keeping the rules. "Stop talking" he reminds the others when they are supposed to be focusing on a work sheet, but he is happy to join in off-task conversations at other times. He appears to exploring the question of whether the rules are fair and just. When a discussion while colouring in a work sheet turns to who is the fastest,

Joseph argues that there should be no rush ("like (at) dinner-time") and no race, and adds wisely: "If I win a race and all of you are trying, it's not…What if I was ten and you were five?". Some of the educational games at school provided an opportunity for the children to discuss fairness. On two occasions Joseph participated in a familiar competitive game, but because resources are lost no-one can win.

> ### Bingo Game Where No-one Can Win (phase three)
>
> The understood goal of the bingo game was to win by filling all the spaces on the card as they are called out or shown by the person 'in charge'. However, in this case, Letter Bingo, there are not enough letters (they are lost) for anyone to complete their board. Echoing the phrase that was familiar at the kindergarten, the teacher nominates one of the children to be 'in charge'. The girl 'in charge' says: "I'm still the judge cos no-one actually had them all". They start again, and the girl-in-charge looks at the letters before giving them to chosen participants, then puts them all down for the children to pick up the cards they need. Still none of them can complete but since two other children have three spaces missing, while Joseph has two, he decides "I've won actually" and tells the teacher that there is no letter 'I'. She suggests that they make one. The observer notes that 'The game is easy; the children appear quite happy to have it turned into a girl-with-the–power game'.

> ### Letter Bingo Two (phase three)
>
> On a second occasion, two days later, a small group of children go into an anteroom with a teacher aide for reading. They read a story together, then Joseph is nominated by the teacher as the person 'in charge' of the 'Letter Bingo' game. The teacher aide allocates the boards. Two children are given two boards, and one of them says "Oh, she (one of the children who has just one board) will win". Teacher aide: "Doesn't matter". When she leaves, the two children each put a board back, to make it even. Joseph refers to one of the spare boards as "Mr Nobody" They run out of letters, and nobody fills their board. Joseph: "Mr Nobody won: he got four'.

This activity works as educational design in the same way as worksheets for which the educational purpose is a mystery and rules or meanings outside the classroom don't apply. Joy Cullen and Alison St George (1996) referring to research on children's early acquisition of scripts for classroom life, have described the agenda of Year One classrooms as fundamentally about 'doing school' (a focus on routines, doing assigned classroom tasks and following procedures): an orientation towards work rather that learning as understanding (p. 16). We were interested, and disconcerted, that Joseph – and most of the other children – found this aspect of curriculum design unsurprising. Presumably they understood that this is just an easy letter-recognition exercise poorly disguised as a competitive game, and, under Joseph's leadership they did not take the competition seriously, because it was unfair.

LAUREN

When we first met Lauren she was living with her mother in her grandmother's house. Early in the project she and her mother moved into a new house with her mother's partner and we visited her there. When asked what she would like Lauren to get from her experiences at the early childcare centre Lauren's mother replied:

> Social interaction, because she is an only child and we're around adults quite a lot although we have lots of friends and cousins over in the weekend. Social skills. And one of the things I've really noticed is that she's quite cautious in all areas and I think that is a good thing but in some situations I think she could overcome [things] better and I would hope that at daycare that she gains more confidence with that. (Parent interview, phase one)

She added: "Some things she doesn't do and she becomes, not lazy, but safe and she's always talking about things like smoke alarms and fire alarms and will they go off and what will happen... she's very concerned about danger". Lauren had been nervous about animals, especially dogs and horses, and the family had been working together to assist her to overcome her fears. Lauren's mother's partner, commented:

> There's a paddock up the road, and, until they started doing works up there, there used to be a horse. About every second night we would go for a bike or scooter or skateboard ride up there and go and see the horse.... Now, if a horse is a metre away, she'll be happy to stand and talk about it.

Her mother added:

> And then about four or five weeks ago her dad [who Lauren still sees regularly] took her to the A & P (Agricultural and Pastoral) Show so we chuckled to ourselves and said "Good luck" and he knows too, and she rang up very excited: 'I've just ridden a pony'. (Parent interview, phase one)

At the parent interview Lauren's progression towards trying something new was described. At one stage she became quite timid about going into the sea, having enjoyed it when she was younger. By the end of the project she had overcome this reluctance and had joined the Nippers – junior life guards who meet together for beach activities on a Sunday morning. Lauren was learning to swim, and at the end of phase two she told us: "and I have sticks I put in the deep water and then I have to try and go under the water and I have to try and get it... (and) I can float on my back". After four months at school her mother described Lauren's participation in a triathlon where, out of three junior classes, Lauren was one of only two children who could swim across the pool.

Lauren might be described as an inquirer, who asks questions about situations, events and rules that puzzle her and, sometimes, make her afraid. We have interpreted this as a journey towards resilience. A key feature of her childcare experience, reported in this chapter, is a culture of puzzling and trying to make sense of the world in enquiring conversations. Her teachers responded to her questions with respect, explanation, reassurance, and information. So do her family.

> I've always had that philosophy... that if (she's) asking I need to give her that information. And it was just tonight on the way home "Now Mum, that car in front, why is the roof low?" and she started asking questions about design. "Why has your shirt only got one sleeve?" because it was an off-the-shoulder thing and I said "That's the way it's made and that's the design of it. Some people would like that so that's why they make it, so somebody might buy it". And it's interesting that she asks those questions because we just take that for granted. She does ask a lot. (Parent Interview, phase one)

During phase one all except two of nine episodes and conversations observed were with one of the teachers and a small group of children. Six of these episodes of joint attention referred to events and situations beyond the here and now. Four of them question childcare routines, gender norms, and reasonable rights and responsibilities: the schedule at the centre, what boys do, the rules of cricket (at the centre) and appropriate social behaviour in a group. One episode was a discussion with the researcher and another child about the fairness of taking balloons away from someone without negotiating first, and another was an interaction with another child, Daisy, as they discussed whether the play area was a 'girls-in' site or a 'boys-in' site. The conversation topics were initiated by Lauren in every case except for a discussion about 'practising' initiated by a teacher and included at the end of this case study. During the cricket game episode Lauren complained that the children were being too noisy; a teacher explained that children are permitted to make loud noises outside, and they discussed three strategies when the situation is annoying: discuss with a teacher, use your words with the other children, or move away. She then tries the second strategy by asking Liam to please give her back the bat. This doesn't work, and the teacher comments that it was quite 'reasonable' for Liam to decide that she had completed her turn with the bat because she had moved away and sat down. Commenting on the strategy of giving children responsibility for dealing with other children who were annoying them, the teachers said:

Teacher 1: I think we've always had a culture of framing it in a positive – it's not "You can't do this" or "You don't do this", it's "How can we do this together" and how can we sort problems out and have it as a positive thing, and giving the responsibility back to the children to take charge of it.

Teacher 2: Now with so many of our children you can say "You've got so many solutions and words that you already know to go and talk to that child about them. I'll stand here and help you if you need me" and just with that you can see (them understanding) "I can do this".

Puzzling about sadness

Lauren's puzzling about sadness appeared on two occasions during our observations in phase one.

Carpentry (phase one)

In one episode, Lauren is at the carpentry table with a teacher and other children. One of the children describes their construction as a traffic light for cars, and the subject turns to safety on the road. The teacher comments

Teacher: You have to stand on the footpath and make sure there's no cars coming.

Lauren: Why?

Teacher: Because if you step on the road you might get hit.

Lauren: Run over. Do you know what. I saw some flowers on the road because there was a boy on the road and there was no adult with him and he get run over and there was no adult.

Teacher: That's really sad, isn't it?

Lauren: Yeah.

Teacher: The boy must have died there.

Lauren: Yeah.

Teacher: It's really sad.

Lauren: Why it's really really sad?

Teacher: Because that little boy's not going to be alive any more.

The teacher then introduces the role of a hospital, the fact that people who have died from other causes are taken there, and the notion of an 'autopsy' where 'they find out what made them die'. The conversation is interrupted by a child who talks about the cut on her finger.

On another day, and perhaps linked to this topic, Lauren has a passing conversation with one of the researchers about a pretend 'nest' that she has constructed. The researcher asks if there is a mother bird in there with the little birds, and Lauren replies: "She flied away and left them alone and didn't look after them". Researcher: "Is she coming back?" Lauren: "Never again because she died". Researcher. "Oh. How did she die?" Lauren: "Because she got run over by a car".

In another episode, when Lauren is recounting an amusing event about cooking with her Nana, with whom she often stays, Lauren says: "Why is it sad not to see me when I stay home with Nana?" (although sadness had not been mentioned in the conversation). The teacher replies: "Because we miss you. But you're having so much fun with Nana".

Puzzling about gender norms

The next episode shows Lauren in conversation with other children exploring and disputing gender concepts.

A 'Girls-In' Space (phase one)

Lauren and Daisy are playing together, apparently constructing what they call 'girls-in' space and 'boys-in' space. Lauren says "I have to have my guitar because I'm going to play on it because I'm a boy, eh". Daisy wants this to be a girls-only space. The expression "girls in" and "boys-in" appears to have been invented by Daisy to exclude the boys. Lauren, who wants to take on the

---

role of a boy, suggests that it depends on the day of the week, so Daisy has the last word: "It's a girls-in because it's Wednesday". Alongside Daisy's analysis of 'boys-in' and 'girls-in' spaces, Lauren has decided to define the role of being a boy as someone who plays a guitar. She announces that she is a boy because she is playing the guitar ('strumming' a long unit block).

Lauren: This is a listening song and we have no guitars, just listening. The boys played the guitars. I'm a boy and I play the guitar. (to another child nearby, a boy): Are you a boy? Do you want to get your guitar out and play? You can come and play. You don't have to do it because you are a boy.... I have to have my guitar because I'm going to play on it because I'm a boy, eh.

Daisy: No, this is only girl ones. ... girls-in. (They argue about whether it is a boys-in and a girls-in, or a girls-in only)

Lauren: No, it's boys-in and girls-in. You say boys share their 'in' with girls don't they, and on Friday girls use the oven eh, so it's Thursday so the girls put their instruments in the boys-in, eh.

Daisy: No, it's a girls-in because it's Wednesday. [It was indeed a Wednesday].

It all seems to get too complicated to progress the play, and at the end of this discussion, Lauren introduces a story-line about monsters. Lauren: "I'll be a monster and you can be the..." Daisy: "And I pretend I cry at you okay?". This negotiation is satisfactory, and the play continues. This interest in the markers of gender, in particular her exploration of being a boy, will be stepped up in phase two as she finds a number of strategies to enable her to change into the childcare centre's supply of boys' spare clothes.

Flying

Both the teacher and Lauren are jointly contributing to a pretend story-line as the teacher pushes Lauren and another child on the swing.

"Have you got your seat belts on? ... You're on an aeroplane taking off slowly...Are you on a plane? ...". Lauren reminds her that she will be scared of the noise if it's a little plane, and when the teacher says that sometimes you can see the pilot if it is a really small plane, she asks "what's a pilot?". Lauren talks about flying to Wellington (a one hour flight) when she went on a flight with her dad, and was met by her Poppa.

Questioning the schedule at childcare

(i) Pick-up time. Questions about pick-up times are responded to with patience and information by the teacher. She explains the connection between the times and what the children will be doing. She then shows Lauren the roll, and explains that it tells the teachers the pick-up times.

> *Pick-Up Time (phase one)*
>
> (Jarvis sounds unhappy).
> Teacher: That's Jarvis. Maybe he's a bit sleepy. He's having a sleep with us today.
> Lauren: Why?
> Teacher: Because he's staying with us longer so he's having a sleep.
> Lauren: Why is he going to be staying here longer?
> Teacher: I'm not too sure, but his Mum asked us if we could have him til 3 o'clock, so maybe she's got some more jobs to do. She needs us to look after him a bit longer.
> Lauren: When his Mum going to pick him up?
> Teacher: Three o'clock.
> Lauren: When is three o'clock?
> Teacher: Well, when we finish lunch it will be 12.30 and 3 o'clock is a few more hours after that so we have a play and then we have afternoon tea and then we play for a little bit longer and then she will be here. It's after afternoon tea, a short while after. Because your mum comes about 4.30....
> Lauren: Do you know what? Do you know what Lizzie said when I was on the swing: her mum's coming at five.
> Teacher: Five o'clock do you think?
> Lauren: Yeah.
> Teacher: ...maybe I can get some things out today, an old clock perhaps I can show you the different times and the numbers and how we tell what time of the day it is.
> Lauren: When is Daisy going home?
> Teacher: Well, this is what we have a look up on here Lauren, on the roll, and it will tell us what time all the children will arrive at the centre and what time all the children are supposed to leave so I can find Daisy's name and it tells me that she's going home at 4.15pm.
> Lauren: Yeah.

(ii) The routine yesterday. While in the previous episode Lauren was puzzling about the rationale behind what would happen in the future, in this episode she is reflecting on a past event.

> *Too sleepy for Afternoon Tea (phase one)*
>
> There is a discussion between Lauren and the teacher. Lauren asks her "You know yesterday I didn't have any afternoon tea?" The teacher is genuinely interested in this. "Why not?"
> Lauren: Because I didn't have any.
> Teacher: Were you not feeling hungry yesterday?
> Lauren: I was but I was too sleepy.
> Teacher: Too sleepy? Oh, you're so right because I remember you having a sleep on this couch right here that you're standing on. Do you remember that?

Lauren:	Yeah....
Teacher:	Were you too sleepy to eat were you? Was your mouth too tired? Your jaw just couldn't open and shut?
Lauren:	What is jaws?
Teacher:	What do you think it might be?
Lauren:	I don't know.
Teacher:	It's got something to do with your mouth.
Lauren:	Eat.
Teacher:	Your jaws are like your gums that your teeth come out of, so you're feeling it with your fingers – feeling your jaws and they open and shut – that's your jaws. Can you feel them closing together when you shut them? Interesting isn't it?

[Lauren then quizzes the teacher about what she is having for lunch]

Puzzling about the weather and the solar system

These questioning practices continue in phase two, two months before she is about to turn five and start school. But Lauren is more likely in this phase to interact with peers than she was in phase one. Of the fourteen episodes in phase two, five are interactions with other children only: a game with Bob the Builder cards and three other children (most of the time a discussion about whose turn it is), an episode of pretend play with another girl in which Lauren is the big sister ("I'm going to school", returns from school, hands baby to play partner, "Baby's crying Dad", "It's morning time now"), an episode when she intervenes on behalf of a younger child who says the boys are annoying her ("No, that's not okay Robbie"), an episode when she plays on the bikes with Sheryll, and an episode in which she joins David in concrete-making play in the sandpit. This latter was originally David's enterprise, but she is absorbed in her assistant role, and her few comments include: "I need some more water, thanks mate... Thanks mate, that's enough...... Thanks mate".

Lauren continued to question adults in phase two. In one episode a conversation begins when a teacher is looking at a book about the house-building down the road, a book that has been made by the teachers for re-visiting and discussion. Sheryll tells the teacher that she is going to squash (the game) with her father that night. They talk about how it's a really fast game and you have to be really quick, and the topics shift from the rules of squash and who plays it, to the teacher's lunch, to showers (of rain), how the sun got up in the sky, what makes Jarrod's hair stand up, and where two of the other teachers are. In twelve minutes of this extended conversation between a teacher and the two children, there were 130 conversational turns; Lauren contributes forty-seven of these, and twenty-three of her contributions are questions. All of the questions are carefully answered by the teacher. Here is a small section of that conversation:

Raining Outside (phase two)

Teacher: It's pouring down.

Lauren: Oh no, we can't go to the concrete truck [on the building site down the road] now.

Teacher: No we can't, not while it's raining but it might be just showers.

Lauren: What's showers?

Teacher: A shower is when the rain comes but the wind blows the rain away so it doesn't rain all day. It means that it rains for a little bit and then it stops and then it rains.....

Lauren: How did the sun get up in the sky?

Teacher: That's a really good question Lauren, and do you know what, I don't know the answer. It's just always been there.

Sheryll: I do.

Teacher: I don't know how earth was made, and I don't know how all the planets were made.

Sheryll: It spins around.

Teacher: It does. Earth does spin around in space...

Lauren: Well why? Well my mum knows.

Teacher: Does she? How does she think the sun got up in the sky?

Lauren: She thinks it just moves like that [moves her fist up from the table].

Teacher: It does move, yeah. But how did it get there the very first day the sun came?

Lauren: Just get over to the other side.

Teacher: It's an interesting thing to think about, isn't it.

Lauren: Like it gets over, if it was raining in [this town] then it would be, and in Australia it would be sunny. So it moves over, so it moved over to Australia.

Teacher: Oh, you are right maybe. Do you know what, the sun, when it's raining the sun is always up in the sky.

Lauren: Why?

Teacher: It's always, it's hiding behind all the rain clouds so it's always up there but it just can't get through the rain clouds.

Lauren: How come?

Teacher: It can't be shining because the clouds are blocking all the light, not all the light because otherwise it would be night time.....

Lauren: Why if there was all the lights [blocked] then it would be night time?

Teacher: That's right, if .... the sun is on a different part of the earth, so it might be night time in New Zealand but it might be day time in America perhaps.... [She says that she will bring a globe and a light to the centre the next day to illustrate this].

Lauren appears to be developing a working theory in which the sun and the rain alternate (move over) between Australia and New Zealand, while the teacher is inviting the children to imagine an alternative theory about sun and rain clouds. Sheryll contributes the information that the explanation is something about the spinning of the earth.

Puzzling about having a baby

Lauren has heard about the teacher having an ultrasound scan several days ago, and she knows that one of the teachers is having a baby. In this episode she comes running inside with Teddy up her T-shirt, has a conversation with another teacher about when she, the teacher, had her baby.

Having a Baby (phase two)	
Lauren:	Did you have medicine when you had the baby?
Teacher:	The baby got a bit stuck when it was trying to get out.
Lauren:	Did it hurt?
Teacher:	No, they gave me some special medicine.
Lauren:	And how did they get it out?
Teacher:	They had to cut my belly.
Lauren:	With a knife?
Teacher:	A special doctor's knife called a scalpel.
Lauren:	And how did they stick you together again?
Teacher:	Just like using a needle and thread. Like we do here.
Lauren:	Did it hurt?
Teacher:	No, I didn't feel it cos they gave me some special medicine so I didn't feel it.
Lauren:	Can you still taste the medicine?
Teacher:	No. It was quite a long time ago because (the baby) is big now.
Lauren:	The doctor will have to cut me because the baby's having trouble getting out.
(She takes teddy out from under her T-shirt) There. It came out.	

The teacher tells this story to Lauren's mother, and she adds to it: "Lauren said "Oh, I don't want to have a baby Mum, because it would hurt and the doctor ... I don't want them ... about the body, she's very interested in that, isn't she?"

Puzzling about being a boy

The theme of making sense of the descriptors of 'being a boy' continues in phase two. Lauren is frequently changing her clothes, searching amongst the childcare clothes to find boys' short pants, although the rule is that you must only change into childcare clothes if yours are wet and you don't have your own to change into. She has developed a number of strategies to resist this rule. On one occasion she says she wants to play rugby and her long-sleeved shirt will be too hot (she doesn't then play rugby); on another occasion she goes outside to briefly play with 'gloop' (like finger paint) and gets some paint on her clothes, providing a reason to change; on a third occasion she, Mike and Robbie use the spare clothes drawers as 'dress-ups' and they search for interesting boys' shorts: "cos we're going to Auckland to the zoo eh? To look after the animals" (a popular TV programme is about zoo keepers at the Auckland Zoo). Robbie holds up a skirt. "That's a dress!" says Lauren. Teacher: "In Scotland men wear dresses". Lauren: "You mean Māori people?" Teacher: "Yes, they do too". One day she arrives at childcare with a parcel of returned and laundered childcare clothes: "Put these in the daycare drawer. All the shorts, shorts, shorts".

In the following transcript she is defining being a boy as having shorts on. Lauren has gone inside and changed into stripey shorts. She and Greta are pushing the bikes down the slope. She greets John and Carl, who are also on bikes.

> **Only Boys Wear Shorts (phase two)**
>
> Lauren: I'm going racing... These pants fall down on me..
> Greta: Come on, you're coming with me?
> Lauren: Oh yea. I'm coming with you.
> Greta: I'm just going to find a park.
> Lauren: Yea, Hey man hey John, hey little rabbit. It's Christopher here. Hi little bunny rabbit.
> Greta: Come on.
> Lauren: Hi John. Hi Carl. Hi John. I'm a boy cos I've got shorts and a t-shirt on. I'm a boy cos I've got shorts on eh?
> John: Come on, hop in here.
> Lauren: Oh, yeah mate (gets onto a bike) ...... (To researcher) Only boys wear shorts at school cos the school thinks it looks handsome. [Runs off to play on the climbing equipment].

Asking questions at school

We observed Lauren on three different days after she had been at school for four months (interrupted by a month of summer holidays). Episodes included: writing (Teacher: "At printing time we're concentrating and we don't speak. ... Find your best 'e' and give it a tick"), reading (colouring in a worksheet after matching letters to pictures), reading in a group, singing practice in the hall, estimating the number of marbles in a jar, and a dice game (snakes and ladders). On the second day (St Patricks day), the day was similarly scheduled: colouring in a shamrock, hat parade day in the hall, writing about the hat ('My hat is sparkly and I tried to put pom poms on'), a running record test, completing a 'd' worksheet, writing 'a story about Dad or Grandad' ('My dad does my hair in a little pony'), and a worksheet for matching pictures that have the same initial letter sound. The teacher tells the researcher that Lauren has made a breakthrough with writing.

Questioning the story. As in many of the classrooms we visited, there is little opportunity to actually tell a story. For instance, in a lesson on Writing about Dad, the teacher says: "When you write your story about your Dad or your Grandad...make sure you've got a capital letter and a full stop. That's what I'm looking for today. Think of your story before you go away [from the mat]"). Lauren does ask a few questions, as in the following, but it interrupts the small group reading time:

Story Time (phase three)

Teacher:	This story's called bedtime – it's the Wizard's bedtime.
Lauren:	Is he a naughty person?
Teacher:	No, he's a wizard darling.
Lauren:	What's a wizard?
Teacher:	He's like a magic man. Like in The Lord of the Rings. Did you see that? ...There was a wizard, and he could do magic tricks. [She reads on] Who's on the bed here? It looks like a giant, and what's he taken to bed with him? A bone.
Lauren:	Is a giant really scary?
Teacher:	Are there really giants?
Lauren:	No.
Teacher:	No, well, they're not true. Here we go ... (she reads the story)

Lauren also tries to liven up the meaning of the story in a big group story-reading time, perhaps calling on her interest in accidents hospitals and danger.

Big Group Story Time (phase three)

Teacher:	Let's read this one. It's called "The" – you know what this is? – "The Tree House" (some children join in with the reading). Try it again.
Class:	The Tree House....
Teacher:	It's an owl... And he's telling you that this is his house. [She point to the words and invites the children to read].
Class:	Here is my house said the owl.
Class:	Here is my house said the bee.
Class:	Here is my house said the bird.
Class:	Here is my house said the koala.
Class:	Here is my house said the -.
Lauren:	White-tail!
Another child:	Spider.
T:	Well, it could be a White-tail. Has it got a white tail?
Class:	No.
Teacher:	Let's see if it starts like White-tail.
Lauren:	(shouting) No, cos it's got 'spider'.
T.	Let's start again. We'd better go back.
Class:	Here is my house.
Lauren:	(quietly, to herself) I just mainly said that.
Class:	Said the spider.

We might admire this disposition of Lauren's to take a critical and questioning approach to story-lines. However, when there are seventeen other children interacting in a group reading episode, this can be irksome for any teacher. Her mother commented that "She's actually a child that unfortunately makes a bee-line for mischief-makers.... And I was like that at school too". Our clue that this curiosity and critique has become a facet of a disposition is supported by its appearance in spite of unfavourable circumstances, but wise children also recognise opportunity, and 'read' the classroom for those occasions when they can ask probing questions and introduce trouble to the narrative without jeopardising the good will of the teacher. Some of Lauren's interests in telling a good story may, where the curriculum is crowded, have to wait until the business of writing independently is achieved, and she can write her own.

LEARNING IN THE MAKING

Disposition-in action: work in progress

This section summarises our interpretation of the three dispositional components, introduced in chapter two, translated from the triadic definition of a learning disposition, our observations, and the literature on the continuity of learning as authoring, recognising opportunity, and connected knowing. All three of these components combined together as a work in progress towards the children being ready willing and able to ask questions.

Authoring. Lauren's inclination to ask questions was in no doubt: her authoring of questioning conversations occurred at all phases of the project, and at home. The clue for us that Joseph is ready to ask questions about entitlement (about who should ask the questions and be in charge of what happens next) at school came from his being willing to: question his entitlement to have an ordinary conversation at mat time, question the justice of a competitive game that no-one could be said to legitimately win, and question the teacher's binary of soft and mechanical toys. These were not situations that he has experienced at the kindergarten; it seems that he may have a more general, big picture, view of fairness and entitlement and he can recognise what it looks like in a different context. There is a sense in which by phase two he is asking questions of himself at the kindergarten; once Mahesh has gone to school Joseph can take more of a leadership role. By phase three Joseph has recognised opportunities to be an 'in-charger', to take the lead, and to (mildly) critique the status quo, but he is disappointed that reading has not come easily, and he recognises that this is the major agenda in school. His interest in the 'big picture' and his concern for 'fairness' have remained themes for him, moving from one context to another and appearing stronger because they still appear in places where there is not much room for them. His intense and affective engagement with the trolley play, and his inclination to communicate his opinions were also examples of taking authoritative action.

Recognising opportunity. In early childhood settings and school Joseph is learning to recognise the different ways in which he is being positioned by peers and by teachers. This accumulation of episodes is allowing him to: become attuned to opportunities when he can be an 'in-charger', develop his thoughtful concerns for fairness, and recognise (and perhaps construct) those projects that provide him with an interesting and enjoyable balance of challenge and skill. Part of this is recognising relevant similarities and differences. In her classic 1977 study of children's drawing, Goodnow comments (p.15): "Without ways of analysing similarity and difference, we cannot begin to ask questions about how what we observe (for instance features of drawings) relates to, for example, experience or age". We might say the same about recognising opportunities to learn. Joseph appeared to be developing criteria for what was safe, dangerous and 'naughty' at the kindergarten by tacitly analysing similar and different events. At school he is respectful in class, gets on with the tasks assigned, and chooses his moments to question what might be the classroom norms. Lauren knows that she is welcome to ask questions at the childcare centre and at home. In both cases she will be responded to carefully and thoughtfully. At school Lauren's mischievous introduction of a troublesome meaning to the story of the Owl's House (the entry of a poisonous white-tail spider) was not censured; indeed the teacher accepted it as a valid possibility, but she made it clear that the agenda on this occasion was decoding a script. Making sense includes having the sensitivity to occasion – as well as the ability and the inclination. But an 'occasion' needs to be, at least occasionally, available.

Connected knowing.   In these case studies, subject-knowing and disposition-knowing were very closely entwined. Both children were using their past experiences to ask questions about the present and about possible selves. Joseph may be developing criteria about: when one is entitled to take the lead and make the decisions; what risks are optimal; and what circumstances or rules are fair for all? Lauren is asking questions about the way that the world works, how are babies born, and she is questioning cultural norms like what does gender mean in social practice. Joseph's interest in technology, utilised in pretend play in the kindergarten, and enhanced by library books at home, provided him with the knowledge to question the teacher's lesson frame. Lauren's interest in sad events, gender roles and signifiers, and white-tail spiders and the weather and the schedules at the childcare centre means that she asks questions about these matters. Both children are developing working theories in areas that interest them, and both the domains of interest (entitlement, risk, fairness, scheduling, the sad and scary, weather) and the facets of a resilient disposition, to puzzle over and to seek meaning, travel with them from phase to phase, from their homes to their early childhood centres and to school.

Design

We highlight here two features of educational design that were inviting children to build resilience by asking questions. The first of these, affective engagement with peers, appeared in the previous chapter on resilience as well. The second is dialogue and teacher expectations.

Affective engagement with peers.   In phase one Joseph does not appear to be able to pursue interests (for instance the sea animals example) when he is called away by a friend who is deemed by both of them to be 'in charge' of the agenda. By phase two however, Joseph is his own boss in more episodes, designs his own projects, and inserts technical interests into pretend play (exploring how to make a lock from a coat hanger, for instance) and physical play (calculating the speed and turn in order to safely negotiate a steep driveway in a trolley). These episodes of affective engagement (a mixture, in this case, of excitement and fear) appeared to be very motivating, and they may have their equivalent in participation in team sports, a year or so later. It was his mother's philosophy that:

> if he's happy, he's happy learning. ..... Because I think you want them to be comfortable, enjoy this learning experience, make these relationships, be socialised in different ways, and then, when they're like that, obviously they'll learn.

Dialogue and teacher expectations. For Lauren, during the childcare phases of this project, the curriculum design encouraged her disposition to puzzle about the ways of the world. The teachers were willing and patient mediators for her quest to make meaning of events and topics that do not appear to make sense to her: sadness, accidents, gender, and time, for instance. The teachers value these dialogues, and they have a generative agenda (one that they hope will contribute to life-long dispositions) of their own for Lauren, introducing knowledge that might put puzzling events into perspective and strategies for coping with distress, re-constructing stories as a mode of making sense, and reminding her that some things matter and some things are less important. In one episode Lauren tried to intervene when two younger children were fighting over a teddy bear; she was adamant that Vera had it first, a claim that was vehemently denied by the other claimant; the teacher said to Lauren: "It's not a big problem. It's a *soft toy*" (at the time none of the three children were convinced by this argument).

The teachers at Lauren's childcare centre present a view that the meaning of work and play at the centre should be transparent: there is a roll that tells you when people arrive and leave, there is a structure to the day that enables a certain amount of prediction, there are principles and rules that make managing complexity easier, and there are adults who will listen. The teachers treat Lauren's questions seriously and explain their words, provide knowledge, reassure, admit that they don't know, and introduce some principles of learning. On one occasion, when Lauren writes her name at the childcare centre, the teacher took the opportunity to revisit an earlier story, written three weeks earlier, in which a teacher assisted Lauren to write 'butterfly' on the computer, and her own name on paper. She seizes the chance to talk to Lauren about 'practising' as a good principle for learning:

Teacher: Wonderful writing Lauren, that's fantastic. You did a very clear [points to four of the letters]. ...
Lauren: Look what Lizzie did.
Teacher: Lizzie's been practising as well, she has too [points to two of the letters that Lizzie has written]. And Daisy's been doing lots of practising too, hasn't she?

Lauren: Where? [The teacher explains that this Learning Story does not include an example of Daisy practising, but that she often writes her name, and her parents' names, on her paintings].

Lauren: Oh ... Does Robbie do some [practising writing]?

Teacher: He's doing a little bit of practising isn't he?

Lauren: He likes riding on the bikes better eh?

Teacher: He does. There's lots of different activities that the children can do.

Lauren's disposition to make sense of things that interest and excite her by asking questions of those who might know, may depend, at school, on her recognition of some rather narrow windows of opportunity until she can read and answer questions for herself. Our research suggests that learning in the making, with learning dispositions in mind, is about developing 'dispositional milieux' as places and people and artefacts that afford, invite and provoke those ways of being and acting and knowing that will contribute to life-long learners who are communicative, kind, creative and curious citizens. The strengthening of the disposition is also about responses in-the-moment, a feature of Lauren's childcare centre and her family.

PROVOKING IMAGINATION

Exploring Possible Worlds

> Children's pretend play is not an early distortion of the real world but an initial exploration of possible worlds. Moreover, as they think about those alternatives, children consider them in a coherent and consequential fashion. In that sense, pretend play is not an activity that is doomed to suppression but the first indication of a lifelong mental capacity to consider alternatives to reality. (Harris, 2000, p. 28)

The two case studies in this chapter are about children beginning to consider alternative worlds, and at the same time to develop new lenses through which to interpret and imagine the world. Maxine Greene in her book entitled *Releasing the Imagination* comments that "imagining things being otherwise may be the first step toward acting on the belief that they can be changed" (Greene, 1995, p. 22). The design of educational environments can provide opportunities for this disposition towards imagining things being otherwise, and for learners "to use imagination in a search for openings without which our lives narrow and our pathways become cul-de-sacs" (Greene, 1995, p. 18). Elliot Eisner, himself a painter, also writes about the imagination in education. He comments that:

> Marrying the arts and cognition has not been all that common. We tend to think about the arts as trafficking in the emotions, while the sciences deal with matters of cognition. I reject such a dichotomy and regard any practice done well as potentially artistic in character. Thus, the practice of science – when practiced well – is an art form. So is painting. (Eisner, 2005, p. 2)

This chapter highlights the value of the arts as well, including drama, and the case studies describe 'multimodal' approaches to making meaning. Carey Jewitt (2008) has reviewed the themes of multimodality and literacy in school classrooms, and claims that the mode chosen to represent knowledge is integral to meaning and learning. She writes about the learning potentials of teaching materials and says that multimodality "attends to meaning as it is made through the situated configurations across image, gesture, gaze, body posture, sound, writing, speech and so on.... (*modes* are) organized sets of semiotic resources for meaning making" (p. 246). Many of the modes available in early childhood settings, affording meaning-making through projects and imaginative dramatic or fantasy play, have been documented in this book; they are not readily available in other educational settings. In a number of early childhood settings in New Zealand, with the assistance of peers and teachers – and rapidly-advancing and increasingly-accessible digital technologies – four-year-olds are taking photographs and making movies (Carr, Lee & Jones, 2009;

Clark & Moss, 2001). Glenda Hull and Mark Nelson, writing in 2005 about 'the power of multimodality' (with a particular interest in literacy and digital multimodal texts) comment that "multimodality can afford, not just a new way to make meaning, but a different kind of meaning" (p. 225) and they add that they feel a certain urgency about this and like-minded projects because of the print domination in schools and universities (see also New London Group, 1996, and Kress, 2003). In our view, a love of and disposition towards multimodality, together with the skills of 'braiding' or 'orchestrating' multimodal texts (Hull & Nelson, 2005, p. 225), can be provoked in early education – before literacy becomes established as silos of writing and reading print-based texts, art activities are squeezed into a crowded curriculum schedule as an extra, digital technology relegated to an hour in the computer lab, or theatrical endeavours programmed as formal events once a year.

SARAH

At the beginning of our study Sarah had been attending a full-day childcare centre from the age of two and when we met her she was in the 'nursery' section of the same early childhood centre complex. She was the only child of a professional couple, and her mother described their family as "a unit of the three of them, plus the cat!". The cat provided the impetus for an imaginary theme, as 'Super Kitten', that accompanied Sarah through all the phases of our observations. Sarah was included in many of her parents' work experiences, including travelling internationally. While Sarah was involved in the school's 'after school activities' her mother commented that as working parents it was very difficult for them to manage having friends home to play after school and she felt that this had made it slower for Sarah to establish relationships with the children in her class – the culture of the families in the area was for children to play at each others' houses after school – but Sarah had a very close friendship with another child at the centre, Donald, and this was supported both in the early childhood centre and at home, as the children's mothers knew each other.

Imaginative dramatic play with objects

Early childhood centre observations and interactions with Sarah, alongside the other children at the centre, indicated that she was deeply engaged in dramatic play on a daily basis. Sustained and supported dramatic play was a feature of this centre, and, notwithstanding the interruptions for refreshment breaks, the children were mostly able to have long uninterrupted periods for play. In phase one Sarah appeared to be comfortable engaging with others, although she was more often deeply engaged in dramatic play with objects and toys rather than with the other children. In four of seven episodes, Sarah was playing with objects or equipment, initiating a storyline, with other children entering the play for short periods. One of the early childhood teachers commented:

And she's so social at the moment, like she's right in there chatting in the social wee circle and really playing. But I also see her as someone who actually doesn't mind if she's not being social. Because she's very social with objects, like she's very dramatic play with ... little objects and things, she gets right involved in her own little world. And if someone wants to play alongside and with her, that's great. But if they don't, that doesn't worry her either. She's quite self-contained in that way. So like – well a lot of the time I used to see her playing on her own and now she's becoming quite social with it. But I still --- she seems to be quite happy either way. You know, she's not someone that has to have a best buddy with her all the time[11]. (Teacher interview, phase one)

Sarah appeared to have very clear ideas and goals for her play and was able to continue that play around other children and their goals and activities, despite apparent attempts by other children to take over the authoring, and interruptions as they borrow or move her 'characters' around. The following are excerpts from a one-hour episode during phase one that illustrates her imaginative play with objects.

Duplo homes and families (phase one)

Sarah is at the Duplo table with Abbi. There are play houses, cars, furniture and duplo people. Sarah is putting a 'person' figure in and out of a car. She is talking mostly to herself with only occasional comments to Abbi, as Abbi moves into Sarah's zone of play:

Sarah: That's a grown up. And I need a car. I need a car with a trailer for the rest of my kids. (Abbi bends to pick up characters around Sarah).

Sarah: No I need – I can do my own one. And this one is driving this one. With the kids at the back. And there's one kid is driving with grandpa and the dogs staying ... (She takes the characters away from Abbi and carries on ignoring her).

Abbi: Hey!

Sarah: No, those are ... there already is one on your side. ... We got a doggy and ... they know the baby's at the back. The baby is at the back lying with the girl and the other one is holding the dog. ... Excuse me, can we come in? Yes. Can we come in? ... Knock-knock is anybody home? Hmm. Oh, guess I have to open it. Ooo owww with the door. You stay outside while I open it. ... Can you give me a shoe, please? Can you get me a shoe? You can't steal my things, okay. Thank you. Grandma shut the door.

Abbi tries to engage by handing characters to Sarah. Sarah acknowledges this by giving the new character a role in the script that is occurring. After a few moments of this Abbi reaches over for a character of her own:

Abbi: I need to borrow him for a minute, can I? (she reaches for a character).

Sarah: No. You can have that one (handing her a different character. Then she continues talking to herself and the characters). Ooh, Harold my boy, where is Harold? Got Harold to bed. That's Harold's bed. And Harold is in his bed because it's nearly night time. "Excuse me, I want to go to bed" (speaking in a different voice) "waaa- waaa-

---

> waaa. Waaaaaah. Hmmmwaaa". And here's a mattress. Then I don't get my baby. "Where's my baby? And I hold it up. I hold my baby". And the record is playing and they are asleep. It's going g-g-ggg-ggg-gggggg. Hey that's ... otherwise Harold is awake and he needs to be sleeping.. Put the table ... where's the table? Where's the green table? Oh here's the green table. No. I need it. My table.

This pattern continues with Abbi adding characters and Sarah making it 'fit' into her script. Twenty-five minutes later Abbi moves off and Sarah continues talking, now alone with the Duplo. She continues to move around the people, acting out the story. A teacher moves over to talk with her looking at the characters tucked up in beds:

Teacher: Is everyone asleep Sarah?
Sarah: Yes. (Tania enters the room and joins in.)
Sarah: You can have one of them, this . . .
Tania: Mummy, Mummy.
Teacher: Are they going on a trailer?
Sarah: And then this one is sleeping upside down.

Tania reaches for another character.

Sarah: No, that's what I need.

Sarah looks around at the characters and carefully selects two which she hands to Tania. Two other childen arrive, and one of them makes off with the play television. The teacher intervenes. Teacher: Oh we don't want the TV to go do we?

Sarah: No.

The teacher asks for the television to be put back.

Gordon arrives, and after some joking interaction about the toilet Sarah grabs at the walls as Gordon starts to knock them down. Instead of making a fuss she redirects him to the importance of the walls by continuing the story.

Sarah: The other one is sleeping there. He's behind the door. Yi-hi-how. No. No breaking the house little boy. It's staying up because my hand is on it *(giggles)*.

They then continue the story line and after a few more minutes Gordon moves out of the room as Tania returns to the room and moves over to the table where the Duplo is set up. Tania touches a wall and some of the bricks fall down – she laughs as they fall to the floor.

Sarah: You breaked the chimney silly girl. (using a voice of one of her characters).

Tania pauses and then picks up a character and engages in the storyline also. Gordon returns holding the television. The three of the children continue to play for another twenty minutes before Sarah is left alone once more, where she continues to play with the characters – and as the characters – before tidy up time is called for all the children.

Cats and super kitten

Sarah's play with Donald in phase one centred around cats and dogs as the main themes. They appeared in different contexts – cats and dogs in *outer space* one day, and in the *woods* on another day. We observed Sarah both 'being' a cat, and 'creating cats' and other children being 'cats' in her dramatic play games. In a phase two episode the story line was a complicated plot of travelling in space to arrive at a planet where Sarah and Donald have captured a kitten, put it into a cage (designed for dragons) and celebrated by finding a chocolate and strawberry shop from where they ate till they exploded. The play included the use of cardboard tubes as props for telescopes, chairs as a space ship, and some interruption of the story-line as Donald attempted to take over the direction of play; Sarah, however, managed to remain in charge of the script. Super Kitten play continued when the researcher visited two days later. Both Sarah and Donald wore cat tails (on elastic around their waists) to signify their role, and although to a listening outsider the 'cat' element might not have been always clear, Sarah added the occasional reminder to Donald; she says "Remember, I take.... Meow, meow, meow" and Donald replies "Cat biscuits". Before the following episode Sarah says "Remember we're magic kittens".

Magic Kittens in Space (phase two)

The story line so far has been a complicated plot of traveling in space to arrive at a planet where Sarah and Donald have captured a 'beautiful kitten', put it into a cage (designed for dragons) and celebrated by finding a chocolate and strawberry shop from where they ate until they exploded. After recovering from this adventure, there is a pause and then:

Sarah: I can read your mind!

Donald: We're in space.

Sarah: We're in the space ship. Want to go. No one takes me back to home.

Donald: Is that your telescope? [Tubes had been used for telescopes from the beginning of the game].

Sarah: I've got two telescopes now. (holding up another tube and grabbing at the one Donald is holding out).

Donald: My telescope! My poor little telescope – you're lost.

Sarah: (giggles) Oh that was good. (giggles and screeches). I'll just do another [show]. I'm going to get the batteries out this time. That's the right end.

Donald: Why Sarah?

Sarah looks thorough her telescope. She puts her feet up on the seat of Donald's chair and he pushes them away.

Donald: Do what I say or you're not playing the game.

Sarah gets up and walks away to the door, and then back to her seat as Donald turns, making a "taking off" sound. Danny is sitting in the front seat, pretending to drive. Sarah is screwing her face up as she returns to her seat. Donald moves his chair back with Sarah and she helps Donald arrange his chair.

Donald: Pull it closer.

They both sit and look through their paper tubes and the game continues for another 25 minutes. Neither refer to Donald's attempt at subverting the game to the way he wanted it played, and after sitting closely together for some moments fiddling with the 'telescopes' the script continues led by Sarah.

Sarah's own interpretation of this game, when shown photographs of this episode, echoed both the fun of the game but also the sense of clarity of themes and Sarah's own script in the play:

Sarah: Hmm. Well we're looking after interesting things and this is a space ship on a planet, so a planet and doing interesting things.
Researcher: Oh you're on a planet?
Sarah: Yeah. And a space ship and looking out at interesting things with the telescope.
Researcher: You and Donald played that game for quite a long time, what was interesting about that game?
Sarah: Because . . . because we can then pretend what we need. We can pretend something what we're seeing. Yeah. Like Donald pretended he saw a big, funny space ship coming. Funny.
Interviewer: Oh right.
Sarah: He had two [telescopes]
Interviewer: Really? So what else happened in that game?
Sarah: Um, Donald forgot which telescope was his.
Interviewer: But you remembered?
Sarah: Yeah. I told him. (Interview with Sarah, phase one.)

The resources in this centre supported both the complexity and the length of the play. The children had uninterrupted time to continue the drama, and freely available and accessible junk material and furniture to enable the construction of the setting to be maintained as the game shifted in theme and topic. Sarah's favourite character, Super Kitten, appeared to be a consistent role for Sarah, enacted both at home and at the centre. Sarah's fifth birthday cake at home was constructed in the shape of the head of a cat. When Sarah positioned herself as 'Super Kitten' her interactions with the other children increased and she often led or directed the scripts of the game. In three of four very long and sustained episodes of dramatic play in phase two, a Super Kitten script engaged Sarah in complex interactions and dialogue. In Super Kitten play Sarah was able to assert her own scripts and storylines with both Donald and any other children who moved in and out of the play.

Transferring Super Kitten to the school classroom

Seven of the eight episodes from the school phase of Sarah's observations involved instructional activities that Sarah was expected to complete in a set amount of time, with prepared activities, and required outcomes. There was no space for episodes of dramatic play. On one occasion, however, she introduced the imaginary Super Kitten enabling her, for a moment, to introduce some continuity of theme in a setting where she found the tasks of reading and writing mysterious. The episode is one of story writing.

Story writing (phase three)

The teacher has given directions about writing in their story books. She hands out the books and the children head off to their assigned tables. Sarah spends some time searching for a pencil sharpener, and as she finally sharpens her pencil over the rubbish bin near the teacher's desk the teacher comments "You should have been writing ages ago. Quick as quick". Back to her desk, Sarah sits and opens her book, holding her pencil, swinging her feet. She looks closely at the writing on the previous page. Then she gazes at the art work on the wall. She looks down and writes 'is' and talks to the girl on the other side of the table. She talks about her invisible kitten under her chair, and turns her pencil upside down and rubs out what she's written. Sarah has explained to the children at the writing table that Super Kitten is under her chair. "It's invisible so you can't see it." The children at Sarah's table all look under the table. But the teacher moves alongside the child opposite Sarah, and Sarah begins to look down onto her own book. She peers closely at the book. The teacher moves away again (all children are now looking as though they are attending to their writing), and Sarah leans her chin on the book (grins at the researcher) and then picks up her pencil again. The three girls start talking – spelling 'ing'. Sarah asks: "Is it the one with the two lumps?". … Sarah remains unengaged with writing. She calls out: 'Me', as the teacher goes by. The teacher stops and helps Sarah find "me" in the reading word list. As the teacher begins to talk with another child at the end of the table Sarah leans over and watches. She picks up her pencil and begins to write. She then begins to draw a picture above her writing. …

Sarah: My rubber's awesome (to a boy going past). It can't rub off that much but it can rub off this much.

She demonstrates to the child opposite, on the other child's book. Some children are moving around the room. Sarah and two others talk together at the table.

Sarah: (to one of the children at the table) You're awesome at writing

She stands up and continues to draw in her book, swapping pens and pencils and colouring in her drawing very carefully (she has drawn a person with long hair). She continues drawing – using many colours. Then she begins to add more colours to the drawing on the previous page from another's day writing.

Already Sarah had learnt that 'being a student' means to be seen to be concentrating on the required task – taking the stance of being "carpentered to the desk" as a signal of attending to one's work (McDermott, 1976, cited in Davies & Hunt, 1994, p. 404). She drew on a strategy of praise of another's work to engage them in conversation, and used what little control over the situation that she had to move around the table, sharpening her pencil, looking for her sharpener etc – all of these engaged others in her interactions. The visual imagery that Sarah called upon to remember 'ing' – "Is it the one with the two lumps?" (a question, perhaps, about 'n' or 'm') – demonstrated the sense that Sarah was making from this act of 'writing' and using imagery as a tool to help her remember what the shape of letters and words looked like. Sarah carried this same strategy – using the picture to assist her – into her emerging reading in a reading instructional activity.

> ### Reading instruction (phase three)
>
> As this episode begins it is reading time and the class has been divided into different level groups. Sarah has completed five minutes buddy reading, and then for nine minutes stood watching a boy using a reading programme on the computer (this was used as a choice activity during reading time). There are two student teachers, the classroom teacher and the Reading Recovery Teacher working with the children, and a small group of children has moved to another classroom for buddy reading with the older children. Sarah is directed, by the Reading Recovery Teacher to do her allocated 'reading task' with the Student Teacher. Together Sarah and the Student Teacher sit on the floor in the book corner and Sarah reads the book "*Big Things*". As she reads she puts her finger under each word. She looks at the pictures to help work out the nouns – Ambulance, Bulldozer etc.
>
> Sarah: Fire T..r..u, it's a Fire Engine?
> The Student Teacher sounds out the word 'Truck' and Sarah looks again at the picture but repeats: 'Fire Engine'.
> Student Teacher: What can you notice at the end of every sentence?
> Sarah: A full stop.
> Student Teacher: What can you notice at the start of every sentence?
> Sarah: These (and points to a capital A).
> Student Teacher: A capital A.

Thus, on this occasion, the rules of reading words and letters and recognising sentence structure took priority over making meaning. Sarah's expertise in developing story-lines using verbal text with props has not yet found a place in the school context. However, when the researcher discussed with Sarah her experiences with learning to read and write, Sarah was ready to construct herself as capable and competent. She commented on the 'unfair' nature of the rules of writing, the affordances of a task that was yet to be mastered.

> Researcher: Have you had some books that you really like to read that you feel that you're good at reading?
> Sarah: I know a few. I keep forgetting what the words are. I know some of the words. Because I know how to do a lot of letters. I'm really good at my letter signs. But 'cause sometimes I forget that some go to the bottom and some go to the top. It's the unfairest thing that some letters start at the bottom. (Interview Sarah, phase three)

Sarah balances her 'I keep forgetting' with the fact that she does 'know how to do a lot of the letters' and with the systemic unfairness of how letters are constructed and written. [A year later, Sarah's mother told the researcher that Sarah was now an enthusiastic and competent reader and writer].

A multimodal task at school

A multimodal class project of making a model of a *fale* (a traditional Samoan house), in contrast with some of the writing episodes, was an enterprise that connected with Sarah's prior experience: travelling in the Pacific. This extract from a lengthy episode illustrates Sarah's focus and leadership.

> ### Making a Fale (phase three)
>
> One class activity had real connections for Sarah: a construction from sticks, popsicle sticks, card and string of a *fale*. The class had been looking at 'Samoa' as a theme and had over the week been doing a range of activities associated with this topic. The room had a wonderful display of interesting objects that families had shared, and that the children had gathered and made over the week. Leading up to the activity we observed the children had drawn a plan earlier in the week and were ready to construct the *fale* in pairs. Wikipedia had provided the information that "a *fale* (pronounced fah-lay) is a traditional Samoan thatched roof house. Traditional *fale* do not have walls, or they have thatched blinds surrounding the living quarters", and provided some pictures. Sarah had spent some time in the Pacific with her family, so this project was one that connected to her lived experiences and as an activity not only made sense, but enabled her to demonstrate her 'expertise' at orchestrating a number of diverse props into a meaningful task or object. Sarah receives praise for her plan, and remained focused on a tricky task in collaboration with another child. Although there was not much flexibility it did need concentration and dexterity, and Sarah was able to be the authoritative leader.
>
> Sarah: There you go, you do that. ... No-no, you have to hold it while I push. No, you hold the card. Now we make another big hole. Okay. Hold it while I make a big hole.
> Fiona: I don't want to do it.
> Sarah: You don't know how to do it, and I do.
> Fiona: Sarah ...
> Sarah: Look. Cool.

When we spoke with Sarah's teachers about this activity they commented on her 'high engagement'. They emphasised her skills with scissors: "there were lots of fiddly bits in there":

Researcher: And so how do you think Sarah's engagement and participation went into that?

Teacher: Good. ... High engagement. She's really good with scissors, cutting and just wee fiddly bits and stuff because there were lots of fiddly bits in there. So she was – in the pair [of children she was working with] she was probably – yeah – the higher one of the two. Yeah. And she has good ... small motor skills. (Teacher interview, phase three)

HENRY

During this research study Henry lived with his mother and his younger brother. His parents had separated just as the study began; the father had moved out of the family home and Henry still spent regular time with him. Henry had a set of grandparents who lived in the same city, and one grandparent in another city not far away. He was close to all his grandparents, and another family upheaval occurred when one grandparent died in an accident just before the study began. By phase two, Henry's mother had enrolled in a College of Education as a part-time student. Henry's father worked as a tradesperson. During our study Henry was attending a kindergarten programme five mornings each week. he had been attending the kindergarten since he was two (this early childhood centre provided a programme three afternoons a week for the two- to three-and-a-half-year age group). Several of the children within Henry's group of peers had also attended this afternoon programme and three of these children were amongst the children that he played with the most. By phase two he was close friends with Stephen, whom he had also met at the early childhood centre, and the two of them played most of the time together, although three of the eight episodes in phase one included play with other children.

It's pretend. We're pretending...

There were eight longish episodes in phase one, over two days. All of them were outside: one was a restaurant in the sandpit (initiated by another child), four involved treasure maps, and three were episodes where Henry pretends that the early childhood centre is under water (but he has a plan). There were two common themes throughout all the phase one episodes we observed: constructing and averting possibly dangerous situations (water, fires, sharks and tree monsters), and treasure maps,

Danger and uncertainty.　　Prior to our arrival the kindergarten had had a visit from the Fire Brigade, and had also been running a theme around sharks; these experiences were also appropriated by Henry and the other children during our observations. Fire truck badges as an option for the research jackets contributed to the fire play props in the initial part of the observation period. The fantasy that the outside playground was flooded with water permeated much of the imaginative play. The teachers in this centre did not have any idea where this notion might have come from, but they did not as a rule place many restrictions on the use or movement of equipment and water around the kindergarten if it was important within the context of the play. Henry's mother commented on Henry's persistence in areas outside dramatic play as well:

> Henry does like to challenge himself, to push himself further, he will really persist now until he gets it right – he used to get frustrated and upset and give up if things didn't work out straight away … but lately he is being a lot more patient, even if it doesn't go right straight away – he will really stick at things now and for a long time. [She gives an example involving blocks, and another about learning to use swings at home.] – I think he is a really good problem solver – he is quite persistent – he does like to work things out for himself – he gets annoyed if I try to do it for him, he wants to be able to do things himself. (Interview, phase one, Henry's mother)

Henry used this fantasy of a flooded playground as a way of introducing challenge, danger and uncertainty. In phase one he was usually the one who articulated the danger and sought a solution; in phase two the theme of danger continued, but Henry had to work much harder to retain the authorship. Much of the imaginative play in both phase one and phase two involved an element of considering and acknowledging both the 'real' and 'pretend' in order to 'make sense' as well as to play out a good story. He shifts back and forth from pretend to the 'real' "we're just pretending" in order to keep the plot line going and the other players involved. When the story-line is interrupted by a play partner who resists Henry's imaginary tactic – as in 'The Restaurant' and the 'Fire' episodes – Henry insists that the tactic is "pretending" and can proceed.

The Restaurant (phase one)

Henry has been involved in a 'Restaurant' activity in the sand pit area organized by Peter and Liam. Two teachers and a group of children, including Henry, have been engaged in this activity for some time. Peter was the key player in organizing the event, while Henry (who became involved on invitation from Peter) has entered fully into the pretend play. When the observation of Henry began, the teachers and children had moved away from the sand-pit area. Henry, however, has remained behind in the sand pit by himself and continues to busy himself with the oven and the various pans and dishes filled with sand that are lined up along the sand pit edge and on a small wooden table sitting in the sand pit. He starts organizing the abandoned party food, making new cakes/pies and putting trays in the oven – he is talking to himself, and making adjustments to the oven knobs, checking that things are cooking. Henry has filled up some paper patty cups with sand and he hands one to the researcher.

Henry: Here, this is for you, it's a cup cake – it has pink sugar on the top......

Researcher: (pretending to eat it) mmmm, yummy.

Henry: Do yah like it?

Three boys have wandered over; they are standing in the middle of sandpit amongst the dishes and start knocking and kicking them over. Henry notices and stops what he is doing.

Henry: No, careful, you're standing in them. It's a restaurant.

Ben: That's not a restaurant.

Henry: It is a restaurant. Yes it is, look. These are the dishes. We're pretending it's a restaurant.

Ben: 'Tis not.

Henry: Well you don't know, Ben. You weren't invited to the party.

Ben: Was so, so. Don't care.

Henry appears to be unsure of what to do next. He retrieves a plate with patty tins that have escaped being destroyed and attempts a conciliatory move with Ben, by attempting to enlist him in the pretend plot-line.

Henry: Can I.... Here, do you want some cake, these is .... cup cakes (Henry holds out the plate towards Ben. Ben takes it from Henry and drops it straight on the ground.)

Ben: That's not a real cake.

Henry: 'Tis. It's pretend. We're pretending it's a cup cake.
Ben walks away towards the bars. Henry looks at the remains of the party, doing nothing for a few seconds, then follows and joins Ben and some other boys on the bars. They all play together amicably until Tidy Up Time is called.

Putting out a Fire (phase one)

Henry is brandishing a piece of clear plastic tubing (a Perspex tube) in order to put out a 'fire' in Ricco's sand building. Ricco, who has been previously involved in sword play with other children using the Perspex tubes tells him that he can't do that because "That's a sword". Henry responds "You're not my friend now Ricco" and Ricco still says that the tube is a sword, and hoses for putting out fires are in the shed. Henry 'sounds determined': "No. Yes. I can use this. I am pretending it's a hose". He continues to use the tube as a hose, but shifts the direction of the play by inviting Ricco to join him on a 'ship' ("We need this ship to get through, to get through the water cos this is all water, even the sand pit is water").

Water Danger (phase one)

In a phase one episode that we have called 'water danger' Henry is standing inside the doors of the kindergarten, discussing the imaginary geography with Ricco: which parts of the kindergarten have turned to water and which parts are still designated as land. They are trying to get to the sandpit, and to solve the problem of how to get there when they have just declared most of the outside area to be 'water'. Ricco decides that it is possible to walk around the edge of the woodwork area to get to the sandpit as this is 'dry land'. Ricco starts to head off when Henry calls out after him.
Henry: Oh, no, the sandpit is water as well, the sandpit is water as well, come
        back.
Henry doesn't seem to think they have worked out the problem satisfactorily, or maybe is annoyed that Ricco created a solution too soon, so he creates another problem to be solved (the sandpit is now water as well).
Ricco: (calls out to Henry) No no it's not. It's okay. See.
Ricco has reached the sandpit and is collecting up spades and a digger.
Henry runs after him and reaches the sandpit.
Henry: (talking to self) Oh, oh, it's okay. We builded a bridge eh. This is a
        bridge here.
Henry finds a way to solve the problem of now being 'in the water'. The play continues.

Like Sarah, Henry prefers to be in charge of the script (and the scene-setting). The theme of rescue from danger continued ten days later when Peter and Henry were in 'the fort':

The Fort (phase one)

The fort is a playground climbing structure that the children can play both in and on; it includes a bridge from one section to another. Peter climbs down and heads towards a grassy area. Harry has designated the grassy area as flooded.

Henry: (shouting): No, no! Well, is that swimming?
Peter: No.
Henry: Well we're stuck I'm afraid, stuck forever.
Peter: But I'm stuck here.
Henry: Well there's a board to come back over here.
Peter: Is that not water there?
Henry: Well (thinks about it).... Yes.
Peter: Oh, well I can go that way.
Henry: Hey no, that's the water and that's the water,
Peter: Is the grass water?
Henry: Well we're pretending that's the water. (The boys dressed up as policemen come by).
Henry: Were stuck – policeman. We're stuck.
Henry moves off the fort to join Peter and the children with police hats on the lawn. The conversation turns to the microphones in their research jackets, and they come to find the researcher to ask for more microphones for the policemen. This theme of 'being stuck' will recur a year later.

Treasure maps. A treasure map theme had been initiated by another child at the kindergarten, Peter, who had brought from home an interest in Peter Pan, Captain Hook, pirates and treasure hunts. Henry then became engaged with these story features, adopting and adapting the notion of a treasure map and leading the direction of the play. According to the teacher who spent most of her time in the outdoor area and therefore around the children who were involved in these episodes, Peter had watched the Peter Pan movie at home and started coming to kindergarten and talking about Peter Pan and Captain Cook and this became part of his play with the other children. Peter insisted he was Peter Pan much of the time and started calling the teacher Captain Hook, often referring to her as Captain even when he was not engaged in any 'Peter Pan play' (she appeared to accept this quite happily). Peter's interest in Peter Pan had been going on for about three weeks prior to the researcher's arrival. This teacher often engaged in extending the children's ideas around dramatic play; Henry had become interested in the notion of the Treasure maps, but not in the Peter Pan play. At the end of phase one Henry's mother commented after looking at the data from phase one:

I have really noticed Henry's imagination developing this year and I'm really pleased, he has been really into it at home as well. He starts a story going, and it's all imagination – from his imagination. He starts a story and he gets his brother involved in it (although he's a bit young really – laughs). He just follows along with it) but he (Henry) is so patient, very patient with him – its lovely to watch,.... but it lasts and lasts, the story keeps going over a really long period of time – it can keep going for days. I don't know where half of it comes from, it's quite amazing. Yes, I listen in, I listen in from the kitchen or when they are in here and I'm in here busy cooking tea, it really fascinates me. Sometimes its going along, and I think, 'oh that is from so and so' (or maybe something from TV) or something will be – that thing about Africa and we were talking about Africa, and he wanted to find it on the map, and we were looking at Africa on the map, and then it comes up in his game, but most of the time it's – 'Oh, where did he get that from?' I'm pleased because I worry that he watches too much TV sometimes, and I have worried about that a bit – it's important that his imagination is developing – because he is a child who likes knowledge and facts. It's important that he does play and use his imagination as well I think. (Interview with Henry's mother, phase one)

Henry's actions indicated that a treasure map was of great significance for him. It was a powerful artefact that Jay Lemke might describe as having affording *and* semiotic (symbolic) qualities (Lemke, 2000): the physical presence of a *treasure* map focused and afforded the plot-line of the play, and the symbolic nature of a treasure *map* implied that the person who holds it has the knowledge. Both these aspects supported Henry's authorship of the play. A treasure map appeared in four episodes over the two days of phase one observations. Henry kept this artefact as a central part of his role.

It's Treasure Time (phase one)

While Peter had initiated the treasure map play previously, in this Treasure Map episode the suggestion comes from Henry. Peter and Henry are inside together and stand near the table with bits and pieces set out on it for the children to use in craft or dramatic play. Henry picks up a sheet of shiny wrapping paper from a local chocolate manufacturer. It is like cellophane with the trade name together with associated pictures and writing printed on it).

Henry: Shall we, shall we make a treasure map Peter?

Peter looks around for something the same, then moves over to the collage table to look – he finds a piece of shiny paper and starts to walk back to Henry with it).

Henry: No, not that one Peter, here I'll help you.

Henry goes to the collage area and finds Peter a wrapper the same as his.

Henry: Here Peter, here it is, have this one, it's the same as mine. Now we can do it. Let's roll them up. Let's roll them up like this.

Henry is rolling his paper up and Peter starts to roll his map like Henry – they are standing in the middle of the floor and both rolling their sheets of paper up.

Henry: Here Peter. You do it like this, I'll show you.

Henry demonstrates to Peter how to roll his map from the corner on an angle so that it gets longer. – Peter looks closely at Henry and then starts rolling his map the same way – he finishes and then holds it in front of himself. Henry finishes his and holds it up in the air, Peter does the same.

Peter: There's mine, it's the same as yours eh Henry?

Henry: Yep. Mine is bigger than yours. (Peter laughs).

Henry: Let's go. Let's go find the treasure.

> Peter and Henry walk together to the door. Henry is calling out to anyone who might be listening.
> Henry: It's treasure time, it's treasure time. (Calling loudly).
> Peter unrolls his map and holds it in front of him, Henry does the same. They move outside to the sandpit. The two children dig in the sandpit, using spades and digger, filling a truck with sand, and every now and then referring to the map and saying "Ha, ha!".

Ten days later, on the second day of observations, treasure maps are still being used in the play. By now Henry and Peter are looking for treasure, tree monsters and sharks. Ben joins them in the sandpit.

> ### Flowers, Trees, Monsters and Treasure Maps (phase one)
>
> Henry: We're looking for treasure. We are looking for everything that's on this map.
> Henry starts bending over and looking in the sand, moving it with his hand, Peter and Ben do the same. Ben picks up a small flower that has probably blown off a nearby blossom tree.
> Ben: Flowers, flowers. It's a flower.
> Ben shows Henry, Henry stands up, looks at it and then looks at his piece of paper.
> Henry: Yep, flowers on this map. Well we're looking for everything that is on this map.
> They move to an area of the playground under some trees.
> Henry: Yep, there's trees on here, and we have monsters on this map. Yep, we have tree monsters on this map. (Calls out to Peter) Peter, watch out – that's a bush monster, that's a bush monster.
> Henry finds a stick and uses it like a gun. Ben annoys him and breaks his stick.
> Henry: That's not funny. Peter, he's trying to shoot me. Ben, you ruined my map.
> Ben: Well, I ... You're not allowed guns.
> Henry: Well, it's just a pretend gun. It's okay if you pretend.
> Peter suggests that he and Henry return to the swings, and they do.

Who made the clouds? and she's not a real dental nurse

Two short conversations in between these episodes also appeared to be about Henry considering an imagined world "in a coherent and consequential fashion", as Paul Harris comments in the quote at the beginning of this chapter. One is a conversation with Ben about whether God made the clouds, and another where Henry is waiting to have his eyes and ears checked by a nurse and says (loudly, but to no-one in particular) "It's not a real dental nurse – she doesn't have glasses".

> ### Who Made the Clouds? (phase one)
>
> Henry, Peter, Ben and Michael have been playing in the fort, they decide to head back towards the kindergarten to collect something. The group heads off together, Ben picks up a piece of branch.
>
> Ben: Hey look what I found, that's the biggest, that's the biggest stick we found now isn't it?
>
> Henry: Yeah.
>
> Ben: Let's throw it over there.
>
> Henry: Yeah.
>
> Peter: And one day I saw a big big stick and it was who made this? ....and and and nobody was as big as it.
>
> Ben: Only God is.
>
> Peter: God, who's God?
>
> Ben: God's up in heaven, that's our father in heaven.
>
> Peter: Oh.
>
> Ben: And God is bigger than dinosaurs – 'cos God make you and God didn't get bored, he made the world.
>
> Henry: Yeah, and the clouds.
>
> Ben: No he couldn't make the clouds cos God would fall down them.
>
> Henry: Well, are - what about giants? God could make giants – then he could make clouds.

The logic of this conversation is not entirely clear, but Ben appears to be arguing that the existence of clouds would have to precede the existence of God, because otherwise God (who lives in the clouds) would fall down. Henry, on the other hand, may be arguing that if God made giants first then they would hold Him up sufficiently to make the clouds. In any event, and perhaps we should not try to cloak the conversation in logic, they appear to be puzzling about the unseen, the uncertain, the possible, and the impossible: a rich conversational topic indeed.

> ### It's Not A Real Dental Nurse (phase one)
>
> Henry and Tyler have been sent inside to wait for their turn with the Public Health nurse who is checking the children's hearing and sight. They are having a discussion about whose turn it is next, Henry insists that it is his turn next. Henry and Tyler are quiet for a minute watching another child have an eye test. Peter comes in to find Henry and Henry explains they are waiting to have their eyes checked. Peter, sounding a little concerned, says "But I don't need mine checked eh?" A teacher tells the waiting children (Henry, Tyler and Peter) that the nurse will let them know who is next. There is a long silence. Henry says loudly (apparently to no-one in particular although he may have been trying to be reassuring): "It's not a real dental nurse – she doesn't have glasses." Henry had recently been to the dental nurse, and according to his mother the dental nurse did have glasses.

Continuing the exploration of possible worlds a year later

A year later, there were nine episodes of extended involvement over three mornings, and in five of them the pretend play continued. Disaster and heroics have been left behind, but the notion of being 'stuck' remains. In one of the episodes in phase two, when Henry and Stephen are playing with trucks at the dough table inside, Henry cries out: "Oh, it's stuck. HELP! Help me, I'm stuck. No, don't, I can do it myself" (when his truck gets 'stuck' in the 'mud' at the dough table).

In the five dramatic play episodes, the pretend play scenes are less fantastic, sited more often in 'closer-to-the-real' worlds: family, digging a swimming pool, trucks stuck in mud, working at school, and cooking in the sandpit (one pretend episode in phase one was also about a restaurant and cooking). Henry refers once to being 'scared', but it doesn't have any of the danger and urgency of the storylines in phase one.

> ### Digging Swimming Pools (phase two)
>
> Henry, Stephen and Tim children are digging swimming pools. Stephen stops and watches Henry. Tim has started putting sand in the hole that Henry has been digging:
>
> Henry: No don't, don't hide it, don't do that Tim. Oh yuck. I'm scared of this.
> Stephen: What is it?
> Henry: It's only the end of the bottom.
> (Henry has dug down very deep and has reached the bottom of the sandpit).

On a brief occasion between longer episodes, Julie rejects a fanciful story by Henry and, provided with some more plausible modifications by Stephen, he changes it to make it sound more possible in the real world of builders and building.

> ### Who Built this Building? (phase two)
>
> Henry and Stephen are on the swings, and Henry has put a toy on the ground beside the swing. Julie comes over and touches it.
>
> Henry: Hey, that's mine. Don't even touch it.
> Julie: Well, this is mine.
> Henry: Is not your's. It's kindy's.
> Julie: It's my kindy.
> Henry: Well it's my kindy cos I built it. You know who built it? I know, cos I built it.
> Julie: Did not. You didn't build it. Can't.
> Stephen (in the swing beside Henry, corrects this story to make it possible by insisting that it would need to have included a Dad): No, Henry. Cos, with your Dad, you need the Dad.
> Henry: Oh yeah! Well, do you know who built this building, it's me and Dad.
> Stephen: And me, and me eh Henry?

Henry:	Yeah, cos you were at my house the day that we built it, eh Stephen?
Stephen:	Yep. (Julie leaves)
Henry:	Hey, she's gone. She's left it (the toy on the ground). Good.

Friends fight you know, sometimes they do

The notion of being a friend had appeared once in phase one; there are now a number of comments that weave comment on friendship into dramatic play – helping each other and being a friend – or, more precisely, *not* helping each other and *not* being a friend.

In the Sandpit (phase two)

Henry:	Oh help, I'm stuck in here. Maybe I need to dig a bit deeper. (Stephen tries to help). I'm really getting into a trap here. No, don't, don't [help]. No.
Stephen:	Oh no, I'm stuck in a bloody big pond... look, look at me (This time, Henry tries to help). No, I can do it myself.
Henry:	I'm stuck bad.
Stephen:	Do you want me to help you?
Henry:	No, I don't want help, cos you won't let me help you so I'm not going to let you help me.

In a later phase two episode Henry and Tim are arguing over which hole in the sandpit, dug previously, belongs to Henry. Henry comments: "But Tim, remember when we were friends the other day." (Tim: Yep.). There are many more niggling conflicts between the children in this phase, as the children quarrel over whose turn it is on the flying fox, and who will author the storyline. Henry tries to maintain the peace by using humour – 'silly' names like 'dumbhead' and 'bumhead' – which usually works with Stephen (but does not always work with other children in the turn-taking agenda on the flying fox). In the following episode Henry and Stephen are sharing these 'silly' names and laughing together. In the same episode, Henry takes a philosophical view about the nature of friendship.

Fighting and Friendship (phase two)

It is towards the end of the morning and Henry and Stephen are digging holes in the sandpit. They have been playing together for most of the morning, involved mostly with the flying fox, the fort, or in the sandpit. Their play has been interrupted by regular but brief periods of conflict.

Henry: Hey we are fighting a lot today aren't we Stephen?
Stephen: Yeah, we fighted all day eh?
Henry: Why – why are we?
No answer from Stephen, he is pushing his truck deeper into a hole in the sand.
Henry: Cos we are just being silly eh – silly dumbheads.
Stephen: Yeah, dumbheads. (Laughs)

> Henry: Bumheads (laughs – Henry continues pushing his truck in the sand
>   – making truck noises)…….. Friends fight you know, sometimes
>   they do – so we can, you know.
> Stephen: I know. Hey, I know, how about we make a bridge – have this
>   bridge here.
> They continue to play in the sand, and to argue about the direction of play.

Like Peter in the earlier conversation about God, Stephen is not interested in Henry's puzzling about difficult questions (in this case, 'Why are we fighting a lot today?'). On another occasion, Henry comments on the play: he says to Stephen "We're having fun, eh?"

Making up the rules

In another of the phase two episodes, Henry takes the lead to shift the storyline from the imaginary and fantastic (dangerous crocodiles and flooding) to the more 'real' domestic (you be the Mum and we be the brothers).

> ### From Crocodiles to Mums and Brothers (phase two)
>
> Henry is drawing with chalks on the concrete. The notion of the playground
> being flooded is still part of the play culture here, and it is introduced by
> Stephen to try to entice Henry to play with him.
> Stacey: There's crocodiles in there.
> Henry: Are not.
> Stacey: (more urgently) There are crocodiles in there.
> Henry: I can fight them.
> Stephen: No, no I know what this could be.
> Henry: What?
> Stephen climbs off the crate and moves back over to Henry, Stacey follows.
> Stephen: This could be a swimming pool.
> Henry: Yeah.
> Stacey: And remember we – we could get togs.
> Henry then introduces a whole new game plan. There are a group of girls
> nearby with dolls and prams and Stacey had been involved with them prior to
> being distracted by Henry and the chalk. This same group of girls have been
> nearby with the dolls and prams on each of the observation days and Henry
> often engages in conversation with them in passing, often addressing the girls
> as 'Mum' when they are pushing prams.
> Henry: (to Stacey) I know. You be the Mum and we be the brothers.
>   Stephen be a brother, I'll be a brother and you be the Mum.
> Stacey: Nooooo, you be the Dad – you be the Dad cos there's just gonna
>   be one brother.
> Stephen: (attempts to keep the other game going) Hey, excuse me excuse
>   me – oh no, there's crocodiles in that one there (talking at the
>   same time as Stacey).
> Stacey: There is – but you will be the brother (to Stephen) – and me and
>   Henry be the mummy and the daddy.

Henry:	(to Stacey) Can I carry that pram for yah?
Stacey:	Nope – carry Susan's, get Susan's.
Stephen:	(to Susan) excuse me, excuse me can ....
Henry:	(speaking at the same time as Stephen) Susan can I carry your pram?
Susan:	No.
Henry:	I'll carry it up the bumpy stairs for yah, Mum.
Susan:	I can – I can do it.
Henry:	No it's too hard – how about we can both do it?
Susan:	No I can do it.
Henry:	How about we both do it?
Ashley:	okay – are you the brother?
Henry:	Yeah and so is Stephen.

Susan and Ashley step aside a bit to allow Henry and Stephen to assist, Stacey manages her pram by herself while Henry and Stephen help to push Susan and Ashley's prams over a series of planks and obstacles.

Finding physical challenges

Two of the episodes in phase two were centred on a new flying fox that had recently been set up in the playground. The activity included negotiating turns, and the children had introduced an imaginative notion of 'winning', which considerably complicated the turn-taking procedure. *Not winning* seems to mean you haven't done your best or achieved anything spectacular on the way down so you need another turn to attempt a better run, whereas *winning* means you have been successful and so can relinquish the rope to someone else. However, the decision seems to be actually based on whether the player wants to gain some extra turns or is happy for the next person to have a turn. For example, in the following, Henry is at the flying fox and joins in the discussions regarding whose turn it is next. Henry reaches out for the flying fox rope that is being held by Amy. A teacher remains nearby, and also invokes the notion of 'winning' to assist with the allocation of turns.

The Flying Fox (phase two)	
Amy:	It's my turn.
Henry:	No it isn't – well you can have a go after this one.
Amy:	Are you going to win this one next?
Henry:	Yeah.
Henry:	Give it to me. Can I have a go Amy?
Stephen:	Can I have it Amy?
Henry:	Give it to me. My go.
Amy:	I didn't win though.
Henry:	Well can I ... You won! You won! (enthusiastically).
Teacher:	You won that time Amy. Give Henry a go now, he's been waiting so patiently.
Henry:	Give it to me. (Amy passes the rope to Henry).

> Henry: Yeah, after me. I'll tell you when I win. (He has a turn). I won, I won. (Henry takes the rope back to Amy who has several turns in a row).
>
> ....
>
> Later Henry uses a knowledge of high numbers in an imaginative flourish to emphasise that he has been waiting for a long time for a turn.
>
> Teacher: Stephen, just give Henry a couple of goes Stephen cos he's been waiting a while.
>
> Stephen: How long have you been waiting?
>
> Henry: About six hundred and ninety nine hours.
>
> Stephen: Six hundred and ninety nine hours!
>
> Stephen and Henry laugh together.
>
> Stephen: Let's go together.
>
> Both Stephen and Henry have a turn together on the flying fox. They then negotiate several turns each in a row.

Helping others at school

When Henry goes to school these imaginary flourishes to turn-taking have to be abandoned.

> More of the 'kindergarten Henry' was evident in his outdoor play on the adventure play ground, still keen to test out and practice his physical skill and competence and keen to push himself further – but he was a lot less willing to play any key role in negotiations for turns on things (unlike at the kindergarten) and tended to hang back and wait patiently for his turn. The children using this equipment were very mixed in age and the older ones tended to be running the show. Henry seemed to be aware of his place in the pecking order and either waited for a turn – sometimes missing out – or moved to a part of the apparatus that had less competition. (Field notes, phase three)

However there are social situations in the school classroom where Henry uses his imagination to 'read' the classroom culture, recognise the viewpoint of other children, help others, and to work collaboratively in group art activities.

> ### *Handwriting (phase three)*
>
> It is handwriting time, and the children have been instructed to collect their handwriting books and take them back to their table. Henry collects his from the teacher and goes back to his table to sit down. He looks through his printing book. The next free page is set up with ruled lines and the letters L, r and the number 8 set across different lines. He waits until all the other children are seated at his table (there are five children, including Henry). He starts drawing over the existing letters – then moves on to the number eight. The teacher notices Henry working quietly and he gets some public praise (and a tick by his name on the board). He looks pleased, then goes back to his work. He has written two new eights on a fresh line, then he draws back

> over the ones he has already done *'there that's right'* (talking to self). He helps another child "Here, watch this. This is how you do it".

In another episode Henry reduces disruption in the group by giving Scotty a choice and then praising him.

> ### Managing the group (phase three)
>
> The children have all been sent to their tables to start a drawing, Henry quickly gets his book and sits down at the table. The teacher tells the children she will be keeping an eye out for the best table today and they will get a reward. Henry looks at Scotty who is being the most disruptive.
> Henry: Hey Scotty, hey Scotty (he gains Scotty's attention). Scotty, Scotty, do you want me to get you a pencil (he leans towards the pencil container and pulls out a handful). Here is some, which one do yah wanna use? (he starts laying them out and examines them. (Scotty is now looking at the pencils). Hmm. This one is broken, this one is a bit broken, this one is only small. (He looks back at Scotty). Which one do you want? (Scotty chooses and Henry passes Scotty the one he wants.) Good choice Scotty.
> Henry chooses one for himself and starts concentrating on his drawing. The table now settles down and all get on with their drawings. No table received a reward, and it is not mentioned again.

Presumably the children have learned that 'getting a reward' is a code instruction for 'settle down', and they do not actually expect it to mean what it means outside the walls of the classroom.

Being multimodal: From treasure maps in phase one to art work at school

Has Henry begun to leave the construction of possible and impossible worlds behind? This was always going to be a challenge at school. But, as we will see, there is a pathway in the school classroom for this, and Henry grasps the opportunity with enthusiasm. Henry had been attending a pre-going-to-school programme for three months before his fifth birthday, and by the time he started school he was familiar with the school classroom, the teacher, the routines and rules. When interviewed just before he started school he was particularly unimpressed with the amount of time spent 'on the mat': 'it was too long and boring' and 'you have to be more quiet and sit still'. However, he reported that he got to do more 'art stuff'.

Researcher: What things do you like best about going to school so far?
Henry: We do lots of art stuff.
Researcher: Ahh, so you like doing the art stuff?
Henry: Uh huh – it's more fun.
Researcher: Oh, so it's more fun – what kind of art stuff do you get to do?
Henry: Uuhh – drawing ... and paintings with dye and stuff.
Researcher: What kinds of things do you get to draw?
Henry: Just ummm (pause – doesn't answer).
Researcher: Ah, so do you get to draw whatever you want?

Henry: Uuh – well you can draw pictures about a story.

Researcher: Ah, so the teacher reads you a story and then you get to draw something about it?

Henry: Yup.

(Interview with Henry, phase three)

When visiting the school, the researcher noticed that there was a large amount of art work around the room and a lot of it contributed by Henry. She commented in field notes that it was 'very bright, detailed, quite sophisticated and imaginative'. Henry made a point of showing the researcher all his work around the room and the teacher also reported that Henry engaged in any art work very enthusiastically. She also noticed that he was also particularly good in any group art situations, great at coming up with ideas, talking about them and initiating them. In this third phase Henry has not been required to shut down his imaginative powers. The mode of meaning-making has shifted from dramatic play to art. The teacher commented that Henry was very open to others' ideas and willing to incorporate them with his own; she said that he had definite ideas but was willing to set those aside in the interests of the group. Henry is apparently more willing now to set aside his desire to be always the initiator and author of imaginative ideas. Conversations with the teacher and observations indicated that Henry was achieving a reputation amongst the teacher and the children for being a knowledgeable expert in a number of areas. The other children in the class would sometimes comment 'Henry knows' or 'Henry will know'.

> During mat time activities Henry did always seem to know the answers to things, although he did not always put his hand up with the answers; he would mouth the answers quietly to himself, and often waited for the other children to have a go at answering and sometimes getting it wrong before he would offer the right answer. (Field notes, phase three)

Perhaps the balance had now moved to separate out the imagined, in art, with the real, in supplying knowledge about the world. Neither Stephen nor Peter has followed Henry into this school, and Henry does not have a special friend. Joint storying as a favourite activity is now replaced by activities associated with art, and he has also developed an interest in numbers and puzzles. The teacher comments as follows, suggesting to us that Henry's experience at negotiating with others in the early childhood years has 'paid off' in the school context.

> Henry is really into art, he really readily engages in any art activities in the class room – and very enthusiastically.... (He) comes up with really good ideas, he'll initiate ideas and contribute them to the group without any problem. (Researcher – do you have any examples of this?) Well yes, when we were making the model (for the show) Henry was one of the children who was very involved in that activity, he was one of the main players so to speak – some of the other children lost interest quite early on but Henry stayed involved and enthused about the project all the way through, but yes, he'd offer lots of good ideas: "Hey I know, I know, how about we do this like

this". He does have strong opinions and ideas, but I really appreciated, what is great I think about Henry, is that he could take others in the group, (their) ideas on board as well, he would put forward an idea but if another child had a different idea he was really good at – he was really open to going with that idea as well, the potential for conflict was there but Henry was quite adept I think at averting conflict – he could let go of an idea if it wasn't received enthusiastically – or his idea might have been ignored initially but he would often find a way to add ideas from the other children into his own. He would make suggestions that would somehow incorporate the different ideas into his own. (Teacher interview, phase three)

Imagination in story writing at school

In the early months of school, Henry did not find reading or writing particularly engaging. The invention of imaginative stories that engaged him at the early childhood centre is not possible here, because the children are required to write most of the text of their stories, and Henry is very much a novice at writing.

Writing (phase three)

Henry manages to turn a requirement for a 'real life' written story into a more fantastic told story about danger and rescue. The children have been sent to their tables to do creative story writing; they have previously spent some time on the mat, with the teacher encouraging them to think of writing about something they have seen or done the day before. Henry is asked what he is going to write about and he says he is going to write about a cat that gets stuck up a tree. Henry is at the table with his book open. He draws a tree and something in the tree, then stops and looks around at what the others are doing. He talks to the girl next to him about her picture. He then goes back to looking at his page. He turns back to a previous story and starts re-writing over the words. He stops and looks around. He turns to the researcher sitting behind and shows her his book. He shows her that he only has three pages left. He picks up his pencil and starts drawing a scribbly line around his tree, stops to look at it, then speaks out loud with some excitement:

Henry: Oh look, oh yeah, I have a hurricane now, that's a hurricane a hurricane has blown up around my .... oops. (The pencil flies out of his hand; he laughs). The hurricane blew my pencil away.

Boy opposite: (laughs) I haven't seen a hurricane – that doesn't look like a hurricane.

Henry: They are like big tunnels yah know – and they can suck yah right in – like this (demonstrates with his hands in a circular motion, making swooshing/sucking noise) ha ha – that would blow the cat down from the tree – yes siree. (Both children laugh).

Henry (picks up his pencil): I'm going to draw more cats that get stuck in the tree – oh yeah, they blewed in with the hurricane (laughs to himself).

> The children are told to be quiet, the teacher claps loudly and addresses the whole class, tells them to work quietly and to get on with their own stories. She says she will be around to help. Henry stops talking immediately and looks down at his book. He appears to be trying to concentrate, starts to write some letters, writes three letters (*the*) then stops and waits. The teacher has reached Henry's table, she helps another child while Henry watches and continues to wait. The teacher comes to see how Henry is getting on with his story; she bends down beside Henry.
>
> Teacher:　　What is your story about again Henry? – what are you going to write about?
>
> Henry:　　Oh um, a cat, a cat, the cat that's up a tree.
>
> Teacher:　　Ok, lets start down here. Let's write your story down here. You have made a good start (She helps Henry with writing 'cat' and 'tree').

LEARNING IN THE MAKING

Disposition-in action: work in progress

This section highlights the three dispositional components from a triadic definition of learning disposition and the literature on the continuity of learning as authoring, recognising opportunity, and connected knowing. Although we have separated them here, partly to illustrate a disposition-in-action as including inclination (authoring) and attunement (recognising opportunity) over and above knowing and being able, these three components combined together as work in progress towards the children being ready willing and able to explore possible worlds.

Authoring.　　Both Henry and Sarah's case studies provided examples of the four- to five-year-old, over time, deeply involved in exploring imaginary (possible and impossible) worlds. This facet of an imagination disposition appeared in phase one and almost a year later in phase two. And for Henry it appeared in phase three at school both legitimately (in art activities) and illegitimately (against the requirements in a story-writing session). A parallel agenda, or dilemma, for Henry at this time, especially in phase two, was trying to manage a balancing act between 'being in charge' and 'being a (collaborative) friend', a dilemma that nearly scuppered his imaginative endeavours and only seemed to come to some sort of temporary resolution in the more structured environment at school, where there was little opportunity to be in charge and many opportunities to work inside a group. We describe this resolution as temporary, since this is – as Jerome Bruner suggests – a dilemma that follows us through life:

> A self-making narrative is something of a balancing act. It must, on the one hand, create a conviction of autonomy, that one has a will of one's own, a certain freedom of choice, a degree of possibility. But it must also relate the self to a world of others – to friends and family, to institutions, to the past, to reference groups. But the commitment to others that is implicit in relating oneself to others of course limits our autonomy. We seem virtually unable to

live without both, autonomy and commitment, and our lives strive to balance the two. So do the self-narratives we tell ourselves. (Bruner, 2002, p. 78)

Recognising opportunity.   The link between possible selves (chapter eight) and possible worlds is very close. Henry's interest in being the leader and being a friend – both of them possible selves that we have suggested are always in tension – is localised when he considers possible worlds. The contexts of scary and fantastical flooding and fire call for *superheroes*. In phase two, the scenes or worlds that Henry has devised began to include more players. It is not clear whether the scene changed because he wanted more players, or whether it was the other way around. In any case, he adjusted his story-lines and possible worlds to accommodate the interests of a wider range of children. He began to set up the more familiar digging swimming pools, constructing buildings, and family play: These contexts call for *mates* and *mothers* and *Dads* and *brothers*. The shift is illustrated in the 'From Crocodiles to Mums and Brothers' story. At school his capacity to 'read' the classroom culture and recognise the viewpoint of others is deployed to help others in the school tasks. At school, too, the opportunity to imagine possible worlds through art was available and he participated in this alternative mode with enthusiasm. For Sarah, the objects and playthings that were key partners in phase one became secondary supports in phase two when she and Donald spent time elaborating on their Super Kitten scripts. By phase two, as well, Sarah had adapted her style to allow Donald to occasionally direct the story-line: both of them were improvising from one moment to another, as they co-constructed a plot-line that shifted rapidly from capturing a kitten to finding a chocolate and strawberry shop in space to using telescopes. At school Sarah's imaginary worlds found little space; she was hampered by her writing ability (so was Henry but an alternative, art, was valued and available). However, a writing episode did provide her with an opportunity to work in a focused way on a drawing, and she still constructed a moment to introduce Super Kitten, although Super Kitten had now (temporarily?) become peripheral to the classroom agenda of 'doing school'. The task at school of collaboratively constructing a *fale*, with Sarah as the leader, had resonance with similar construction tasks in the early childhood centre. Although Sarah was not the author in the same way, she participated with enthusiasm. Henry's disposition-related knowing of how to have thoughtful conversations about God and friendship may have depended on the opportunities to develop close relationships that the early childhood centre had provided.

Connected knowing.   The *fale* school task – and the Pacific Island theme that surrounded it – made a connection with Sarah's knowledge of materials and architecture from visits to the Pacific Islands with her parents. Disposition-based knowing included her ability to weave a complex story-line and to act out the parts using different voices; she had dramatic talent. At school, this disposition to explore possible worlds would be backgrounded as she waited for her writing skills to catch up. Henry's accumulating knowledge about disasters – floods, fire and hurricanes, for instance – thread their way through all the phases. At school, his storytelling ability may shift beyond the art area – to text or digital modes – as his skills increase. The cat-up-a-tree-in-a-hurricane story indicates that he still enjoys plying his skills at inventing good stories.

Design

A number of features of the educational design in these case studies appeared to afford, invite, engage, provoke – and constrain – this facet of imagination. Although the classrooms provided little opportunity for imaginative story-telling, Super Kitten and imaginary hurricanes appeared at the writing tables in spite of the constraints created by the children's writing ability. It was a disposition that could not, yet anyway, be suppressed. There were two themes of design which more or less provoked the children to explore possible worlds in the early childhood centres and classrooms where Sarah and Henry worked and played. The first was the resources and tasks that provided opportunities for pretend play with objects and with other children, and the second was the valuing of multidisciplinary and multimodal approaches to making meaning. The two were closely connected, since pretend play in the early years is usually multidisciplinary and multimodal, and the opportunities for elaborated pretend play also included a valuing of imagining possible worlds (and possible selves) by the teachers. Henry's teachers were willing to be labelled 'Captain Hook' and to include the children's imaginative (if confusing) notion of 'winning' in their discussions of turn-taking at the flying fox.

Resources and tasks. Pretend play episodes were closely tied to *place*: for Sarah the room where Duplo play was housed was a place in which she appeared to be at home, providing the props with which she could play out her pretend scenarios. Her Super Kitten play with other children was enabled by freely available junk play and furniture that could be moved; at school Super Kitten was consigned (literally) to reside under the table. For Henry and his friends the sandpit and the outside play area at kindergarten evoked rich imaginative geographies where there is flooding, hidden treasure, monsters, and family homes. In both the centres the teachers provided space and resources for imaginative play outside as well as the usual dress-ups and furniture inside. All the early childhood programmes in this study valued and encouraged the children's improvisations; Henry's kindergarten invited the imagination by providing a table of 'bits and pieces' that might be useful for construction materials or pretend play props, and Henry was alert to their possibilities; Sarah's centre enabled her and Donald to move the furniture around and make telescopes, and the blocks available for play in phase one included 'people' and 'animals' that assisted the construction of a complex world. During the early childhood centre episodes we observed for Sarah and Henry, the teachers took a back-stage role: they provided resources, and in Henry's kindergarten they kept a 'weather eye' on the flying fox negotiations, allowing the children to develop their own negotiation skills but intervening when it appeared to be unfair. A teacher was on hand during the one episode we observed where Henry was miserable because Stephen had disappeared. She offered an alternative interpretation

("Maybe he's playing a (hide-and-seek) game with you. Are you meant to find him? ... Where have you looked?") and added a sympathetic "It's been a tricky old day today hasn't it?" when Henry reiterates his view that Stephen "just wants to trick me". The teachers in Henry's kindergarten had introduced sources of new knowledge – the Fire Brigade and sharks – that also became catalysts for play themes and these were appropriated and adapted with alacrity by Henry. In one episode when Henry was in the sandpit a teacher was nearby working with a number of children to construct a large sand shark. The teachers' pedagogy in both these early childhood centres was one of appreciating and supporting imagination as an important aspect of learning in the making.

Valuing the multidisciplinary and the multimodal. This second theme was also taken up in chapter five, where David, Leona and Jeff were initiating and authoring projects in which problem-solving was multi-disciplinary and multimodal. The two early childhood centres that Sarah and Henry attended interpreted multidisciplinary imaginative worlds as worthy of pursuit. An episode at school for Sarah, constructing a 'fale' (a traditional Samoan thatched house), provided similar opportunities for her to orchestrate the use of different resources as had her constructions of 'homes' with duplo blocks in phase one. Although language is important, gesture, the use of props, and accompanying physical activity are also often central to the collective development of an alternative world. At school, the grandiose multidisciplinary episodes of imaginative play were not available to Henry and Sarah, but Henry began to develop an interest in art, both individual and group, and Sarah became engaged in the technology project which included drawing a plan and leading a group to physically construct a *fale*.

PROVOKING IMAGINATION

Storying Selves

People tell others who they are, but even more important, they tell themselves and then try to act as though they are who they say they are. These self-understandings, especially those with strong emotional resonance for the teller, are what we refer to as identities. ... We take identity to be the central means by which selves and the sets of actions they organize, form and re-form over personal lifetimes and in the history of social collectives. (Holland et al., 1998, p. 3, & p. 270)

This is the second chapter on imagination as a learning disposition, and the final case studies chapter. We have called this chapter 'storying selves', and it highlights the notion of identity that will be central to the final chapter. The two case studies – Yasin and Aralynn – describe children's developing disposition to reflect on, and construct, stories about who they are and where they belong. For both these children – and for all the children in this study – the family is the touchstone for their conversations about identity. Katherine Nelson and Robyn Fivush (2004) have argued that identity is created by sharing the past with others in time and in relation to others, through autobiographical memory.

These functions [social and cultural] allow individuals to create a shared past with others from which an individual personal past emerges. The human ability to create a shared past allows each individual to enter a community or culture, in which individuals share a perspective on the kinds of events that make a life and shape a self. (Nelson & Fivush, 2004, p. 500)

Early childhood centres and school classrooms widen horizons beyond the family, and introduce children to a range of possible identities or, for this book, multiple possible dimensions to their identities as learners. Chapter two introduced early childhood centres, school classrooms and homes as 'figured worlds' in which people fashion their sense of self (Holland et al., 1998; Boaler & Greeno, 2000): with a similar function to Bourdieu's 'fields', they are cultural spaces where people come together to co-construct meanings and activities, and in which social positions and social relationships occur. Such figured worlds assign significance to certain acts and value some outcomes over others. "Figured worlds draw attention to interpretations by actors – students and teachers for example – and to the rituals of practice" (Boaler & Greeno, 2000, p. 2). A source of identity is thus participation (in a figured world). During conversations we recognise in each other something of ourselves, which relates to our mutual abilities to negotiate meaning. Wenger (1998) points out that identity is not about self image, but rather about a particular way of being in the world and an outcome of a negotiated experience within membership in communities of practice. "We define who we are by the ways we reconcile our various forms of membership into one identity" (p. 149). Encounters in 'figured worlds' or 'communities of practice' offer information which is tagged in various ways "as important, relevant, O.K. to ignore, reserved for group X, best approached by method Y, no room for error, O.K. to be original and so on" (Goodnow, 1990, p. 277). Wenger suggests that the ability to apply learning flexibly is fundamentally a question of identity:

> The ability to apply learning flexibly depends not on abstraction of formulation but on deepening the negotiation of meaning. This in turn depends on engaging identities in the complexity of lived situations. I would argue that the problem of generality is not just an informational question; it is more fundamentally a question of identity, because identity is the vehicle that carries our experiences from context to context. (Wenger, 1998, p. 268)

YASIN

Yasin's family immigrated to New Zealand from Bombay when he was a baby. He lives with his mother and father and has a brother two years older. His grandmother also lived with them when Yasin was young and his mother was taking a one-year course on design. The grandmother returned to India when Yasin was two, and came back to visit when Yasin began school, to help 'settle him in'. They have no other family in New Zealand but belong to a small Indian community of about forty families who share the same religion and follow the same religious leader.

For most of the project Yasin's father was a sea captain for an Indian shipping company. This involved travel to all parts of the world and meant he was at home for two months at a time and then away for two months. He was home during two of the three visits we made to the family. Languages were highly valued in Yasin's home. In the two years that we knew Yasin he was learning Spanish, Arabic, and Mandarin at classes outside school and home, and at home they were speaking English and Gujarati – "and Hindi from the movies".

> Then when they grow up, they've got the languages. We are becoming a global village nowadays. I was just reading, banking jobs, the first qualification is a foreign language – nothing else. We feel very strongly that twenty years down the line, in the year 2025, when these children will be in the workforce, at that time the world population, the way it's going, there will be a predominance of people who will be speaking Mandarin, obviously, because China's got a large population. And the Spanish-speaking population is on the rise, especially in the United States and South America as well. So that is the reason we want them to learn Spanish, so that when they go in the job market in twenty years, they should have an advantage over other people competing for that same job. They will communicate with more groups of people, they will understand the culture of the particular group of people. Everyone has their own particular culture – what is right for me may be

wrong for you and vice versa. That is very important for me. I wish they could learn Russian too, but it's too much for them…Not only that, what is more important is that both of us feel that they should not just be learning to read in a conventional way, from left to right. Arabic is right to left, Chinese is up to down. So that's our aim. (Parent interview, phase one)

There was also a focus on the visual arts in the family. During the project, Yasin's mother was a dress-maker who specialised in Indian garments for weddings and other occasions. She ran her business from the house, and had designed for her mother in Bombay. Both boys attended art classes. Yasin's mother said to us:

When you do art, it changes your whole mental status. You see, artists will never get angry so fast. You are not stressed out. You know, (in the future) he will do things at his own leisure. (Parent interview, phase three)

By the end of the project Yasin also attended Saturday music lessons, enjoyed playing soccer and attended after school swimming and tennis classes. His father was not working on the ship any more; he was running a grocery shop and commented that it was becoming difficult to keep all these activities going. Telling stories was a routine at Yasin's home; his father regularly told imaginative stories to the children in the evenings, stories with a practical message. He wove stories around an imaginary character, the Mad Butcher (the name of a butchery chain; there was a Mad Butcher shop close by). In a recent story, for instance, the Mad Butcher was on a hang glider, and then fell down; this story was about safety in the sea. The children provided their own contributions to the stories.

This case study is about the ways in which the early childhood centre connected with these experiences and this social and cultural capital from home to provide opportunities for the authoring and revisiting, by Yasin, of stories about the past, about places away from here, and about the future. These stories, together with imaginary stories attached to his paintings, provided a rich array of 'storied selves', as Yasin took up opportunities to explore his identity as a family member and as a learner.

Stories about the self in the family have a place in the early childhood centre

Yasin began his formal early childhood attendance keen to story himself as a brother, and to revisit his memories and knowledge of family life in Bombay. He attended a kindergarten, in the three-afternoon programme during phase one, and in the five-morning programme during phase two. During phase one, eight episodes of focused activity were recorded. On five of these occasions Yasin introduced his family into the conversation. The Head Teacher at the kindergarten knew the family well; she had visited their home when Yasin's older brother had attended the kindergarten, and Yasin had himself often visited the kindergarten when his brother was attending. One of these five conversational episodes was initiated by photographs taken by the researcher of events on the previous day; the researchers invited one of the teachers to look at the photographs with Yasin, to talk together about the episodes they had observed the previous day. This was not an unusual task, since the children would sometimes revisit photos and stories in their portfolios with the teachers; the teacher's purpose on this occasion was also to assist Yasin with language development (supplying the right names for things), and to establish whether he has understood the art processes that he had been working on. In this conversation, 126 of the 232 conversation turns were about Yasin's home life, taken there by Yasin on every occasion except the first, when it was introduced by the teacher. His brother is a consistent background theme to the conversation, as a reference point ("You'll have to show (brother) how to make them"), as a standard ("My brother doesn't know how to make a puppet anyway"), as a link to the past ("when my brother attended this kindergarten"), and as a lucky person who got lots of things at his birthday party and has a 'book rack' (book case) in his bedroom. There are glimpses of the construction of multiple dimensions to identity here as Yasin and the teacher weave stories together: Yasin as a younger brother, a future parent, and an artist (in Yasin's words, a 'stamper-boy' or print maker who makes stamps or seals). The teacher used a number of strategies: (i) establishing common ground for a conversation about expertise that uses the brother as a reference point and provokes a discussion about India, (ii) re-telling together a story about the family, (iii) building on a conversation where Yasin introduced the notion of self as a parent, (iv) talking about home, and (v) providing the language

Establishing common ground during conversations. The following episode, documented by the researcher, was one in which Yasin was deeply engaged in making puppets with the teacher. He was making puppets by gluing felt animal shapes onto the end of popsicle sticks with a glue gun. The children then contributed to a shadow puppet show behind a back-lit screen.

Puppet Making (phase one, excerpt)	
Yasin:	Teacher, Look, look.
Teacher:	Oh, you've been designing over there. What have you been making over there?
Yasin:	Puppets.
Teacher:	Some little puppets. Did you try them behind the screen? You come and show me what they look like behind the puppet screen. If I turn the light on, you can show me what they look like. You can show me the shadows or the outline of them. There you go. Now you stand behind the screen and I'll have a look and see. Oh I can see the shape of your animal. What other animal shape have you got? Oh I can see your monkey and the other monkey. Shall I hold it and you have a look?
Child.	I see a rabbit.
Teacher:	I'll hold it and you have a look.
Teacher:	Hello, what's your name? Oh where's my friend. Oh here it is, two little monkeys. (Chants) Two little monkeys swinging in a tree. Teasing Mr Alligator, you can't catch me.

The following is a conversation, later, with the teacher about this Puppet Making episode:

Yasin: And my brother doesn't know how, my big brother doesn't know how to make a puppet anyway.

Teacher: Oh, he doesn't know how to make puppets.

Yasin: No.

Teacher: But you do.

Yasin: No, I don't need to use the puppets with someone helping me, I need to use it alone.

Teacher: You can do it yourself now, you don't need someone helping you. Maybe you'll have to show (brother) how to make them then. Do you think you could show him how to make them?

Yasin: But I showed him my monkey puppet.

Teacher: Oh, you showed him your monkey one.

Yasin: Yeah.

Teacher: And what did he think about that?

Yasin: He thought it was good.

Re-telling together a story about the family. One of the key artefacts in the photographs is the glue gun, and Yasin remembers an earlier occasion (perhaps a year earlier) when the family gave a glue gun to the kindergarten. The teacher remembers it too, and together they begin to reconstruct the story.

Yasin: Yeah. My Mother – we had a glue gun and we gave the glue gun to this kindy.

Teacher (sounds surprised): You did, too. That was a long time ago. Did your Mummy tell you that?

Yasin: Yeah.

Teacher: That you brought a glue gun for kindergarten. I think you might have been... how old were you when you did that, um..

Yasin: Three and a half.

Teacher: Three and a half – I think you might have, when (brother) was here. When he came to this kindergarten, did your Mummy bring it?

Yasin: No.

Teacher: No? When you were older?

Yasin: No, when I was three and a half.

Teacher: Oh, when you were three and a half – I remember that.

Yasin: But first I was three and...

Teacher: First you were three and then you were three and a half.

Yasin: Yeah.

Building on a conversation that introduced self as a parent. The conversation topic moves from ages to birthdays, and being older. Yasin shifts the topic to being a parent, and the teacher builds on this.

175

Yasin:	She [mother] said … I will be a parent.
Teacher:	You will be a parent. Oh, when you're bigger, you will be a parent.
Yasin:	Yeah.
Teacher:	What do you think you will do when you are a parent?
Yasin:	I will work.
Teacher:	You will work. What work do you think you might do?
Yasin:	Work on the ship work.
Teacher:	Oh, you might go on a ship and do work like your Dad. What work does he do on the ship?
Yasin:	He does, he makes stuff and …
Teacher:	He makes stuff. You might do that when you are a parent.

Talking about home. The discussion turned to 'book racks' at home and at the kindergarten. The teacher supplied what appears to be the correct word (book shelf) but this information was ignored by Yasin. The teacher asked about his favourite books (a mermaid and a space book). He has explained that the new 'book rack' is in his brother's room. And he added "And there are so many books to read".

Introducing reference to India. Another episode in the same day involved a conversation between Yasin and the teacher where the teacher's mentioning a pattern board from India provides the entry point for Yasin to talk about his grandmother and her shop in India.

Stamping (phase one)

Yasin makes a stamping pad and some stamps, and has stamped patterns onto paper. He now takes a rubbing and decides to rub a pattern over the top of the stamps.

Teacher:	Oh, there's your stamps and you've got your stamp pad.
Yasin:	And this is.. now I need to draw.
Teacher:	What are you going to do?
Yasin:	Now I need to draw on that.
Teacher:	You're going to draw on it. Oh, what's on this side? Oh, you're going to get the rubbing patterns from here. From the rubbing board, like you did last time. Remember when you did the rubbing on that one, and now you're rubbing on this one. This is another board.
Yasin:	Where did you get this from?
Teacher:	Oh, I got that from Pasifika [a local festival of the arts]. This is a Pacific Island pattern board.
Yasin:	My teacher…
Teacher:	And this one is an Indian pattern board from India. So you can see the patterns emerging.
Yasin:	My Nana has a bigger shop.
Teacher:	A shop – in India? What does she sell in her shop?

Yasin:	It's very big.
Teacher:	What things does she sell in her shop?
Yasin:	She sells nothing.
Teacher:	Nothing?
Yasin:	She just works there.
Teacher:	Oh, she works there. Oh.
Teacher:	(returning to the topic at hand) You're going right over them. Want to choose a different colour now?
Yasin:	Now I want to do on the other one. Now I want to do on this one.
Teacher:	Try some other paper on there. Get another piece of paper, maybe a thin piece so the pattern comes out clearer. Try this one. Oh, actually, try this one down here, these ones. Which colour would you like to try?
Yasin:	This one. I would like to try like this.

Being an artist: a 'stamper boy' and a painter

A stamper-boy. Yasin took a stamp pad and then using the animal shapes on sticks as stamps. He pressed a stamp onto his hand, and one onto his cheek. He says "Now I can make a stamp, teacher. I am stamper boy! Teacher, I can make puppet into stamp. " A year later the following Learning Story was written by one of the teachers and added to his portfolio.

> ## Making a Stamp Pad:
> ### A Learning Story in phase two that connects with an episode in phase one
>
> Yasin makes a stamp pad from a sponge cloth (cut to size), plastic container and paint and is trying to make a patterned stamp. First he drew a face, using a felt pen, onto a plastic bottle top. When he tried this out on the paper, he couldn't see the pattern. He then drew a face on a piece of paper and attached that to the plastic top. This didn't work. I showed Yasin the Pasifika patterned rubber stamps and drew his attention to the raised base with the pattern. Yasin looked carefully at the pattern and exclaimed, "I know how they made that, they carved it!" We talked about how he would need to find something with 'texture' or a 'raised pattern'. Yasin found a textured metal top, which he glued to the plastic. He attached a stick to the top and proceeded to try it out on the paper. Yasin made another stamper for his brother.

Painting flowers, and adding a story. A second occasion of sustained involvement – as well as the puppet-making and stamping – occurred when the environment was set up to invite the children to try still life painting. The teachers set up the environment, gave encouragement, and provoked close attention by providing focus cues, and making suggestions about the selection of resources. All of these strategies were accepted by Yasin as helpful.

> ### Painting Daffodils (phase one)
>
> A vase of daffodils is set up in the middle of the table with yellow, orange, green and blue paints. Yasin and two other children spend thirty minutes working in this area on their paintings; other children come and go.
>
> Yasin: I don't know how to draw flowers.
>
> Teacher: You don't know how to draw flowers? Have a look at the petals and see what shape they remind you of.
>
> Yasin: Look at my flower ... Look.
>
> Teacher: I can see your petals and the flower head. Mmm what about the stalks of the flowers, the stems, Yasin – what about the stems they stand up on?
>
> Sally: I've put stems on them.
>
> Teacher: See how if I hold up the flowers like that see the stem.
>
> Sally: I've got stems on mine.
>
> Teacher: Some people call them the stalks, you have a look.
>
> Sally: I like to call them the lines.
>
> Teacher: They're quite straight and narrow these stalks, different flowers have different stalks. Daffodils have very long narrow straight stems like that.
>
> Yasin: This is me, and there are my ... I am hiding and nobody can see me ...because.
>
> Teacher: Where are you hiding?
>
> Yasin: Hiding in some bushes.
>
> Teacher: In some bushes!
>
> Yasin: I'm also eating popcorn.
>
> Teacher: Popcorn!
>
> Yasin: Oh, oh look!
>
> Teacher: I'll hold it up over there and you can have a look at it, you can see your patterns. Look I can see your daffodils here. Are they the two daffodils, those ones, and is this you, hiding in the bushes? Oh is this the bushes here? Oh, I can see him behind the bushes.
>
> Yasin: I'm picking the flowers behind.
>
> Teacher: Oh you are picking the flowers up behind the bushes – oh. I'll write a little story. Yasin drew. ...
>
> Sally: (to the teacher) Look!
>
> Teacher: Oh, look at your design. Can I just write a story for Yasin ... drew two daffodils and some bushes, Yasin was hiding behind the bushes. Is that what you were doing – picking flowers were you? Then I'll write this up and I'll write the date there and the same date on the picture so that I can remember, so that I can write the story about your painting that goes with this one. And I might write it up on the computer.

Sharing information about home in phase two

In phase two, almost a year later, the family are still used as referents, but not so much 'out of the blue'. References to an imagined other place are more often *connected* to this place. In one episode, Yasin is sitting at the dough table and has a long conversation with a teacher; other children contribute. The topics of conversation range over cooking and eating at home (Yasin: "I love cooking curry"), the fact that Yasin is wearing his cousin's jacket ("He gave his big hero jacket to me"), his brother ("Guess what, my brother doesn't like wheat"). He reminds the teacher about what country he comes from. The teacher, whose family originally comes from a Pacific Island, says that India is a big country. She uses the dough and a piece of paper to illustrate the relative sizes of a Pacific island, New Zealand, and India. She opts to value the construction of a working theory (New Zealand is bigger than India) rather than to correct his geography.

The Size of India (phase two)

The teacher asks him which part of India he comes from.

Yasin: I don't remember.

Teacher: But you are from India eh? I've got...

Yasin: And you're from...

Teacher: I've got only a tiny tiny island like this, very very very tiny island but India is big big like this piece of paper.

Yasin: (gestures) It's like big as this.

Teacher: Yeah. That's right.

Yasin: And if it's like this it would be New Zealand because New Zealand is bigger than India.

The teacher asks him if he has seen it on a map, and he says 'Yeah', and adds "My Dad, my Mum, told me".

Being a soccer player who knows the rules

In one of the extended episodes playing soccer in phase two there is considerable discussion about the rules and about possible infringement of the rules. In this extract Yasin explains the rules to the teacher after she has asked for his advice.

Playing Soccer (phase two)

Yasin: There go the...oh man! You are not allowed to come too close to my goal...break the soccer rule. No-one's allowed to break the soccer rules.

Teacher.   Are we allowed to use our hands in this game?

Yasin: No in soccer you're not allowed to use your hands unless you're... Use your feet not your hands..then kick it. (Later, when Sam kicks) Good one Sam.....Jack do you want to be in my team? You can take the kick. You can take the kick. If you're in my team I'll let you take the kick.

Jack: OK I'll be in your team.

Positioned as the teacher

Finally, there is an extended episode (forty-one minutes) in which Yasin is positioned as the expert, teaching others. The teacher hears that Yasin has been working with clay at his (outside) art class, and on the home visit the previous evening (with the researchers) she saw a photograph of a fish that he made. She sets up a table outside with clay. Yasin became the expert, giving advice. However, he will only make fish because "it's a fish that you (were) allowed to make", and he is critical of one of the others for making a house. Interestingly, although the teacher talks about stamps and stamping patterns, Yasin ignores these options (in spite of being interested in stamping): he is apparently in 'making a fish like the art class' mode. The teacher positions Yasin as the teacher and says "Yasin says we need a sharp, sort of, some form of cutter because I saw a photo of what Yasin made….just watch Yasin as he's thinking about what shape he wants. He's going to cut a shape out". The other children appear more ready to experiment than Yasin, to his dismay. He finally suggests that the other children go to his art class in order to be properly taught:

The Art Class (phase two)	
Yasin:	Why don't you all go to my art class and you'll see my…?
Teacher:	Why don't you bring a pamphlet about your art class and then the other children would know about it? And they could.. they'd know the details of when it is, what time.
Yasin:	Then they could also go to my art class.
Teacher:	That's right. What do you do at your art class Yasin?
Yasin:	Do art.
Teacher:	Do art. What sort of art do you do?
Yasin:	Like sometimes I can do pictures.
Teacher:	Sometimes you work with clay and you made a fish. And other times you..?
Yasin:	But sometimes my brother does better things because he's older.
Teacher:	Yasin will talk to you about it. What sort of work you can do with this clay and I'll go and get the sharp, plastic knives …..

Home is left behind at school

Shortly after the clay episode, Yasin went to school. During both phase one and phase two episodes references to home and family were woven throughout his participation at the early childhood centre and by phase two these references were more usually contingent on the activity. Five months later, the researchers observed Yasin at school in this new entrant classroom over two and a half days. Home and family were never directly mentioned, although in an episode of learning about 'materials' Yasin contributed ideas about fabrics (e.g. velvet) that was a feature of his experience at home where his mother worked with a range of fabrics as a dress-maker and designer. There were therefore a number of constraints on the imaginative identity work that he had developed at kindergarten. There were twelve episodes from school that lasted over ten minutes. The six longer episodes (over twenty minutes: writing the letters of the alphabet, two story-writing sessions, a lesson from the teacher on materials, a small group reading session, and a thirty minute practice for an item for Assembly) included no opportunity for imaginative input.

Story-writing

In an interview after Yasin started school, his parents commented on his progress.

Mother: They're [Yasin and brother] doing quite well at languages. The only thing that Yasin is having trouble with, is his writing.
Father: He can draw, but he's not interested in writing.
Mother: He's told the teacher "Why do I need writing?"
Father: They use computers now.
Mother: [He says] "There are phones, there are mobiles, there are computers – you don't need to write". (Parent interview, phase three)

The following extract from a story-writing episode shows Yasin very competently answering teacher questions, making the connections between the athletics experience and focusing on the story writing agenda. The teacher introduces the task: "Yesterday you had athletics and today you're going to write a story about it …... How did you like it? Did you enjoy yourself and what did you do? Did you run in a …?" The children start work, and she comments on the writing of one of the childen who has started with "I like to …."

Story Writing (phase three, excerpt)	
Teacher:	I like to run. No …...I don't want just "I like to", something that you did. I don't want everybody "I like…". I want to know what you people do.
Child 1:	I run in the race.
Teacher:	Good that's a good story. You start with, what's that word?
Class:	I
Yasin:	We skipped in the sack.
Teacher:	OK go and find me the word skip. What's the first letter in skip? (She takes him over to see the word skip).
Yasin:	S. (He writes 's')
Child 2:	I run and jump.
Teacher:	And what do you put at the end?
Child 2:	Full stop.
Teacher:	Remember your full stops and don't press so hard with the pencil. I ran in a race. Okay. Quickly, remember also your spaces.
Yasin:	Teacher, do I have to do an idea with the race? …. (The teacher helps other children, then returns to Yasin).
Teacher:	'Skip' does start with the letter s, and there is something, one more letter which makes the sound 'k'.

Yasin:	c
Teacher:	Good and there is a k too, all right. Skip, small i, p should come under the line. And we skipped in a ...., there is an s, there is a k, good. Did you like it? (Yasin nods) Yes, okay, write 'Yes' here. Y-E-S.

Yasin was at his most animated during a lesson on 'materials'. Here was an opportunity to refer (if obliquely) to home (his mother's work with fabrics), and to display his expertise.

	Knowing about Materials (phase three)
The teacher writes 'Materials' on the board.	
Teacher:	We're talking about materials. What's a material? What do I mean when I say material?
(Yasin puts his hand up) Yasin?	
Yasin:	Table cloth in three colours.
Teacher:	Yes .... From material.. that's right. .... What else? Something else? What other materials? Yasin?
Yasin:	Velvet.
Teacher:	What's velvet?
Yasin:	A material.
Teacher:	Velvet. Velvet is a type of? Cloth. .....
Child:	Colour.
Teacher:	Is colour a material? Do we make things with colour?
Yasin:	Paper.
Teacher:	Paper excellent. Paper is a ?
Group:	Material.

Yasin has brought his home to school, although this is not a public entry: just as Sarah brought Super Kitten in chapter seven, and in chapter five, Leona brought her family – more publicly – into her story-writing book.

ARALYNN

Aralynn's case study is an appropriate final story. It belongs in both chapters about imagination: imagining possible worlds, as well as in storying selves, especially in phase one where Aralynn was a leader in dramatic play. It also belongs in a discussion about reciprocity, as she adapts her interactions to the perspectives of others in dialogue when the group includes children who are younger. She engages with authority in gardening projects at all three phases, and she lives in a family that encourages her to ask questions about other people and other cultures. For Aralynn, gardening, storying, and taking care of others, were opportunities for storying a self in the figured worlds at every phase.

Aralynn was born in Melanesia; her parents had met at a New Zealand university as undergraduates and then moved to the home island of Aralynn's father. When Aralynn was two years old the family came to visit New Zealand for a holiday, but the political situation in the Island changed and it was not safe for Aralynn and her mother to return. Aralynn's father had a unique job in the Island and felt unable to return with them to New Zealand until a replacement for his skills could be found. He did visit, for Aralynn's birthday, the funeral for a grandmother and for other blocks of time. These were very special times for the family, and Aralynn's mother commented that they missed him terribly. She had a full-time job in an office. At the end of phase two, the father returned permanently (and after phase three of this project they moved to a bigger house, with a new baby). When the researcher met the family, Aralynn and her mother were living in a small house that her mother had bought and was renovating. They both loved the garden and shared gardening together.

> Aralynn's mother: Aralynn spends a lot of time in the garden helping me. She likes gardening. That was probably right from the start, mum was always in her garden and she was out there and helping her in the garden, so she does a lot of gardening, likes to get involved in the seeds and that, waters the garden and . . .
> Interviewer: I can see you've put a lot of energy into your garden already?
> Aralynn's mother: Yeah. Yeah. I've got an awful lot to do. Like it was a bit of a wreck when I first got here so . . .Yeah. So we like gardening. If I had my choice I wouldn't work and Aralynn would probably be in a kindergarten of some sort where she'd be spending some time with me in the mornings or afternoons and the other times with other kids, and um, I would be running a nursery. If I had the time and money. That's what we would be doing. (Parent interview, phase one)

This love of gardening was a key feature of their lives. Aralynn's maternal grandmother lived in a rural setting and in phase one Aralynn and her mother spent every weekend at the grandparents' home. Before phase two her grandmother died and this was a time of great grief for them all. They continued to visit her grandfather, but this was reduced to only once or twice a month, and being at their own home more regularly allowed Aralynn and her mother to put more time and energy into the garden at home. Aralynn had attended the early childhood centre on returning to New Zealand, beginning in the Nursery for a few months before moving to the full-day centre as a two-year-old. By the time the project began, four-year-old Aralynn had become a key 'assistant' with the settling in of new children, and took particular care of the younger ones in the environment – watching out for them, and taking their hands to cheer them up if sad. She was an 'old hand' at the early childhood centre and was regularly deeply engaged in activities. In phase three Aralynn was attending a very large primary school.

In phase one at Aralynn's childcare centre, Sleeping Beauty was a key theme in both the girls' and the boys' play. In phase two Aralynn appeared to be more frequently taking on a role of *a helper* – there were several episodes of her helping the teachers and the other children – but she combined her interest in story with this helper role, and 'read' stories to other children. Pretend play, with Aralynn as script-writer, continued in phase two with a cast of younger children. Her skills and dispositions as a story-teller continued at school where she enjoyed dictating and writing stories on themes that interested her. Alongside these pretend play and storying themes were a number of episodes, and comments from family and teachers, that referred to Aralynn's capacity to imagine the perspectives of others: her grandparents and the younger children at the centre in particular. And in phase three, at school, connections were made to Aralynn's love of gardening and nature, in her morning talks and an activity about growing beans.

Negotiating dramatic story-lines and actor roles in phase one

There were four very long episodes of imaginary play, and one short episode of focused drawing for Aralynn in phase one. The first episode is typical of the three pretend episodes. It was an imaginary play episode about 'Princess Aurora'. A group of the older children had been playing "Princess Aurora" for several days. They had watched the Disney movie from home – on television or at a movie theatre. A favourite book that one of the teachers had been reading aloud to the children for several days was of fairy tales. Braden's favourite game was "Spiderman". In turns one to four in the following conversation Aralynn is trying to establish that they are not playing Spiderman, and Braden negotiates about this by arguing that there is *another* Spiderman who will be perfectly acceptable.

Spiderman and Aurora (phase one)

Aralynn and Braden sit side-by-side in the 'family corner' talking, and during the episode Tania and then Abbi appear to take on minor roles in the drama. Negotiation of the story-line and who will play what, was a major feature of the episode, since there appeared to be a number of stories in mind: Spiderman, Sleeping Beauty, Princess Aurora, Big Sister, and Saving from Trouble. The multiplicity of themes are introduced early:

Aralynn: I'm not playing that Spiderman.

Braden: We aren't, we're playing the other Spiderman.

Aralynn: You said we aren't playing Spiderman.

Braden: No we aren't playing Spiderman with you, it's the you-know that we're playing.

Aralynn: The movie – she isn't it?

Braden: (referring to the Sleeping Beauty story) She got dead, alive, then dead then alive and then stay alive, eh? Save her.

Aralynn (introduces a character who never appears again): She's getting dead from the action man. Ah, get my book. Action man's a good guy. Save her, she's (...) coming.

Braden: She is, she's in a (...).

Aralynn: I know where, exactly where she is. She's – I know where she is. She's my sister, can you say this to Braden? (To Tania) Are you sick?

Tania: No.

> Aralynn: But she's Sleeping Beauty, she's sleeping – she's Sleeping Beauty.
> Braden: Are you Sleeping Beauty?
> Tania: (rejecting the role of Sleeping Beauty) No I...
> Braden: Okay then you've got to die.
> Aralynn: But remember I'm [saving?] her too cos of I'm Aurora.
> Braden: And I save you cos I'm Spiderman. Can I save her ...
> Aralynn: I don't live with you, I live with these two, don't I?
> Braden: And I do as well, eh? I live with you guys as well, eh?
> Aralynn: No.
> Braden: I live with you guys as well. I live with you guys as well, eh Tania?
> Tania: Yep.

This weaving of fantasy scripts and co-construction of story-lines is a complex task. The children work away at it in a moderately amicable manner for fifty minutes. Adults became involved only twice. The first time was when Braden goes to fetch a mattress and there was a dispute about who and how many can lie on it. Aralynn brings one, and there is a discussion about whether one can be shared. The teacher asks "What game are you playing?" Aralynn: "Sleeping Beauty" and the teacher agrees to bring one more mattress. On the second occasion Aralynn asked a teacher for a coloured popsicle stick, and she brings back a handful. (One of them will later be used as a surgeon's knife to "cut the Prince's ears open"). There is a dispute about their equitable distribution and the teacher assists with the negotiation: "They're for everyone to use, Aralynn, OK?" Aralynn: "But Braden got all of them". Teacher: "Well, what about having four each". This seems to be a satisfactory solution, and Aralynn assists with the counting and distribution. The dramatic play stops when 'picnic time' is announced.

Aralynn, Braden, Tania and the other children have been engaged in such pretend play episodes for a number of months. Aralynn has become skilled at taking the lead to decide on the (shifting) theme, and to assist with who will play the characters, but Braden is usually also a co-director, and the story-line must be constantly negotiated. It becomes even more difficult when the other players – who are necessary for the drama to unfold – have their own views about whom they will be and what they are prepared to do. The teachers' practice afforded this pretend play, providing the time and the props and supporting the children's themes through the choice of stories they read; during the researcher's visit a teacher was reading the children a story about Tarzan and Jane, which includes 'a scary chase' and an escape from danger. On the whole, they only intervened to see to the fair allocation of resources.

Aralynn adapts her storylines for younger children

By phase two Aralynn was one of the last four-year-olds still at the centre; her mother explained how she helped care for the younger children.

> She's the big kid. Which I think she enjoys. I think she enjoys being that big kid. Like when I got there yesterday to pick her up to take her to after school

care, she was reading a book to Danny – I'm not sure which Danny – she was reading a story to him. And she said: "Look, my mum is here I have to go now. Will you get one of the adults to read to you?" She was just talking as an adult – just what you'd do you know . . . and he seemed to lap it up. She was loving it and he was loving it too so . . . And she likes reading some books to me too. She likes — she usually likes me reading, but she reads a book that she's really familiar with, she likes to read it to me, and she doesn't like not being able to remember the words for it, so she likes to carry that on at home... She used to do that with her Nana too. She used to read to Nana and tell Nana what was in the story, yeah, which was nice. And it's nice to see her doing that with wee kids and having the patience to do it with kids. And the other kids have patience to let her do it because . . . you know what kids are like. I mean you know they grab and pull and they want a turn and stuff. And they always sit there and listen to her, like wee google eyes kind of thing.... So . . . they must be amazed that she can read all the words, its just lucky they don't know she can't. .... But it's nice. (Parent interview, phase two)

During phase two the teachers looked to Aralynn more than before for 'helping tasks'. She had been involved in helping to settle a new child, with no English, and she would walk around the centre holding her hand while the new child's caregiver left her for increasingly long periods. She had also developed a firm friendship with Emily, and they were frequently deeply involved in dramatic play. There is less competition for role now, and Aralynn has adjusted her story-lines. In the following episode she appears to have found a theme that engages the younger children: being animals. Aralynn introduces the story-line, and Emily adds ideas. Aralynn includes Danny and livens it up by trialling the voices of being a cat and using baby language. She also reminds the younger children that they are 'pretending' not to know how to say the words.

	Being Animals (phase two)
Aralynn:	Remember. I know, I could be a cat. You don't – you don't mind me being a cat any more cos all the times I've been a horse now, haven't I?
Emily:	And you've...
Aralynn:	Yeah. Cos cats love milk, don't they?
Emily:	... lie down there ....
Aralynn:	Yeah. Do you want to play with us Danny?
Child:	....(indistinct)
Aralynn:	All right.
Child:	You're allowed to play okay Danny?
Child:	.... meow means ....
Aralynn:	Meow. Meow. Meooow.... Meow-meow. .... Pretend I don't know how to say 'kitty' so I say 'kwitty', don't I?
Child:	You can't say 'mice' so you say 'micey'.
Aralynn:	Yeah.

Perhaps Aralynn is seeing this play much more from the perspectives of the other players: including their contributions, using themes that she knows they will enjoy (animals and animal noises), and reminding them that she is 'pretending'.

Taking on the perspective of another

Aralynn's 'reading' to the other children in this phase was noted by her mother. A key thread for this period is her 'helping' – which her parents trace back to the care and attention that they have given her grandparents – first the grandmother who died, and now the care of the grandfather who is alone. Parents and the teachers at the early childhood centre and the school frequently talked about Aralynn as a 'helper' with a disposition to care about others. Her mother commented:

> I can't think of anything else really different that she does (from phase one to phase two). She copes with my father very well. That's one thing. Since mum died she's – you know dad is always the quiet one and mum was full of life and things, but now since mum died dad is still quiet but mopey, she copes with him very well, she handles him very well. She knows when to step back and she doesn't let him get away with anything … she'll tell him if this is what you do, you know, she handles him very well. (Parent interview, phase two)

Writing princess stories at school

By phase three Aralynn's new entrant class had been divided and the sixteen older children (including Aralynn) had been moved to a very small classroom space. Aralynn's school classroom provided her with the opportunity to continue to develop her more complex princess story lines. Although she was also learning to read and write, in this classroom the teacher appears to be more concerned that the story will make sense to someone who reads it, rather than with the detail of the writing, spelling and punctuation. Here is part of a transcript from school, where Aralynn was writing – and dictating – a story about climbing a beanstalk to Princess Land (the beanstalk being a required item in the story, since the class have been growing beans). This was a new genre of story-telling for Aralynn, and the teacher was reminding her that a written story must make sense to the reader. In her first comment the teacher is puzzling with Aralynn about meaning, and she rather reluctantly concedes that you *could* dress up as a windmill. However, the teacher wants to explore whether the word 'useful' is appropriate as a descriptor of Princess Land.

Princess Land (phase three)

Teacher: Okay I played in – listen to this – listen to this bit. (Er Samantha, I'll be coming to check you in a minute). …. "I played in Princess World, I sometimes dress up as a windmill but Princess World – but in Princess World there are dinosaurs and Princess Land is very useful". What do you think

	about that? Well you could dress up as a windmill though I mean that's fine, but – you've said Princess Land is very useful. How is it very useful? What makes you write that in your story?
Aralynn:	Cos...
Teacher:	Is 'useful' a good word, is that what you meant? You know when something's useful, what does that mean?
Aralynn:	It means something's really – it's really useful.
Teacher:	That you can use it a lot.
Aralynn:	Yeah.
Teacher:	So is Princess Land very useful?
Aralynn:	Yeah.
Teacher:	How is it useful? What do – like useful is like, (...) is very useful.
Aralynn:	I know.
Teacher:	So what do you mean by – is useful a good word to describe Princess Land? Well if it's useful then you need to tell me what's useful about Princess Land? Cos you know these stories, these are going to go up on the wall, okay, and I want your Mum and your Dad whenever he comes in to be able to read that and understand what you mean by that. So do you think (...) word useful?
Aralynn:	(provides a justification) Well, because there's lots of Princesses in it and the Kings and Queens are useful.
Teacher:	Okay. Uhm ... useful. Okay. Cos that sort of doesn't make – yeah the Princesses are very useful. You'd have to add lots more to make that make sense to your story. So you could either do that or change your word from very useful. ...
Aralynn:	I want to change my word.

The teacher appears to be open to any reasonable argument for the more bizarre aspects of Aralynn's story-lines. They negotiate, and decide that the word 'beautiful' might be better.

	Princess Land (continued)
Aralynn:	(dictating) 'I decided to climb down and I went back to school. I sheltered back down the beanstalk.'
Teacher:	(reading it back to her) I sheltered back down the beanstalk. Does that make sense? ... Okay, so what do you think you could change about that?
	Aralynn decides to finish the story after 'I went back to school'.
Teacher:	It is okay. I think now that will make sense to your story, okay, cos you said about all the other things, there's dinosaurs there, could be or there is in your imagination but now it's a very beautiful place so useful is not really – can you understand why I said that? Right, you're finished now and I'm going to type that.

Perhaps some of Aralynn's more imaginative flourishes have been lost from the written story: perhaps when she said 'sheltering' she had something like 'going helter-skelter' in mind, and if she and the teacher had had the time she could have dictated an explanation to the reader about why Princess Land was useful. But nevertheless this was an educational conversation – Aralynn retained the authorship and was working at the edge of her ability to combine a pretend story with the perspective of someone who is not about to play out the story with her (her Mum and Dad when they come in to read it).

Making connections: growing beans at school

Aralynn, together with other members of the class, grew broad beans in a pot and took them home to plant in the garden. Her classroom teacher commented on her 'real interest' in this task.

> And there's her beans – her broad beans, and she took real interest in that and she was checking her beans everyday. Cos there's four in the classroom still that are very mouldy but nobody will take them home and I dare not throw them out, because they are still looking at them. And that will be the one that looks at them and know it's disappeared. But no – oh good, cos they were really interested and she liked --- like on Science and Nature day, which is Tuesday for oral language, she will quite often bring a plant of some kind, so she really took an interest in the beans. (Teacher interview, phase three)

The teacher introduced the assessment part of the process: a worksheet. This was an 'individual assessment', and, now, helping others is not deemed to be appropriate.

Individual Assessment (phase three)

Aralynn works diligently to cut out the four pictures of a growing bean and to put them in order and number them. But instead of writing the words 'bean', 'root', 'stem' and 'shoot' she cuts up the model-word sheet and begins to paste them onto the pictures. The class is told not to help each other. She is working alongside Hamish.

Aralynn: What?
Hamish: Is that the stem?
Aralynn: What?
Hamish: Is that the stem?
Aralynn: Yeah. The stem? No that's the stem. ... That's the shoot, that's the stem.
Teacher: Don't tell him please.
Aralynn: (Sings) Baby you're my rock star, baby you're my star. Baby you're my rock star. Bean. Bean shoot. No, no bean – bean um, bean, bean root, root, bean root. ....
Teacher: No you don't – this – this is not sharing what you know, you keep what's in your head to yourself this time, you don't copy your next door neighbour, you tell – show me what you know about this, what we've been learning, Hamish. Okay.

When the combination of gardener-with-information self and the assisting-others self are shut down by the rules of summative assessment, Aralynn resists. Hamish needs help, and when she can't get away with talking, she sings the labels. The teacher later commented: "And what – how did she do? I think she could sequence them all, but some [children] could only tell me the parts, didn't then go through and write them all in the right places which was interesting. I think she got about three out of five". No doubt the irony was not lost on the teacher: Aralynn was totally engaged in the bean growing, and at group time could name all the parts of the plant. She was, at home, a gardener. But when it came to the formal assessment worksheet, she got three out of five.

Making connections across the boundaries of school and time: News time

There were different kinds of news time in Aralynn's classroom: weekend, treasures, and nature. Aralynn was an avid contributor to all three, as the following conversations with Aralynn and her parents indicate: conversations that refer back to the past, to remembering the times that Aralynn used to spend with her Nana.

Aralynn's father: One of her things that she really likes is – you know, the story telling time where she just gets anything and she goes there and she talks about it.

Aralynn's mother: Yeah. Her News. Her News for the week. So she likes to take things like...

Aralynn: Like I can bring – I can bring a little nest or bones and flowers and petals and ...

Aralynn's mother: Because Aralynn's Nana and Aralynn used to wander in ...

Aralynn: And I saw a dead rabbit the other day.

Aralynn's mother: They used to get bones and ... and I bring ... Nana used to open up the rabbit's neck and show us the innards.

Interviewer: Yes. I remember you telling me about that.

Aralynn's mother: It's just that the bits and pieces that she found with Nana – like the nests and stuff she takes those along for her treasures and news-time and stuff. So yeah, she likes to take things to school. She's got three days I think – there's treasures, there's nature and there's weekend news, so there's three times that she can either take something, like a story about the fire engine or some of her goodies. And she doesn't take her dolls and she never asks. Its other things like rocks she's got painted or the skull of a – we think it's a possum.

Aralynn's father: Nature things.

Aralynn's mother: And a flower that had a funny petal on it. So its more outdoorsy kind of stuff.

Aralynn: Uh-hmm. Uh-hmm.

Aralynn's mother: And bugs and bits and pieces like that, so she enjoys that. She enjoys being able to show other children and being able to talk about it. (Interview with Aralynn and her parents, phase three)

The teachers at the school confirmed Aralynn's interest in news time:

Classroom teacher: She always brings something for News. And keeps to the topics. Like – so especially for their age because they do find it difficult to bring Science and Nature in and she brings flowers and all sorts of interesting – sometimes radishes that she grew from her garden. I can think of all the other things that she's brought. And she's brought bones of a sheep, it's a skull they found at [area]. And for special News she always brings something different for special news, it was actually a skull as well, it was a whole little skull, last Tuesday. And sometimes on a Tuesday and Thursday she will be the only one that has bothered to bring special or Science Nature news, or there might be one other or there might be someone who wants to sneak in their weekend news or something like that. But she's actually kept to the topic.

Caring about other people

Aralynn's family have strong values about respecting other people and other cultures. During phase two, her mother had spoken about the opportunities to appreciate difference: "You know. And she's got a father who's from a different country and there's different languages, and then there's this whole – all that other side of the family that's different – you know, different from me and my side of the family." And, in phase three:

Aralynn's father: I suppose perhaps one other thing I would really like probably if I had to learn and also in her school environment is actually to appreciate other people and other cultures. You know I used to think one of the things that they should probably do in school settings here is probably at an early age like that to have small talks, like ten minutes or so – say three talks a term by different people from different groups and talk about their specific values and how they do things in different cultures, so that you know, that they would actually learn more about those cultures, because I feel that even though they learn like Māori words and that, it's not sufficient.

Aralynn's mother: Hmm. I think Aralynn is perhaps more aware than some children. She's more aware of people and how they are different. Because she said to me about other kids and how this is what they do at home and this is not what they do and why do they wear that on their head? And you know she talks about their differences which I think is really good. She's – she realises that they don't just go home and do exactly what Aralynn does, she's aware that there are differences in the world and um, yeah.

LEARNING IN THE MAKING

Disposition-in action: work in progress

This section has been included in all the case study chapters. It summarises each of the three dispositional components introduced in chapter two, derived initially from a triadic definition of a learning disposition, as authoring, recognising opportunity, and connected knowing. All three of these components combined together as a work in progress to describe Yasin's and Aralynn's journeys towards being ready willing and able to story selves.

Authoring. Yasin's conversations with teachers at the kindergarten set out the contexts of a cultural self: the country outside New Zealand, India, where his nana and extended family live, and his family in New Zealand who are widening his perceptions of self as a global citizen by introducing him to new languages – Spanish, Arabic and Mandarin – and new skills – art, music, tennis and soccer. He explains the rules of soccer to the other children, and the teacher invites him to take on the role of a teacher in other areas of expertise – art work with clay for instance – as well. He initiates these conversations and the early childhood teacher is able to recognise and assist with the details. By school, however, this cultural self has been left behind. During Aralynn's early years at home, childcare centre, and school she is positioned authoritatively as a caring helper, an adept story teller, and a keen gardener; these selves are spontaneously expressed in episodes of joint attention in all phases of this research. She authors them in different ways, and on several occasions chose to take responsibility as someone who helps others.

Recognising opportunity. Yasin's lengthy storying discussions in the figured worlds of home and kindergarten were welcome, and while in phase one he introduced his family to almost every conversation, by phase two he is introducing home information in response to the topic at hand rather than 'out of the blue'. At school, however, he appears to recognise that spontaneous storying about himself does not have the same public and legitimate space. He seized the chance in a technology lesson to introduce his knowledge from home of the fabrics that his mother sews, but his extra-curricular lessons may have taught him to 'read' a diversity of educational environments, to recognise a figured world in which one follows directions, gets on with the set tasks, and does not try to engage the teacher in discussions about self and family. When in phase two Aralynn was one of the older children at the childcare centre she responded to the invitation from this social environment to adapt her storylines for the younger children. There were no set scripts here; children make it up as they go along and she sees the play from the perspectives of the other players and improvises accordingly. At school, enabled to bring her interests to News Time, she adjusts to the audience again and the teacher comments that "she keeps to the topics".

Connected knowing. Although Yasin does not have opportunities at school to contribute disposition-based knowing about self from the past and home, he is also scripting a self as a school pupil. He knows that teachers expect a contribution to the large group discussions, for instance, and he is able to call on his general knowledge at appropriate times. His teacher told the researcher that "He is very good orally, like he knows so many things. His general knowledge is quite good". For Aralynn, the storying could continue into school, in a smaller classroom than Yasin's. Her subject-based knowing – her love of, and knowledge about, gardening, which began at home with her mother and her grandparents – is also part of the valued school curriculum. The school teacher was enabling her to continue the imaginative princess stories that she had been developing at the early childhood centre, emphasising not so much the possibilities of being a princess but of being a story-teller, when she is reminded that a story for an audience needs to make some sense. At the childcare centre she 'read' books to the younger children, as she had 'read' books to her mother and her grandmother, and the abilities she is developing in caring and kindness are connecting strands throughout all the phases.

Design

A number of features of the educational design in these case studies appeared to afford, invite, engage, provoke – and constrain – this facet of imagination. We have commented here on: the provision of spaces for storying selves, the availability of different modes for telling stories, and a recognition of funds of knowledge from home.

Space and time. The educational design in phase one of Yasin's experience in an early childhood setting provided him with spaces for authoring stories that interested him: as a sibling, a potential parent, an artist, an expert soccer player. He was also invited to venture into new art activities: making puppets and painting flowers. The latter provided opportunities for inventing an imaginative story, with himself as the main character. This was not the teacher's intent – she was focusing on the children's capacity to notice carefully in still-life art activity – but she picked up his cue and promised to write up the story for him. This story – like the Learning Story in his portfolio about Making a Stamp Pad – would provide documentation that can be revisited, an opportunity to re-read his story and to remember his first attempts at painting flowers and being a possible print-maker. Aralynn's childcare centre provided time and resources for her elaborate dramas associated with being Aurora, alongside Sleeping Beauty and Spiderman. In phase two the demography of the childcare centre invited her to be a carer for the younger children, and this was also an opportunity to learn to adjust her side of the dialogue to engage the younger children. Her school classroom still provided her with a space (at writing time) to weave a story about a land where princesses and kings and queens are useful, because she could dictate her story to the teacher.

Valuing the multi-disciplinary and the multi-modal. Yasin's kindergarten environment provided many affordances for children like Yasin who are interested in art: craft resources to choose from, painting and easels available and accessible, visits

193

to the art gallery, and wall displays that provide models that can be adapted. The teachers step up the demand of these affordances by issuing invitations to participate (for instance to do a painting of flowers) and provocations that demand clarification of their ideas, remembering of events, and the completion of tasks. Almost a year after he painted the daffodils (together with himself in the bushes eating popcorn and picking flowers) he discussed with one of the teachers a painting he had completed the day before: a painting of two insects with antennae. Field notes record that he explains that the big one is Yasin and the little one is his older brother and the larger insect is eating the smaller. In phase two he also completed a drawing of a character that he remembered from an earlier theatre visit by the kindergarten children. Aralynn's school classroom did not interrupt her penchant for imaginative stories, but it was placed in scheduled time, with some provisos (in the story-writing observed, the story was required to be loosely attached to the theme of growing beans). Aralynn's teacher reminded her that a story-teller should consider the perspective of those who will read the story: she emphasised meaning, not just the technical skill of getting letters and words correctly onto paper.

Recognition of funds of knowledge from home. There are examples here of the social and cultural capital at home and the social and cultural capital at the early childhood setting or school being 'in synch', through invitations and provocations that bring topics from family and home into the discourses and activities of centre and school. In these case studies, the families constructed, recognised and supported the telling of self stories: the gardener and the artist, for instance. As Maxine Greene said (1995, p. 20), and perhaps as Bourdieu might have said:

> A young person trying to become a ballet dancer is affected in her or his conception of a life in dance by the way those immediately around her or him in childhood talked about such a choice as worthy or impractical, as romantic or somehow suspect.

Aralynn's mother and – especially after phase two when he returns to New Zealand – her father provide models and commentary on the why and how of a caring self. The teachers also appreciate Aralynn's helping the younger children, and the mixed age at the centre provides opportunity for Aralynn to hone the abilities that are part of a caring disposition that she has developed with her grandparents. At school, Aralynn's home had a legitimate place. Her love of gardening was appreciated when they grew the beans, and the teacher valued the way in which Aralynn used News Time as an opportunity to bring interesting stories from home. Yasin's family are providing extra-curricular opportunities for him to learn languages and skills that are designed to set him on the journey towards becoming a global citizen, and the teachers support these initiatives: during our observations one of the teachers positioned Yasin as an expert in working with clay, because they knew he had been working with clay at his art class, and he was on one occasion invited to contribute words in Spanish. The kindergarten teachers used a number of strategies to listen to, invite and provoke his stories about home.

LEARNING IN THE MAKING

> How do actions or events on one timescale come to add up to more
> than just a series of isolated happenings? (Lemke, 2000, p. 273)

What might we conclude from these case studies for the reciprocal relationship between disposition and design, and can we provide any working theories about the trajectory of learning disposition over time? In this chapter we bring together the data on young children's learning from the previous six chapters to construct some commentary on a 'zoomed-out' big picture about *learning in the making* and we connect our findings with the literature that we have found useful in coming to these conclusions and implications.

The case studies provided a 'mid-level' analysis (Gee, 1997) from 'zoomed-in' episodes of learning. Of course, the more we zoom out, with learning dispositions in mind, the more uncertain our working theories become. However, we still see the value of taking the analysis to another level. Allan Luke has asked 'Which grand narratives should count in curriculum making and pedagogy in the national and educational systems of Asia and the Pacific?' (2005, p. 11) and comments 'In the case of curriculum making, radical overskepticism towards metanarratives – and oversensitivity to the local and the individual – can lead to fragmentation and paralysis' (p. 17). He adds that:

> (L)earning to live together in difference, the establishment of an ethics of care
> and empathy, the issues of transcultural and intercultural communication, and
> the direct education of the Other within what was historically purported to be
> homogeneous systems are not designer options for curriculum, pedagogy and
> education, but must be part of any version of new basics (Luke, 2005, p. 22).

We hope that our focus on learning in the making with reference to dispositions towards reciprocity, resilience and imagination will make a contribution to discussions about curriculum, pedagogy and education for the 21st century. In the first part of this chapter we describe the *content* of disposition: the intersection of these three dispositions, together with the six ways in which children in our study were 'doing' those dispositions. We suggest that the intersection of learning dispositions describes a multi-faceted learner self. In the second section we describe the *processes* of learning disposition: a working theory about what might be going on in the "middle" transactional space between disposition and educational design, the space where identity work is done, shaping and reshaping multi-faceted learner selves over time and place. The final section is a commentary on some of the implications of this study for education.

A MULTI-FACETED LEARNER SELF: THE CONTENT OF LEARNING
DISPOSITIONS

In chapter two we argued for three learning dispositions: reciprocity, resilience and imagination. In chapters three to eight we translated those three nouns of disposition into verbs, choosing two actions, or facets, of each disposition to analyse: *participating in dialogue* and *being and becoming a group member* for reciprocity, *initiating and orchestrating projects* and *asking questions* for resilience, and *exploring possible worlds* and *storying selv*es for imagination. These verbs had emerged from the case studies as we became immersed in the data, reflected together on the analysis, and returned to the literature. They were, in practice, often closely interconnected, just as reciprocity, resilience, and imagination are closely connected. Henry's story provides an example of the intersection between imagination, reciprocity and resilience. In an interview during phase two, Henry's mother expressed concern that Henry might have become a bit aggressive or 'bossy'. She worried about this because of the relationship changes and difficulties in their family life over the past year. However, from our observations, early childhood experiences had provided opportunities that may have contributed centrally to Henry's well-being or resilience at this period in his life, when, just before phase one of the research his parents had separated and a grandparent had died. During phase two Henry was involved in more regular conflict: the flying fox recently introduced to the playground, for instance, had afforded turn-taking conflicts as well as exciting physical experiences. Our observations suggested that these situations had provoked Henry to work out solutions that would sustain the play and maintain good social relationships. This desire to sustain the play had been a feature of his interactions in phase one as well, although his response to conflict then had been more often to shift out of pretend play by reminding others that this was 'just' pretend. By phase two Henry was also developing more strategies in response to his new interest in conscripting a diversity of potential play partners; these strategies included shifting the imaginative story-line to more 'real' situations (from the fanciful notion that he built the kindergarten on his own, to including an adult to make a more plausible story; and from storylines that included crocodiles and dangerous flooding to the more generally familiar topic of 'mums and brothers'). This shift enabled the co-authoring of play scripts because the repertoire of possible story-lines was familiar to a wider range of players. He had also become very adept at using humour: introducing large numbers ("I've been waiting six hundred and ninety nine days") to communicate his opinion in an amusing way, or using 'silly' and mildly rude words like 'bumhead' to diffuse situations or prevent them from escalating in order to maintain the play. It seemed that if Henry was in any sense 'working out' the family upheavals of the past year, the people spaces and resources at the kindergarten were also affording, inviting and provoking him to respond to difficulties with resilience and to develop strategies in the domains of both reciprocity and imagination in order to do so.

In this chapter's analysis we follow on from Joy Cullen and Alison St George's study of 'scripts for learning' in classroom life (1996) to suggest that the children in this study were developing self-scripts for learning. These 'scripts' for a multi-faceted learner self were about what learners do and might assume, and what opportunities to look out for. Self-scripts have possible selves in mind. Hazel Markus and Paula Nurius have suggested that 'possible selves' "provide the essential link between the self-concept and motivation ... Through selection and construction of possible selves individuals can be viewed as active producers of their own development" (Markus & Nurius, 1986, pp. 954, 955). These self-scripts give us information about "things to do or not to do, things to say or not to say, in relation to a 'probable' upcoming future", as Bourdieu has said (1990, p. 53). This script metaphor aligns with metaphors of 'actor' and 'author' in the education literature (Lobato, 2003, 2006; Greeno, 2006) and it seemed to work well for describing the learning trajectories of the case study children: many of them were learning through dramatic play scenarios and while they were deciding what Spiderman, mates, and princesses were supposed to do, they were also trying to understand what learners and pupils were supposed to do as well. The notion of a script, too, sits alongside the idea of an early childhood centre as a 'scene'. We were exploring which aspects of these scripts were carried over, improvised and renovated, when the scene and the possible self (for instance, being a school pupil) changed. A script implies a story – although it is an adapted script in response to new languages, new players and new props – and Bruner (2002), Paley (2005) and Sfard and Prusak (2005) make cogent claims for the connection between identity and storying. In this study, we have combined what Holland et al. (1998) have called 'narrativized' identities and 'positional' identity.

> Narrativized or figurative identities .... have to do with the stories, acts, and characters that make the world a cultural world. Positional identity, as we use the term, is a person's apprehension of her social position in a lived world: that is, depending on the others present, of her greater or lesser access to spaces, activities, genres, and through those genres, authoritative voices, or any voice at all. ... Put perhaps too simply, figurative identities are about signs that evoke storylines or plots among generic characters; positional identities are about acts that constitute relations of hierarchy, distance, or perhaps affiliation. (Holland et al., 1998, pp. 127–128)

Acts of positioning in episodes of learning can become narrativised as scripts, available for reference on other occasions. Cullen and St George's study of junior classrooms in New Zealand in the mid 1990s concluded as follows, and thirteen years later these comments are still relevant.

> An implication of this model for teachers is that classroom life needs to support the construction of scripts for learning and not simply scripts for routines and procedures. Accordingly, teachers need to be aware of the dynamic classroom processes which affect children's perceptions of learning, particularly their own role in creating classroom orientations to learning. (Cullen & St George, 1996, p. 11)

In the case study chapters we explored the ways in which episodes of learning in early education centres and classrooms contributed to the shaping of possible learner selves and provided access to scripts about a learner self. Many of these self-scripts 'bumped' up against each other or bumped up against the rules routines and discourses of the context (Clandinin, Huber & Huber et al., 2006). Finding ways to negotiate across scripts (their own and their teachers') was a key learning for the children in the early years. Lauren found that her self-script of shifting to-and-from the signifiers of boy and girl cultural scripts bumped up against the childcare teachers' rules about not using up all the spare childcare clothes: the response was a tolerant view of the rules by the teachers. Yasin found that his story-telling-about-home facet of disposition bumped up against his recognition of being a school pupil and the school classroom practices of only telling stories that the novice writer can write. Lisa's self-script of selectively participating in dialogue in one centre bumped up against the 'shy' self that had been, initially, constructed in another early childhood centre. Joseph's 'friend' script bumped up against his curious, questioning self. Sarah and her early childhood teachers' sense of her as a good student at the early childhood centre bumped up against the discursive practices of the formal learning requirements in school. We observed the complex process as children appeared to select from, negotiate between, and orchestrate, these apparently inconsistent facets of self. The design of the educational practice sometimes assisted and sometimes hindered this process, and families mediated. We would not ask that these contradictions and conflicts *settle*, for they are the stuff of life and meaning-making. Bruner reminded us towards the end of chapter seven that 'a self-making narrative is something of a balancing act'. However, we look to educational designs to assist children to find these balancing acts interesting, and to begin to make some sense of the often confusing and mysterious contradictions and conflicts in participatory practice.

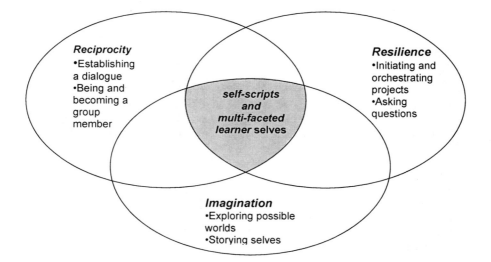

Figure 9.1. The content of learning dispositions: reciprocity, resilience and imagination

Chapter two introduced this disposition-based curriculum content of nouns and verbs. Figure 9.1 sets it out in diagram form. The next section, on transactional and progressive *processes,* builds on it to look at how this content was shaped and re-shaped in transactions over time between disposition and design.

LEARNING DISPOSITIONS OVER TIME AND PLACE: TRANSACTIONAL AND PROGRESSIVE PROCESSES

We have set out some ideas about dispositions as *content* in order to have a foundation to explore the *processes* of shaping and re-shaping learner scripts over time. Disposition, by definition, lasts longer than one episode; it has a history, it looks toward a future, and self-scripts are adjusted and reorganized over time. We looked in our data for "recurring conventions of thinking and behaving and constantly defended values" (Holland et al., 1998, p. 31). Our observations, interviews, recordings and reflections on a series of episodes for each of the case study children's lives in early childhood settings and school classrooms, connected together by us to tell a story, are perhaps 'like smaller streams that feed into a larger river' (Lee, Brown, Brickhouse et al., 2007, p. 333). Are they 'blips' or do they form streams and patterns? This question was asked in a discussion of a study of out-of-school science book club meetings with a group of third grade children:

> (Are) experiences of positioning and being positioned in book club meetings at an early age mere blips in the life of a person? Do they constitute mediating influences that we forget but which nevertheless tremendously influence the direction identity development takes? Or do they play no role at all? ... The repertoires of school are often compartmentalised so that students' otherwise relevant knowledge is not invited and evoked, and the continuity over time is lost to the urgency of the banal moments of everyday life in school. (Lee et al., 2007, pp. 333, 335)

And we return to the question at the beginning of this chapter: 'How do actions or events on one timescale come to add up to more than just a series of isolated happenings?' It is our turn to ask these questions of the succession of learning episodes in a wide range of enterprises and tasks. As we reflected on our data, we returned to Miller and Goodnow's 'person-participating-in-a-practice' as a unit of analysis (1995 p.8), and to Wertsch's description of "living in the middle", as an "agent-acting-with-mediational-means" (1998, p. 24) - and to the work of the many researchers who confirm the central role of relationships between the learner and affordance networks. Here we ask: what happens *in the middle* between the individual and the environment? What happens when a disposition meets a design (an affordance network or a dispositional milieu)?

James Gee provides one overview of these processes. He has written about identity as an analytic lens for research in education, and described four ways to view the processes of identity formation: *developed* from 'forces of nature' (unfolding from genetic inheritance; Gee cites the example of his being an identical twin), *authorised* by authorities within institutions (the ways in which, for instance, teachers and pupils might be positioned), *recognised* in discourse and dialogue (how other people treat, talk about, interact with someone as a 'good helper' or a 'shy person'), and *shared* in the practice of "affinity" groups or communities of practice (Gee, 2000/2001, p. 100). The *developing*, or unfolding from genetic inheritance, plays a part, but the opportunities to learn in homes, early childhood centres, and schools – in the past and in the present – powerfully contribute to identity through Gee's other three processes. In the case studies in this book, teachers and educational environments were authorising, recognising and sharing. In turn, teachers' identities *as teachers* were being authorised by their school structure, recognised in their interactions with other teachers and with the children, and shared in the wider educational sector and community. Families too were authorising, recognising and sharing on behalf of their children, and their own identities as, for instance, *'good'* or *'not good'* parents, have been in turn authorised by a range of authorities, recognised in their interactions with other people, and shared by the wider community and especially the mass media.

We return to Greeno's discussion of progressive themes in understanding transfer of learning, introduced in chapter two. He notes that transfer is "an inherently authoritative action", involving "doing something that one has not been taught explicitly to do" (2006 p. 538). The children, families and teachers in this study drew our attention to these aspects of interaction as well.

For many of the children the tracing of disposition-in-action into new territory was associated with courage – to question the norm (Joseph), to skate along the boundary between the acceptable and unacceptable (Aralynn, Henry and Ofeina), to engineer a gap in the rules (Lauren, David and Samuel) – constructing opportunity in unfavourable circumstances. Greeno cites Rosa Parks as an example of transfer as moral courage; she transferred her participation at school to her resistance in the civil rights movement. He says that authoritative and accountable positioning is about being entitled and expected to move about the environment freely, with access to materials and the authority to use, adapt, and combine those resources in unconventional ways. Connected general knowing, too, might be described as a transactional and progressive process – it is about "knowing general characteristics and large-scale relations, sometimes called *survey knowledge of the environment*"(p. 543). Greeno was writing primarily about subject-based conceptual domains like science or mathematics, but these ideas seemed to fit well for the content of dispositional domains as well. We saw in the case studies that both categories of connected knowing – the subject-based and the disposition-based – were relevant, and we will argue that there are also multilingual, inter-disciplinary and nonverbal multimodal and multisensory categories of knowing or making meaning that were important here. The 'knowing' is often tacit. There are different sites that can possibly become connected too: the early childhood centre, the school, the family, the church, and other sites in the community that include the 'real' worlds outside educational institutions in which concreting, cooking, writing, acting and art-making have value.

Dispositions-in-action: authoring, recognising opportunity and connected knowing

When we came to analyse the dispositions-in-action at the end of each case study chapter, we adapted Greeno's two-part analysis to parallel Perkins et al.'s triad of inclination, sensitivity to occasion, and ability, introduced in chapter two. Greeno's 'knowing' includes recognising opportunity or 'perceived affordance' (2006, p. 542). We separated these two – knowing and recognising opportunity – although they follow on one another's heels. Our research indicated that 'recognising opportunity' was a key process.

Chapters three to eight have described some of the continuities over time and place for: establishing dialogue, being and becoming a group member, initiating and orchestrating projects, asking questions, imagining possible worlds, and storying selves. The transactional and progressive processes that seemed to reflect those continuities were: authoring, recognising opportunity, and connected knowing. All of these three processes are sited in the 'middle' ground between disposition and design, a transactional space in which learning dispositions are strengthened, shaped, weakened or ignored. We had observed the ways in which, some of the time, learners were relating to the educational environment by authoring, recognising and connecting. We separated these three out in our analyses for three reasons.

The first is that we wanted to highlight, with Perkins et al. (1993, p. 4) that "to treat dispositions as solely about motivation would be to take too narrow a view". We, too, wanted to add sensitivity and ability.

Secondly, this analysis enabled us to highlight the ways in which sometimes, for some of the case study children, one aspect of the triad had not (yet?) kept up with the other. Samuel's enthusiasm for reciprocal play became a disposition-in-action in phase two at the kindergarten only when he developed the ability – strategies and languages – to interact with others. The teachers' active engagement assisted him with this. Lauren's inclination and ability to ask about the meaning of life and death was, when she was at school, well ahead of her sensitivity to the appropriate occasion. In the following transcript, in chapter six, for instance, Lauren's school teacher was reading a story to a group.

Teacher: This story's called Bedtime – it's the Wizard's bedtime.
Lauren: Is he a naughty person?
Teacher: No, he's a wizard darling.
Lauren: What's a wizard?
Teacher: He's like a magic man. Like in The Lord of the Rings. Did you see that? ...There was a wizard, and he could do magic tricks. [She reads on] Who's in bed here? It looks like a giant, and what's he taken to bed with him? A bone.
Lauren: Is a giant really scary?
Teacher: Are there really giants?
Lauren: No.
Teacher: No, well, they're not true. Here we go..[reads on]

It was not surprising that in this context, with a group of children waiting to hear the story, the teacher found this constant questioning irksome. However, unless the curriculum is permeable enough to find other recognisable spaces for Lauren's authoritative exploration and curiosity, there is a risk that her question-asking will be shut down altogether, at school anyway.

The third reason for separating the aspects of the triad for analytical purposes was that recognising opportunity, attunement to circumstance, seemed to be the site for critique, improvisation, and questioning the norm. 'Recognising opportunity' may be the leader in this enterprise.

Design in action: authorising, being permeable, and connecting the knowing

At the same time, in the case study chapters, we had outlined some of the design features that appeared to be prohibiting, hindering, affording, inviting, actively engaging, or provoking the dispositions-in-action. In this chapter we have chosen some of these design features, aligning them with the authoring, recognising opportunity, and connected knowing. We had observed the ways in which, some of the time, the educational environment was relating to the learner by authorising, being permeable and connecting the knowing. All of these three processes are also sited in the 'middle' ground between disposition and design, a transactional space in which learning dispositions are strengthened, shaped, weakened or ignored.

We thus describe transactional and progressive processes of *authoring and authorising*; *recognising opportunity* and *being permeable*; and *connected knowing and connecting the knowing*. By 'being permeable' we mean that the educational design is flexible enough to include openings and spaces of opportunity for the children to recognise. These processes are summarised in Table 9.1. They describe a transactional space between incoming dispositions and available design options: where the *disposition* processes of authoring, recognising opportunity, and connected knowing interact with the *design* processes of authorising, being permeable, and connecting the knowing.

Table 9.1. *Transactional and progressive processes in the middle space between incoming dispositions and available design options*

Dispositions in action		Educational design in practice
Authoring	←→	Authorising
Recognising opportunity	←→	Being permeable
Connected knowing	←→	Connecting the knowing

The following three sections outline some of the key features of these transactional and progressive processes.

AUTHORING AND AUTHORISING

When children were deemed to be authoring, we noted in the case study chapters that they were: initiating; enjoying; taking on identities as 'grown-ups', expert readers, writers, soccer-players, drivers and artists; deeply engaged in activities often with a high level of affect (excitement, emotion); inclined to communicate their opinions; focused and persevering, 'locking on' to learning; interested and enthusiastic; balancing desires and goals; taking responsibility and taking on the role of a teacher. Children often appeared to be considering 'possible selves', and the notion of identity, being positioned as an authority, was a powerful mediator here.

For many years Anne Smith has been a strong advocate for the inclusion of children's voices in domains that matter to the child, and the case studies in this book provide further justification for children as authors:

> Children have traditionally lacked voice and visibility, but slowly a recognition of children's roles as social actors who are active co-constructors of meaning and "experts" on childhood is emerging. (Smith, 2008, p. 15)

In our study, authoring was frequently mediated, as authorising and authoritative positioning, by teachers. The teachers in David's early childhood centre talked about giving the responsibility back to the children when they complained about their peers, and the teachers willingly acted as 'resource assistants' for David's projects. At school, he was given permission to adapt the schedule and the school tasks to follow his interests. Being 'in charge', or an 'in-charger' was a key theme for Joseph in chapter six: he took this language with him into school, and it accompanied his leadership role in a mathematical game where he took responsibility to question its fairness. Carol Dweck has described her own shift in view on authoring (learning) goals when she was a young researcher, researching how children coped with difficulty.

> Confronted with the hard puzzles, one ten-year-old boy pulled up his chair, rubbed his hands together, smacked his lips and cried out, "I love a challenge!" Another, sweating away on these puzzles, looked up with a pleased expression and said with authority, "You know, I was hoping this would be informative!"...... What did they know? They knew that human qualities, such as intellectual skills, could be cultivated through effort....I, on the other hand, thought that human qualities were carved in stone. You were smart or you weren't, and failure meant you weren't. It was that simple. If you could arrange successes and avoid failures (at all costs), you could stay smart. Struggles, mistakes, perseverance were just not part of the picture. (Dweck, 2006, pp. 3, 5)

Perhaps Sarah had approached school in the same way ('assuming that you were smart or you weren't'), and expecting teachers and peers to recognise her abilities, and the educational design to invite and reward them. And maybe this is a hazard of an educational system in which five-year-olds enter already established classrooms of new entrant or year one children who have already learned some of the basics. This system has many potential advantages, and we have seen some of them: it provokes four-year-olds who are left behind, given a supportive and familiar environment, to improvise relationships with new and diverse others when the five-year-olds go to school, and it enables older children in first year school classrooms to become the teachers of the very new entrants. But both of these advantages need to be facilitated by authorising teachers, and small classes (as for Jeff, David and Aralynn) help teachers to also invite and invoke relevant prior knowledge.

The children were not just individuals pleasing themselves, their teachers and their immediate family about achievement; for many of them the inclination to be a good learner, or at least a good pupil, over a longer time-scale came from a wide and imperative source. Four of the case study children written up here were from families where both parents were born outside New Zealand, and for whom English was an additional language: Jack, Ofeina, Samuel and Yasin. These families had emigrated to New Zealand in anticipation of a good education for their children, and some of them had sacrificed their own prospects to do so. Grandparents and wider family in the 'home country' were monitoring their achievements as well.

The following are some of the features, from our case studies, of opportunities for authoring in educational design.

Including the social

Writing about collaboration as one of many aspects of a disposition towards engaging with mathematics, Melissa Gresalfi argues that authoring, or exercising authority, helps students to recognise opportunity and make connections between ideas:

> Research on collaboration has documented that working with other children can create opportunities for students to engage more deeply with mathematical content than they might have done on their own. ... Specifically, groups in which students ask for help, challenge one another, and provide support create opportunities for all students to engage more deeply with content. ... In particular, these behaviors allow students to take on more responsibility for making meaning. When students are able to exercise authority for mathematical meaning-making, they are expected, obligated and entitled to explain. This stands in contrast to systems in which students rely on the teacher or the textbook as the authority. The act of explaining and justifying their ideas helps students to become attuned to the opportunities to make connections between ideas. (Gresalfi, 2009 pp.362-363)

Gresalfi suggests that exercising authority collaboratively helps students to organise their understanding around core concepts, and that this understanding is related to more effective transfer of mathematical concepts to other situations. We also suggest, from our data, that a similar process may apply for strengthening dispositional meaning-making, encouraging recontextualising and improvising across time and place and subject content.

Many of the children's episodes of complex play were co-authored and in social contexts. Communication usually took place in small groups (two to four children), and often there were separate areas, spaces and resources to allow children to pursue their joint interests. Early work by Kathy Sylva and colleagues (Sylva, Roy & Painter, 1980) emphasised the value of the dyad as a learning context which encouraged complex play and talk. Most children in early childhood centres had virtually uninterrupted time to initiate and develop complex pretend play themes and knowledgeable skills. Schooling, however, included only brief windows of opportunity to maintain reciprocal engagement, and limited opportunities for collaborative activities or time to establish expertise on complex tasks. In another research project in an early years classroom, the value of 'choosing time' in the early years of school is noted:

> Mark's portfolio tracks his increasingly complex interactions with a diverse peer support group ... When he builds train tracks with Max early in his first year of school the teacher comments "This is the first time I have seen Max play with another child. He usually plays by himself". She adds: "This demonstrates to me just how important 'choosing time' is to these young children beginning primary school". (Carr, Peters, Davis, et al., 2008, p. 61)

During the time when Buzz was observed at school, almost the only time he was able to engage freely in conversation with a peer in the classroom, was during a brief period of News Time. Ofeina experienced similar constraints in the classroom, and the playground provided the context for her social play. In the school classroom she constructed brief opportunities to offer support to other children. For Samuel the school pattern of short, adult-organised and structured tasks mostly linked to reading, writing and arithmetic, were a constraint on group activities, but he found a way (as David had, in chapter five) to maximise the 'choosing time', where he could play with others (and still be near an adult). Anne Edwards and Carmen D'Arcy (2004, p. 149) point out that pupils need teachers "who regard social processes and learners' positions as key features of knowledge sharing and production in classrooms." Neil Mercer writes about a 'dialogic trajectory', and says that:

> We need ways of describing how intersubjectivity (in the sociocultural sense of this term as used by Wertsch, 1984) is pursued, maintained, or lost in the course of classroom talk. (Mercer, 2008 p.38)

These constructions of the importance of social relationships *for learning* in school appeared to be constrained by a view of the curriculum as crowded. In this project the teachers commented on their busy schedules, and the ways in which they had to cover the curriculum.

Teacher: That's one of the things we keep talking about in the meetings. Too many curriculum areas to be covered but that's what they say we have to cover just during the year.
Researcher: Even in the first year of school?
Teacher: In the first year of school.

Discussions and making meaning together are central to acquiring knowledge. And relationships, encouraging an ethos of education where learners struggle, make mistakes and persevere, are at risk in a tightly scheduled curriculum at school:

Student and teacher are new social positions constituted by the classroom community of practice. In most schools, children and adults now relate in an impersonal way, distinct from the concrete particularity, the personal ties of family relationships....The child assumes different modes of subjectivity in the two different contexts. (Packer & Goicoechea, 2000, p. 10)

We ask, with Vivian Paley (in the introduction to chapter four), "Must it be so?"

Authoring opportunities and expectations

There were, nevertheless, many examples in the data of teachers deliberately introduced co-authoring opportunities. Group activities, led by a teacher, were helpful for assisting children to learn some of the protocols of group play. Samuel, after a shaky start, took his new abilities in collaborative play into play with trolleys and trailers. Trolleys were particularly useful for provoking collaborative play: unless the driver was on a slope they needed one person to push and one to drive. Samuel combined his interest in vehicles and his enthusiasm for social interaction when he drove a tractor and trailer around the playground, picking up and dropping off children along the way. The teacher had been actively engaged in an earlier collaborative episode with trolleys outside, facilitating successful 'togetherness': teaching the children to steer, and adding some obstacles for them to steer around. Ofeina's role as a helper was often associated with her skills in, for instance, doing jigsaws (in all phases) and screen printing (at the kindergarten).

Opportunities to create projects were more likely to be available at early childhood centres than schools, but there were a few examples of children being given time to author their own projects at school: David worked for some time with the stickle bricks and Jeff made a 'dice' from a construction set. Leona's primary teacher commented (in chapter one), regretfully, that: "We used to have 'developmental'" (a period of time, usually at the beginning of the day, when children could pursue their own projects). She added that she thought that in the old style of teaching, 'developmental' should precede the work, and free play should not be used as a reward.

Teacher expectations also influenced the opportunities for authoring (Timperley, 2003). It was a major shift in view when Lisa's early childhood teachers reframed her personality from 'being shy' to 'being selective'. When they saw her as 'shy', they perceived their role as being to encourage her to talk to others. One of the teachers said: "I'm not always successful in getting her to talk". By phase two they had recognised that she could indeed competently talk to others, because she had taken on a role as 'a mat-time teacher'. "I was surprised because of the fact that she talks not a lot, that she could do all that". The teachers began to construct her as reflective and selective, positioning her as smart and capable. They stopped trying to persuade her to talk and began to see their role as mutual participants in dialogue, initiated by Lisa.

In phase one Lisa attended two early childhood centres, and in the other centre the teacher spoke of her efforts to build a relationship with Lisa, who would not communicate with anyone during the first few months: "I did not push myself onto her, but I actually tried to make a sort of friendship with her. I think to actually build up her courage so that she had one special person....". David and Jeff both saw early childhood teachers as assistants, not authority figures. Children invited (and in Jeff's case demanded) adults to provide help with their projects while retaining their authorship: assisting with using a screw driver, finding cricket equipment, putting created things in a safe place, finding blankets, making a book. The availability of the teacher to assist with these projects was an important component of enabling the children to overcome obstacles in achieving their goals. Early childhood teachers were on the whole very available to the children for help and advice, even when Jeff made such heavy demands that they became resistant to being at his beck and call. He eventually moved towards being able to complete tasks independently without having to continually ask for adult help.

Including the affective; opportunities for focus and flow

Both Mihaly Csikszentmihalyi and Jay Lemke have researched the value of the affective dimension in episodes of joint attention. When this is optimal, Csikszentmihalyi calls it 'flow' and alleges that the experience of flow acts as a magnet for learning – that is, for developing new levels of challenge and skill (1997, p. 33). Flow tends to occur when a person's skills are fully involved in overcoming a challenge that is just about manageable. Optimal experiences usually involve a fine balance between one's ability to act, and the available opportunities for action, and during these optimally affective contexts, learners are less likely to be distracted. Csikszentmihalyi says that flow is generally reported when a person is doing his or her favourite activity; he mentions gardening, listening to music, cooking, talking to friends. All of these contexts were observed in our case studies. Joseph's hurtling down a hill on a trolley was an example of affective engagement, as he tested the boundaries of dangerous and safe. It included embodied and tacit learning, as did, for instance, Ofeina's skipping. But continuity for these learning opportunities often had to wait for after-school football or cultural dance events. Aralynn's case study in chapter eight provided an example of a number of episodes of affective engagement over time: her caring interactions with her grandparents, her gardening with her mother, her episodes of imaginative play with Braden and others, had provided patterns that may have prepared her to persevere in the episode of story-writing at school that challenged her and pushed her skills to the 'just manageable'. She was a child who followed the rules, but focused and affective episodes of caring for and about others in family interactions, and pretend play with younger children at the early childhood centre, may have provided the pattern that made her willing to give Hamish help with a worksheet *against the rule* and specifically proscribed by the teacher.

RECOGNISING OPPORTUNITY AND BEING PERMEABLE

When children were deemed to be recognising and attuned to opportunity, we noted that they were: choosing, interpreting, 'reading' the classroom, constructing opportunity, responding to the viewpoints of others, being attuned to protocol and implicit rules, seizing a moment as an opportunity, working on a localised assumption (for instance that the teachers are assistants that value the children's enterprises), orchestrating people and resources for their particular or collective purposes; playing the game, weighing up the opportunity, developing local criteria (for instance about what was safe, dangerous, or 'naughty', here), and adjusting storylines to accommodate diverse others. They were improvising as the people, plot-lines, languages, resources, and spaces changed.

Linking children's graphic patterns to conceptual patterns, Goodnow writes about how change is "often a matter of change in the number, the location, and the firmness of boundaries." She introduces this idea by saying:

> The best example of such an approach is the work of Kurt Lewin, who, back in 1935, proposed that we think of ideas and 'life-spaces' as regions, varying in size and proximity to one another as well as in terms of the permeability or rigidity of a boundary. Where boundaries are not permeable, ideas or parts of ideas or parts of one's life simply exist side by side, touching but forming separate compartments. (Goodnow, 1977, p. 58)

In the early childhood centres the curriculum boundaries were permeable: recognisable spaces, and time, were available for initiating ideas and topics, and challenging or questioning what others say. And in some of the school classrooms the schedule was permeable too – providing openings for this. Leona could keep the topic of family in her stories, and Aralynn's teacher went to great lengths to help her to write a story that made sense without the teacher taking over the authorship. In other classrooms – but not all – the storywriting task was mostly about full stops, writing on the lines, accurate letter-writing and finger spaces between the words. This inspired Sarah to comment, in the context of a discussion about her writing, that: "It's just the unfairest thing that some of the letters start at the bottom and some at the top". Early childhood centres also included times in which the teachers maintained the authority (often these were at 'mat times') so the early childhood centres in this study provided children with experiences across a range of positioning. One of the advantages – and provocations – of children having sustained experience in a number of different places is the opportunity for reflecting on this diversity and recognising that positions are not inevitable. As Paul Harris has suggested, citing research on children's differentiated responses to possible transgressions:

> The hurly-burly of the preschool allows the child to cast off some of this excess [moral] baggage, by teaching him or her that although adults may take certain conventional violations quite seriously, their classmates often do not care a fig. (Harris, 1989, p. 46)

Children also learn, from comparing what happens in different places, that responses to behaviour are contingent and variable, paving the way for attunement to new contexts, the recognition of opportunity and permeability.

Spaces for the conditional and the uncertain

One of the features of some of the talk by teachers at two of the early childhood centres, Lauren's childcare centre and Yasin's kindergarten, was the element of uncertainty that appeared to be acceptable in the teachers' contributions. It provided openings for the children to share some of the authoring. Here is an example.

Teacher: That's Jarvis. Maybe he's a bit sleepy. He's having a sleep with us today.
Lauren: Why?
Teacher: Because he's staying here longer so he's having a sleep.
Lauren: Why is he going to be staying here longer?
Teacher: I'm not too sure but his mum asked if we could have him till 3 o'clock so maybe she's got some more jobs to do. She needs us to look after him a bit longer.
Lauren: When his mum going to pick him up?
Teacher: 3 o'clock.
Lauren: When is 3 o'clock? ....

In turns 1 and 5, the teacher uses the conditional qualifier 'maybe', and in turn 5 she replies: "I'm not too sure". Conversations between the teachers and Yasin, in chapter eight, similarly provided space for Yasin's contributions about his family. The following is a short excerpt as he and the teacher try to remember the details of an event together. Yasin reminds the teacher that the family had given the kindergarten a glue gun when his brother was attending.

Yasin: Yeah. My mother – we had a glue gun and we gave the glue gun to this kindy.
Teacher (sounds surprised): You did, too. That was a long time ago. Did your Mummy tell you that?
Yasin: Yeah.
Teacher: That you brought a glue gun for kindergarten. I think you might have been ... how old were you when you did that, um..?
Yasin: Three and a half.

It is a reminder of Ellen Langer's work on mindfulness, where she comments that

A good deal of my research has explored the brighter side of the picture: the encouragement of creativity by teaching facts in a conditional manner. In most educational settings, the "facts" of the world are presented as unconditional truths, when they might better be seen as probability statements that are true in some contexts but not in others. What happens when this uncertainty is allowed in? Does the uncertain information become more available to us later, when the context has changed? (Langer, 1989, pp. 119–120)

In a 1976 study, Carol Feldman and James Wertsch researched teacher talk in classrooms and found that teachers were much less likely to use conditional qualifiers (or 'epistemic elliptic forms') with children than when they were talking amongst themselves. The authors point out that these qualifiers ('maybe', 'I'm not too sure') introduce the speaker's beliefs into the discourse, and they suggest that a likely reason for the infrequent occurrence is because teachers may feel that they need to preserve a social distance, keeping their personal views out of the classroom. Their research suggests that the teachers they worked with were likely to reduce the affective content of their conversations with children, and they concluded that this seems to raise a very basic question of world view: if teachers see their job as being more than imparting information as objective facts, then 'students would learn to navigate their way through a world of variable commitment and variable certainty' (p. 256). 'Maybe' and 'I'm not too sure' provokes imagination and opens the door to other sources of authority.

Dramatic play as an opportunity for recognising, re-cognising and improvisation

As Paley had taught us, self-script constructions were most clearly observed in the children's dramatic play.

> Children early in their lives exhibit the ability and the desire to enter into worlds that they imagine, to treat objects around them as (refigured) objects from those worlds, and to put aside, at least temporarily, feelings, interests, and concerns that are irrelevant to the play world. The play worlds that children create are akin to the more complex culturally constructed or figured worlds that they enter into as they grow older. (Holland et al., 1998, p. 280)

Almost all of the case study children were disposed to participate in dramatic play for at least some of their time at the early childhood centre. Many of the children's dramatic play discussions were about heroes and heroines in media texts (Spiderman, Princess Aurora and Harry Potter) or people of authority in real life (doctors, mothers and builders), and the children had to be alert to the shifting storylines and agendas. These episodes of dramatic play honed their skills and identities as negotiators, and enabled then to 're-cognise' their authority: Leona could shift from being fragile and helpless under Olivia's magic wand to having authority as a veterinarian with Olivia as her helper, dispensing the medicine. Aralynn was absorbed in the negotiations about roles and scripts in her dramatic play with Braden and Tina, and Braden was at pains to argue the case for Spiderman – he seemed to be explaining that there were two personae for Spiderman, the fighter and the saviour, and his intention was to play the latter (which he knew was more acceptable to Aralynn). In Leona and Lisa's classrooms, children played school at school (reminiscent of Vygotsky's example of two sisters playing two sisters: Vygotsky, 1978 p. 94).

Children in this study, in early childhood centres with readily accessible bits and pieces for use in their play (Henry's treasure maps for instance), were learning that objects can take on many different roles and purposes. This is a key notion in Ellen Langer's (1989, 1997) argument that mindfulness and creative thinking are developed when people are invited to consider imaginative uses of everyday objects, are not therefore 'trapped by categories' (1989, p. 11) or always told the 'right' answers or the only way of doing things. Olivia and Leona together adapted a typewriter as a dispenser of medicine, adding a straw and a paper cup. They are learning that improvisation is what good learners do. Dorothy Holland and her colleagues have this to say:

> Under the tutelage of Bourdieu and others, anthropological attention has turned from the analysis of culture as an objectified and abstract system to ... their constant improvisation within ever-changing social and material conditions. ... Improvisations are the sort of impromptu actions that occur when our past, brought to the present as habitus, meets with a particular combination of circumstances and conditions for which we have no set response. (Holland et al., 1998, pp. 17–18)

Improvisation is, by definition, a key feature of attunement and the recontextualisation of disposition. One of the teachers in the study was asked about the use of worksheets. She replied:

> I don't use commercial worksheets. I do occasionally make them up myself. Worksheets usually just ask them to fill in gaps and they're not usually learning anything. I think you have to think about, to evaluate, 'what's the point?' And sometimes it's best for them to do their own work and take it home and talk to their families about it. (Teacher interview, phase three)

Documentation: a public recognition and a site for revisiting and re-cognition

The work of Joanne Lobato (2003, 2006) on learning transfer has included the useful notions of an 'actor-oriented' approach, and 'focusing phenomena'. An 'actor-oriented' approach seeks to understand the aspects of situations that learners find salient, using ethnographic methods. 'Focusing phenomena' are those "features of classroom environments that regularly direct students' attention" to properties and patterns (Lobato, 2006 p.442). Documentation, and assessment generally, could be described as a powerful focusing phenomenon. Writing about school classrooms and mathematical lessons Lobato suggests that:

> What is critical for the generalization of learning is not the number of contextual situations explored but the particular mathematical regularities and properties to which students' attention is drawn and that students notice. (Lobato, 2006 p.444)

Our work suggests the word 'mathematical' could be also replaced by 'dispositional'. Documentation was not the only way in which children were drawn to notice and recognise a learning disposition – teachers' conversations, peer interactions in dramatic play, and families as reviewers and interpreters were important sources of paying attention as well – but documentation was a process that was important in this study, and it worked differently in different places. Permeability is provided by opportunities to revisit the learning over time, to construct 'cohesive, cumulative educational journeys' in which activities and goals can be seen to form part of 'a purposeful educational journey' (Mercer, 2008 p.34).. Making the learning public may provoke the impetus for re-cognition as a transactional and progressive process. We saw in the introduction to chapter two that Sfard (2008) uses the word 'reification' to mean turning something into a noun, a thing that can be acquired. Wenger (1998) uses the concept of 'reification' to refer to the process of giving form to our experience by realising it, turning it into a concrete material object, as in documentation. "In so doing we create points of focus around which the negotiation of meaning becomes organised" (Wenger, 1998, p. 58). He says that participation and reification are two complementary aspects of design that create two kinds of affordances for negotiating meaning:

> One can make sure that some artefacts are in place – tools, plans, procedures, schedules, curriculums – so that the future will have to be organised around them.

> One can also make sure that the right people are in the right place in the right kind of relation to make something happen. (Wenger, 1998, pp. 231–232)

The early childhood teachers in this study had been working with a national early childhood curriculum in which the outcomes for children were summarised as *learning dispositions* and *working theories* (Ministry of Education, 1996 p.44). The strands of outcome in that curriculum are: belonging, well-being, exploration, communication and contribution, and specific outcomes in the document were described as 'indicative' rather than prescribed. The school teachers were working from a curriculum which was based on seven learning areas, and a number of achievement objectives that were required to be achieved at each two-year 'level'. Many of the school teachers in these case studies were using commercial worksheets as summative assessment tools; many of the early childhood teachers were using 'Learning Stories' as formative assessment tools. Learning Stories were narrative accounts of an episode of learning, usually accompanied by photographs; they include an analysis of the learning, often in dispositional terms, and a suggestion of the possible pathways forward (Carr, 2001b; Carr et al., 2004, 2007, 2009). They are housed in portfolios which are accessible to families and frequently taken home. Here is an excerpt from a Learning Story about Lauren, in a netball-playing event. It includes commentary on her 'subject-based' and 'dispositional' competence. It was a group story, personalised for each of the participating children.

> Lauren was very accurate with her goal shooting skills, she enjoyed being involved in the game and her height made it easier for her to reach up and catch those high passes from her team mates then aim for the hoop and shout with joy with each goal that went through. Lauren liked to know the reasons behind calls that were made by the referee and would question until she was satisfied, she would then look to make sure everyone was following those rules and took responsibility to advise players if they weren't. Lauren your

desire to learn and question is a great skill. You are able to convey your thoughts (and) listen and respond until you are satisfied with the information you receive. These are great skills to have Lauren.

This account is addressed to Lauren, and although during our observations this story was not re-visited with Lauren, there were a number of occasions when teachers sat down with the children and re-read stories in the folder – including comments in the stories about the learning dispositions and the possibilities for the learning journey ahead. And the portfolios frequently went home, to be read by families. We have included excerpts from Learning Stories as additional data for Samuel, Joseph and Yasin.

Families as reviewers and interpreters

Learning stories and portfolios that travel between the educational setting and the family invite families to assist children to re-cognise and re-interpret their experiences. Families accompany the children from place to place and over time, acting as reviewers, interpreters and mediators. They provided support for the children when belonging or participation was not going according to the children's expectation, and they acted as a mediating voice when children were trying to make sense of a new environment. In chapter six, Joseph's mother commented:

He noticed that he couldn't read in the same way [as his sister]....But he made one of those quantum leaps, probably mid-year, at six, and now he can read.... He's so excited and proud, because it really was frustrating for him. There was no pressure from us, but he was doing a comparison.

Henry's mother said:

Henry does like to challenge himself, to push himself further, he will really persist now until he gets it right – he used to get frustrated and upset and give up if things didn't work out straight away ... but lately he is being a lot more patient, even if it doesn't go right straight away – he will really stick at things now and for a long time.

Ofeina's mother talked about her ambitions for her children:

I told them, you go to University, 'cos I didn't, I know I should have but I didn't. I worked part-time when I was at school; when I was (in the) sixth form I had to get a part-time job to help out ..... I keep saying to my son "even if they say you can't, you have to do your best".

She spoke several times about the possibility of returning to Tonga:

The thing is that there is no TV [in Tonga] all the time and, you know, there are not many social activities for children. ... Over there you come from school where dinner has to be done, otherwise you just sit and do your homework. ... When I came here we thought, wow, we expected people in

New Zealand to be very bright and (better than us) but it was not that way. It was a shock 'cos they have the facilities like textbooks and computers.

Finding spaces for critique

It was in these *recognising opportunities and being permeable* processes that we recognised moments of critique as incoming dispositions bumped up against – interrupting and potentially transforming – the design. Even in unfavourable circumstances, some of the children found opportunities to critique the system or the practice, without jeopardising their identities as 'good pupils'. There was a sense in which the children '*couldn't not*', and they recognised or constructed safe opportunities. Aralynn 'couldn't not' help others who were struggling, although the classroom instruction was not to do this: her disposition to help others in the group was a very powerful mediator, and she found a way to help, by singing the answers. Lauren 'couldn't not' find a space to mention the possibility of a white-tailed spider to the text during a decoding of print lesson. Henry 'couldn't not' help Hamish in an individual assessment task, although prohibited. These children re-cognised the situations in which they found themselves. Henry had improvised with materials (the treasure map) and relationships (in phase two) at his early childhood centre. In an episode at school he had just learned to write the number ten, and was starting a worksheet where he was required to colour in the boxes that contained ten dots. He begins by writing the number ten several times across the worksheet and he suggests to another child that she, too, could improvise on the required task.

Girl next to Henry: What's that? You're not supposed to do that. Just colour them in.
Henry: I can. I do. I'm writing the number 10. You can do this if you want 'cos it's the number 10.

Children's improvisations in dramatic play often included an element of critique, as they reminded each other of rules and story-lines. We suggested in chapter six that the situations at school in which Joseph was defending fairness and entitlement were not specific situations that he had experienced at the kindergarten (or at home) and 'it seems that he may have a more general, big picture, view of fairness and entitlement and he can recognise what it looks like in a different context'. Perhaps this was an example of disposition-based 'survey knowledge of the environment' (Greeno, 2006, p. 543), in this case of the 'fairness environment', when Joseph reminded the other children in his literacy group that a 'fair' race needed a level starting point: "what if I was 10 and you were five?" in chapter one.

Critique often appeared to be sited in places where all three of the transactional processes were at work. For Joseph, for instance, the clue for us that asking questions had become a facet of disposition was that he was willing to question the format of conversation at school News Time, to question an accepted norm; and he was willing to question the justice of a competitive game that no-one could be said to legitimately win, although the relief teacher had said that 'it doesn't matter'. His inclination increased his sensitivity to occasion, sharpening his re-cognition and recognition of context. Furthermore, his knowledge of mechanical matters became 'connected knowing' when he questioned the teacher's binary of soft and mechanical toys ("you could put a battery into a soft toy"): his subject-based knowing had increased his capacity for authoring and fine-tuned his recognition of opportunity. And his disposition-based knowing about entitlement and fairness, built up from many episodes of interaction, some of which we observed, did so too. This disposition-based knowing was valued at home; it contributed to his sensitivity to context, and to his inclination to take responsibility to resist the status quo.

This study confirms that, when learning dispositions were fragile, the opportunity or affordance network needed to be more demanding: from affording (in the sense of providing a favourable physical or material environment) to inviting, actively engaging, and provoking. When learning dispositions were robust, we traced the continuity of a disposition-in-action even when the educational practice hindered or prohibited it. Gresalfi describes this demand as opportunites that differ in 'force'. She commented that:

> The interaction between the force of an opportunity and whether a student took up that opportunity was an important indicator of the nature of a student's disposition for learning. Specifically, the analysis attended to whether, over time, less forceful opportunities to learn and participate were required for a student to participate in a particular way. For example, students who took up weak opportunities, or who took up such opportunities with frequency, appeared to be constructing a more stable disposition for working with others than students who took up only very forceful opportunities. (Gresalfi, 2009 p.343)

In our data, more forceful opportunities – or a more demanding affordance network – were necessary at early points in a learning disposition journey.

CONNECTED KNOWING AND CONNECTING THE KNOWING

When children were deemed to be knowing in ways that connected across time and place, we noted in the case study chapters that: they were calling on informed interest and competence, referring to funds of knowledge from home, library, church, park and sports field. They were making connections with prior events, remembering, using a range of 'languages'. They were calling on subject-based knowing (often cross-disciplinary and multi-modal), as well as disposition-based knowing (for instance knowing ways to invite others to join in). They were using past experiences, developing general criteria and working theories, and having a repertoire of strategies for keeping the peace and sustaining the group. The knowing was connected across time and place in three ways (in addition to across the phases, and from early childhood to school):
- with resources and tasks that connected with the world beyond the early childhood centre or school classroom,

- as multidisciplinary, multimodal and multisensory knowing, and
- with funds of knowledge from home and culture

Resources and tasks that connect with the world beyond the educational setting

Chapter five emphasised the initiating and orchestrating of projects as a key facet of resilience, and most of those child-initiated projects made connections to communities beyond the here and now. During phases one and two, connections were made with the world beyond the educational setting in a number of ways. One way was via the tasks on offer. A number of tasks in the early childhood centres were mimicking the tasks at home. We did not observe the children cooking, although the Learning Stories in the children's portfolios told of episodes in which the children had been involved in cooking at the early childhood centre. It was recorded for instance that Joseph brought his peach muffin recipe (and his mother) to cook muffins at the centre. Many of the children were involved in cooking at home (Joseph, for instance, had made the muffins on one occasion when the researchers visited the home, and David had made biscuits at home with his father). When David 'cooked' at the centre, he improvised in the sandpit, using a range of resources that served the purpose of pretend play. Similarly, when he made 'concrete' in the sand pit, he drew on experience where he had participated in the concreting of a wall at home. And, over a number of visits from the early childhood centre he had also carefully observed concreting at a construction site down the road. There were also some connecting tasks across phases two and three: Aralynn was enthusiastic about growing broad beans in the classroom and this task made connections back in time and place when she gardened with her mother. Leona embraced the writing tasks at school with alacrity – assisting other children – she had been writing at home and at the early childhood centre. We accompanied Ofeina on her school visit when she was still at the early childhood centre and watched while she looked around the classroom, focused on some paintings and was heard to say, to herself, "I can do that".

The children were positioned and positioned themselves with self-scripts and islands of expertise (Crowley & Jacobs, 2002, p. 333) that had caché in the valued world outside the centre of the classroom. In chapter seven David positioned himself as an expert cook, concrete-maker, and cricketer, and the teacher at school was positioning him as 'a writer', assuming that the actual expertise would follow from the naming of a 'clever writer' self. In the early childhood centres the adults frequently talked to the children about home or about events where they knew children had knowledge and skill. The teacher reminded Yasin about his art classes, and suggested that he might teach the children how to construct with clay – with mixed success, since his view of the creative process with clay was somewhat prescriptive and the children had learned to improvise. Once the children started school, however, explicit reference back to what might have been learned during the early childhood centre experience was never heard, and any attempts by the researchers to talk about it with the children were usually firmly resisted. The children had moved on. Although we felt anguish that a crowded school curriculum was frequently squeezing out opportunities for the shaping and strengthening of learning dispositions, they did not seem to be unhappy about this. They were 'doing school' and gaining the knowledge and skills that they and most of their families recognised as marks of being a school pupil – reading, writing and using numbers – and on the whole they appeared to feel grown-up and confident. Going to school, and acquiring the knowledge that is valued there, is a rite of passage of great cultural significance; we wondered about the loss of opportunities for reciprocity, resilience and imagination.

Valuing the multilingual, the multidisciplinary, the multimodal and the multisensory

Gunther Kress has something to say about the valued knowing that will greet these fourteen case study children during their life-times.

> One might say the following with some confidence. Language-as-speech will remain the major mode of communication; language as writing will increasingly be displaced by image in many domains of public communication, though writing will remain the preferred mode of the political and cultural elites. The combined effects on writing of the dominance of the mode of image and of the medium of the screen will produce deep changes in the forms and functions of writing. This in turn will have profound effects on human, cognitive / affective, cultural and bodily engagement with the world, and on the forms and shapes of knowledge. *The world told* is a different world to *the world shown*. (Kress, 2003, p. 1, emphasis in then original).

He argues for multi-modal genres of communication, genres that we found to be typical of early childhood settings. His particular interest is in the impact of digital technology which we did not see in this study, except in the Learning Stories. However, we know from our work in other early childhood settings that four-year-olds can take digital photographs, download them, add text and voice files, prepare power point presentations, make digital movies, dictate e-mails, and search the internet (Carr et al., 2009). A number of the children in this study were multilingual, and in the early childhood centres, the knowing was frequently multidisciplinary, multimodal and multisensory. We began our study in early childhood centres where these learner scripts were not usually inscribed in the subject domains of science, or mathematics, or literacy or art. Our analytical tools were immediately confronted with the multi-media and multi-disciplinary worlds of Princess Aurora, Harry Potter, gardening, making concrete, group skipping games, and being cats. In chapter four, Ofeina had translated into screen printing some of the themes of interest to her, honing her social skills along the way. In chapter eight, Yasin's paintings included imaginative representations of a possible world in which he can hide in the bushes and eat popcorn. His family and his art work provided a backdrop for conversations with a teacher who greatly valued art as an activity that is woven into the curriculum. Buzz used a range of media – drawing, collages, riding the pedal car, making vehicles with dough, and writing stories – to elaborate and extend his interest in vehicles and driving, which probably originated from his experience of diverse vehicles on his grandparents' farm.

Buzz also shared an interest in the characters and the plotlines in the Harry Potter movies with other children, and the Harry Potter theme occupied them for many days. Having an additional common language, an understanding of who does what, who is a 'goodie' and who is a 'baddie', can assist with dialogue and storyline, as we saw in Jack's case study. Jack could engage with the other children, in spite of their different home languages and their different competencies in English, because they had watched the same television programmes at home.

When they began their school careers, for a number of the children in this study, imaginative story-telling journeys were interrupted by the school requirement that they write the text themselves. In some of the first year classrooms, however, like Aralynn's in chapter eight, and David's in chapter five, teachers wrote up dictated stories. In this way, imaginative stories, honed during pretend play with others in early childhood centres, were kept alive. Henry and Sarah's case studies illustrate the tentative journey towards the 'lifelong mental capacity to consider alternatives to reality' that Paul Harris writes about (Harris, 2000, p. 28), and Henry could continue this capacity at school in his paintings. Body language as gesture, facial expression, and stance is a powerful language in the early years, and Judith Hanna (2008) has reminded us that the language we use determines the way we think: she advocates for the powerful language of dance, and many of her arguments for the multisensory apply to the dramatic improvisations and scripts in these case studies.

Connecting with funds of knowledge from home

We commented in chapter two that recognising the value of "funds of knowledge" from home (González et al., 2005) opens up new possibilities for learning and effective classroom teaching. This was a strong feature of school experience for only one child, Aralynn. Her story, and the ways in which she could connect her 'knowing' from home to school, is told in chapter eight. The curriculum in her first year classroom included three different kinds of news time – weekend, treasures, and nature – and Aralynn was an enthusiastic contributor to all three. The class was also running a bean-growing theme, and this called on her experience and love of gardening at home. In Leona and Buzz's classrooms the teachers talked to the children about their own families, and while we did not hear the children talking about theirs, Leona and Buzz both wrote stories about their families in their story-writing books. At the early childhood centre Yasin talked about his family with teachers who were interested and knowledgeable enough to prompt him; he brought his knowledge about fabrics from home to the technology discussion on materials at school, although his family was not mentioned there. Children entered school with views about justice, confidence in standing up in front of a group at Sunday School, experiences of kindness with a grandparent, sibling relationships as a model of reciprocity, attitudes towards diversity, and much more. Samuel brought his interest in words and books, and this found a place at the early childhood centre and at school. Aralynn's father should have the last word here about the significance of funds of knowledge from home. He commented:

> I talk to her sometimes when it's just her and me, and the [Island] life where people don't have money and all they eat – is you know they have to work for what they get. And she asks 'why?' and 'how?' and I'm sure she still doesn't really understand when I explain things, but those are some of the things as she grows up she'll become more aware of and she'll go: oh yeah, that's why dad told me these things.

SOME IMPLICATIONS FOR EDUCATION

It is our view that children's learning dispositions may be threatened by the onslaught of any school curriculum that is packed with compulsory tasks, tight scheduling and summative assessments – and does not provide even moderately forceful opportunities for learning dispositions in practice or in documentation. Although many of the children in this study were constructing opportunities, children had few entrypoints to continue to explore and strengthen the self-scripts about being collaborative, resilient and imaginative learners in the long term. Although the children found or generated some spaces for these scripts, they were reluctant to question the features of a beloved milestone for the self: being a school pupil. On the whole they embraced its discipline and inflexibility with a mixture of resignation and enthusiasm. These case studies have taught us some working theories about educational design that can usefully contribute to an understanding of the features of a transactional space in which learning dispositions are shaped and strengthened. We argue that if these learning dispositions are to become robust, curriculum and pedagogy in practice - with learning dispositions in mind - need to be more deliberate in early education: in early childhood centres and primary schools. Material affordances may need to be followed by invitations, active engagements, and provocations. Consistent with our view of strengthening the transactional space between dispositions-in-action and design-in-practice, Gunther Kress argues that 21st century children, too, should be involved in the design.

> This (curriculum for participation in a fully globalised economy) will be a curriculum which focuses above all on 'dispositions', a return to quite traditional notions of education – not training – on something akin to the German notion of *Bildung*, but refocuses clearly on the real features of the new globalising world and its demands.... giving the students a full awareness of what might be possible.... Such an education would provide them with the means both for setting their goals and for achieving them in the contexts of their lives. This is the ability for which I use the term 'design'. (Kress, 2003, p. 120)

One of the key features of engagement in these case studies was the affective quality of the episodes of deep engagement. These episodes were sited in relationships, and where the relationship included an adult, the adult often knew enough about the child to provide cues that deepened the discussion and made connections elsewhere. There was often a balance between ability and challenge, and there was usually plenty of time. It was interesting that some of the most deeply engaging episodes in school classrooms involved small class sizes. In Aralynn's class there was a discussion about writing a meaningful story in one of the smallest classes that we met: a class of sixteen children. In spite of other constraints – a very small classroom space, a relief teacher who did not know the children when she took over the class, and the same curriculum demands as in all the other classrooms we visited – the teacher provided an example of an exchange in which Aralynn was challenged to the edge of her ability, while still holding some sense of authorship in the task. In Jeff's classroom, an episode of small group mathematics problem-solving involving the teacher and six children, showed how the teacher encouraged the children to find and articulate different ways of solving problems. The researcher commented on how excited children had been afterwards, and how they had talked about what they had been learning. Such an approach where the teacher could achieve intersubjectivity with the children, would have been more difficult with a larger group. When Lisa moved between two early childhood centres, she was much more talkative and engaged in the centre with more favourable ratios and group sizes, where the teacher could engage in extended conversation and play with the children. In her other centre, the teachers acknowledged that they did not have the opportunity to talk to individual children for very long because of group size.

Research has indicated that small class sizes make a difference for children in the early years (Siraj-Blatchford et al., 2003; Wiliam, 2008), and it may be that it is because a small class invites the kind of dialogue between children and teacher that Aralynn, Lisa and Jeff experienced. In a synthesis of meta-analyses relating to achievement in school John Hattie found small effect sizes from reducing class size, but he adds that "One reason for these small effect sizes relates to teachers of small classes adopting the same teaching methods as they were using in larger classes, and not changing their teaching strategies to optimise the opportunities in small classes" (Hattie, 2009 pp.85-88). When class sizes are small, teachers can more easily add an affective or personal quality to the relationship and therefore the engagement. These case studies emphasise the value of strategies for dialoguing with children and for making connections with incoming dispositions and funds of knowledge – in early childhood as well as in school. Iram Siraj-Blatchford and Laura Manni in the Researching Effective Pedagogy in the Early Years (REPEY) study analysed 1167 adult questions identified in a random sample of four half-day observations in pre-school centres that had been identified by an earlier study as 'effective'. They found that 95.5% of questions asked by early childhood staff in these settings were closed questions that required a recall of fact, experience or expected behaviour, decision between a limited selection of choices or no response at all. Research in school contexts has frequently focused on dialogue as a contribution to understanding of content knowledge, but the principles are the same for the dispositions discussed in this book (Mercer, 2008; Mercer & Littleton, 2007; Wells, 2002). We have argued here that learning dispositions can become connected from one place to another if teachers are aware of the possibilities.

There is no denying that in a research context the audio recording can diminish the quality of teacher talk by reducing the teachers' spontaneity and tolerance of pauses, but it seems that teacher education and professional development have a role to play here. The role for teachers of co-authoring in the development of self-scripts for learning is supported by these case studies and other research that we have cited.

In our view, all three transactional and progressive processes are braided together, but the features of recognising opportunity, and its associated possibilities for re-cognition, were the most powerful. A number of curriculum tasks in early childhood and school are inevitably authored and directed by teachers. However, in a number of early childhood centres and classrooms that we are familiar with, beyond these case studies, teachers are facilitating projects and interests that have been initiated by individuals or small groups. These projects can mimic some of the improvisational quality of the dramatic play episodes that we observed in early childhood centres, a quality that may have provided the pattern for David to feel confident to, in a tentative way, 're-cognise' the teacher's literacy tasks at school. He was used to marshalling and orchestrating the resources he needed in order to complete his tasks: the teachers, mates, water, sand, flour and various items of equipment.

Recognition and re-cognition of learning dispositions can be both intuitive and public. We suggest that the first of these, the intuitive, develops through immersion in a culture where authority is contingent and variable, but everyone is authentically privileged at times. In our view, sitting in the Star for a Day chair does not qualify. The early years are an important time for practising and recognising agency. Holland and her colleagues provide a view about the children's intuitive recognition of the behavioural markers of privilege.

> (Bourdieu) argues that many styles of acting and matters of taste that serve as indices of high social position are more easily learned in childhood. Those who learn activities in childhood perform them in a more natural, less self-conscious style, itself prestigious. Those who learn later usually retain an awkwardness, a more "mechanical" than "organic" sense of the activity. (Holland et al. 1998, p. 136)

However, the authoring of self-scripts can be made public in various ways. We noted in chapter one that in New Zealand at the time of these observations learning dispositions were a key outcome in the early childhood curriculum, and had been for six years. At the time of writing this book, signalled in chapter one, their equivalent, 'key competencies' had been incorporated as mandatory in a revised national *school* curriculum. By now, both the national early childhood and the school curriculum documents have mandated outcomes that combine inclination, sensitivity and ability (Ministry of Education, 1996 p. 44 and Ministry of Education, 2007 p. 12). The school document states: "As they develop the competencies, successful learners are also motivated to use them, recognising when and how to do so and why". Both documents site these outcomes in 'interactions with people places ideas and things' (the school document, p. 12) or 'responsive and reciprocal relationships with people, places, and things' (the early childhood document, p. 43). A diagram in the school curriculum (p. 42) aligns the early childhood strands with the key competencies for school (relating to others, participating and contributing, thinking, using language symbols and texts, and managing self). In the early childhood sector a key resource, *Kei tua o te pae* (Carr, et al., 2004, 2007, 2009) has been issued by the Ministry of Education to early childhood centres and schools, combining theoretical ideas, research literature and exemplars on assessment for learning that aligns assessment with the curriculum. That resource provides arguments for, and examples of, narrative assessments that include family as interpreters and children as authors. These initiatives support the following assertion by Lemke.

> Whatever we offer in the classroom [or early childhood centre] becomes an opportunity to pursue this long-term agenda of identity building; our primary affective engagement is with this agenda, with becoming who we want to be, not with learning this or that bit of curriculum.... (Lemke, 2000, p. 286)

In this study the families mediated this process. They assisted children to interpret and make meaning of new contexts. Typically, families have more informal opportunities to chat to teachers in early childhood, but when more formal artefacts like portfolios are in place they can contribute powerfully to multifaceted learner selves – and take funds of knowledge from the early childhood centre into the home (and to families who live elsewhere). This may be a particular issue where families have not themselves experienced agency, especially, in our case studies, for those families who have migrated to a new country, a new culture, and a new social environment. Those sites in which families do have social and cultural capital are often not represented in the design of educational institutions in their new country, as Liz Brooker has eloquently argued (Brooker, 2002). They may remain represented in the families of the 'home' country, in the church community or at the sports club, with no bridge to the early childhood centre or the school. Families can be assisted to cross these bridges, but teachers will have to take on more of a role in the process if equitable opportunities to learn are to be more than rhetoric. It is too chancy to rely totally on the intuitive.

Learning dispositions and what might be called 'subject-based content' were closely connected. It was apparent in our data that children who had acquired expertise in something were able, in those contexts that invited and invoked this expertise, to use it to call up resilience (Leona and Jeff) reciprocity (Jack and Ofeina) and imagination (Aralynn). Leona could 'turn the tables' of positioning by bossy peers when she displayed sophisticated and admired knowledge about veterinarian practice. Jeff's excitement about numbers helped him to engage with the challenge of new number problems at school. Jack's knowledge of media scripts enabled him to engage in focused episodes of play with others who did not share his home language and whose competence in English was fragmentary. Ofeina received status, and a role in play, when her expertise at screen-printing and skipping was revealed. Aralynn's morning talks foregrounded the connection with other places of great significance to her, and invited her school class to imagine these contexts with her. In each of these occasions, the early childhood centre or the school had a space for the children's funds of knowledge and skill and gave it a place as a public bid for identity. Perhaps, if and when key competencies or learning dispositions are valued in school as well, Lauren's curiosity and question-asking, Joseph's embodied disposition to explore limits and entitlements, Sarah's capacity for imaginative drama, and Yasin's interest in telling stories, will be valued as well, and the literacy and numeracy will take their place alongside multi-disciplinary, multimodal and dispositional curriculum content.

Learning in the making: what might we ask of an educational system over time?

This question was raised in chapter two. We look towards a connected-up education system that fosters learners who can: relate reciprocally with diverse others, respond with resilience and curiosity to adverse and uncertain circumstances, imagine possible worlds and possible selves, and add a critical voice to question and defend social justice and the opportunities for multi-faceted learner selves that we have described in this book. These are learning dispositions, described by some as the contributors to 'life-long' learning. We have analysed the ways in which early education – in early childhood settings and primary schools – is a site in which this journey begins, a powerful site that can be deliberately authorising, permeable, and connected. We have argued that these three transactional and progressive processes are key to keeping learning dispositions on track (albeit via diverse pathways), and we suggest that if educational designs become disempowering, inflexible and disconnected then the learning valued here will falter and possibly fade. These fourteen stories of children learning to live together in difference, take some authority in their lives, and imagine alternatives may provide some frameworks for a critical theory of development and learning that has consequences for education in early childhood settings and school classrooms.

NOTES

These names are pseudonyms, in many cases chosen by the children or their families.

We observed in three kindergartens in phase one when Lisa was observed in two settings: in an afternoon kindergarten programme and a childcare morning programme. The kindergartens in this study were state-owned, providing free sessional programmes for three-and four-year-old children; the younger children attended three afternoon sessions a week and then they 'graduated' as 'nearly-fives' to the morning programme for five days a week. One of the childcare centres was a sessional (mornings only) early childhood programme. The other two childcare centres were all day programmes for two- to five-year-olds; one of these also had an 'under-twos' programme, housed nearby. At the time of the study the childcare centres charged fees. Since the study they now receive additional government funding to provide twenty hours a week free childcare for three- and four-year-olds.

3
The New Zealand government's educational monitoring organization.

4
The fourteen children here were part of a wider study of twenty-seven children in a project entitled *Dispositions in Social Context* (Duncan, 2005; Duncan, Jones & Carr, 2008; Jones, 2009; Smith, Duncan & Marshall, 2005; Smith, 2009).

5
In the wider group of 27 children, English was an additional language for six children.

6
In New Zealand almost every child begins school in a 'new entrant' class on, or soon after, their fifth birthday.

7
One of the authors, Anne Smith, has recently published a paper about Lisa (see Smith, 2009). The paper draws on some of the same data and theory that is used in this book.

8
It is a common pattern for New Zealand children to move to kindergarten (and out of another early childhood centre such as playcentre or childcare) when they are accepted into the five morning a week programme for the older children.

9
mihi = greeting

10
In this case study we have analysed each of three themes for Joseph sequentially across three phases, which differs from the organization of other case studies.

11
This transcript (on pp. 55–56) and some of the material in this chapter have been published in Duncan (2005).

REFERENCES

Albright, J. (2008). Problematics and generative possibilities. In J. Albright & A. Luke (Eds.), *Pierre Bourdieu and literacy education* (pp. 11–32). New York: Routledge.

Albright, J., & Luke, A. (2008). *Pierre Bourdieu and literacy education*. New York: Routledge.

Ames, C. (1992). Classrooms: Goals, structures, and student motivation. *Journal of Educational Psychology, 84*(3), 261–271.

Barab, S. A., & Roth, W-M. (2006). Curriculum-based ecosystems: Supporting knowing from an ecological perspective. *Educational Researcher, 35*(5), 3–13.

Barell, J. (1991). *Teaching for thoughtfulness: Classroom strategies to enhance intellectual development.* New York: Longman.

Baron, J. B. (1987). *Being disposed to thinking: A typology of attitudes and dispositions related to acquiring and using thinking skills.* Boston: University of Massachusetts Critical and Creative Thinking Program.

Belenky, M. F., Clinchy, B. M., Goldberger, N. R., & Tarule, J. M. (1986). *Women's ways of knowing: The development of self, voice and mind.* New York: Basic Books.

Bloomer, M., & Hodkinson, P. (2000). Learning careers: Continuity and change in young people's dispositions to learning. *British Educational Research Journal, 26*(5), 584–598.

Boaler, J. (2002). Learning from teaching: Exploring the relationship between 'reform' curriculum and equity. *Journal for Research in Mathematics Education, 33*(4), 239–258.

Boaler, J., & Greeno, J. G. (2000). Identity, agency and knowing in mathematical worlds. In J. Boaler (Ed.), *Multiple perspectives on Mathematics teaching and learning* (pp. 171–200). Westport CT: Ablex.

Bourdieu, P. (1977). *Outline of a theory of practice* (R. Nice, Trans.). Cambridge, UK: Cambridge University Press.

Bourdieu, P. (1986). *Distinction: A social critique of the judgement of taste* (R. Nice, Trans.). London: Routledge.

Bourdieu, P. (1990). *The logic of practice* (R. Nice, Trans.). Cambridge, UK: Polity.

Bourdieu, P., & Passeron, J-C. (1990). *Reproduction in education, society and culture* (2nd ed.). London: Sage.

Bransford, J. D., & Schwartz, D. (1999). Rethinking transfer: A simple proposal with multiple implications. *Review of Research in Education, 24,* 61–100.

Brennan, & Hayes, N. (2007). Pretend you're mean to me and I....:-Collective reconstructions in play. *Early Childhood Practice, 9*(1), 6–25.

Bronfenbrenner, U. (1979). *The ecology of human development.* Cambridge, MA: Harvard University Press.

Bronfenbrenner, U., & Morris, P. A. (1998). The ecology of developmental processes. In W. Damon & R. Lerner (Eds.), *Handbook of child psychology, Vol. 1: Theoretical Models of Development* (pp. 993–1028). New York: John Wiley & Sons.

Brooker, L. (2002). *Starting school – young children learning cultures.* Buckingham, UK: Open University Press.

Bruner, J. (1986). *Actual minds, possible worlds.* Cambridge, MA: Harvard University Press.

Bruner, J. (1995). From joint attention to meeting of minds: An introduction. Foreword in C. Moore & P. J. Dunham (Eds.), *Joint attention: its origins and role in development* (pp. 1–14). Hillsdale, NJ: Lawrence Erlbaum Associates.

Bruner, J. (2002). *Making stories: Law, literature and life.* Cambridge, MA: Harvard University Press.

Carr, M. (2001a). Seeking children's perspectives about their learning. In S. Taylor & Gollop (Eds.), *Advocating for children: International perspectives on children's rights* (Chapter 3, pp. 37–55), Dunedin, NZ: Otago University Press.

Carr, M. (2001b). *Assessment in early childhood settings: Learning stories.* London: Paul Chapman.

Carr, M. (2001c). A sociocultural approach to learning orientation in an early childhood setting. *Qualitative Studies in Education, 14*(4), 525–542.

REFERENCES

Carr, M., & Claxton, G. (2002). Tracking the development of learning dispositions. *Assessment in Education, 9*(1), 9–37.

Carr, M., Lee, W., & Jones, C. (2004, 2007 & 2009). *Kei tua o te pae. Assessment for learning: Early childhood exemplars.* Books 1–20. A resource prepared for the Ministry of Education. Wellington, NZ: Learning Media.

Carr, M., May, H., Podmore, V. N., Cubey, P., Hatherly, A., & Macartney, B. (2000). *Learning and Teaching Stories: Action Research on Evaluation in Early Childhood.* Wellington, NZ: NZCER.

Carr, M., Peters, S., Davis, K., Bartlett, C., Bashford, N., Berry, P. (2008). *Key learning competencies across place and time: Kimihia te ara tōtika, hei oranga mō to aō.* Final Report to the Teaching and Learning Research Initiative programme. Wellington, NZ: NZCER.

Clandinin, D. J., Huber, J., Huber, M., Murphy, M. S., Murray Orr, A., Pearce, M., et al. (2006). *Composing diverse identities; narrative inquiries into the interwoven lives of children and teachers.* London: Routledge.

Clandinin, D. J., & Rosiek, J. (2007). Mapping a landscape of narrative inquiry: Borderland spaces and tensions. In D. J. Clandinin (Ed.), *Handbook of narrative inquiry: Mapping a methodology* (Chapter 2, pp. 35–75). London: Sage.

Clark, A., & Moss, P. (2001). *Listening to young children: The mosaic approach.* London: National Children's Bureau.

Clarke-Stewart, K. A. (1973, December). Interactions between mothers and their young children: Characteristics and consequences. *Monographs of the Society for Research in Child Development, 38*(6/7).

Claxton, G. (2002). *Building learning power: Helping young people become better learners.* Bristol, UK: TLO Limited.

Claxton, G., & Carr, M. (2004). A framework for teaching learning: The dynamics of disposition. *Early Years, 24*(1), 87–97.

Collins, J. (2008). Postscript. In Albright & Luke (Eds.), *Pierre Bourdieu and literacy education* (pp. 363–373). New York: Routledge.

Comber, B. (2000). What really counts in early literacy lessons. *Language Arts, 78*(1), 39–49.

Coordenacao, De Estudos, E., Pesquisas Sobre, A., Infancia (CESPI-USU). (2001). *Children, youth and their developmental supports. Strengthening family and community supports for children and youth in Rio de Janeiro.* Rio de Janeiro: Universidade Santa Ursulao.

Corsaro, W. (1997). *The sociology of childhood.* Thousand Oaks, CA: Pine Forge Press.

Corsaro, W. (2003). *'We're friends right?' Inside kids' culture.* Washington, DC: Joseph Henry Press.

Costa, A. L., & Kallick, B. (2000). Discovering and exploring habits of mind. Alexandria, VA: Association for Supervision and Curriculum Development.

Crowley, K., & Jacobs, M. (2002). Building islands of expertise in everyday family activity. In G. Leinhardt, K. Crowley, & K. Knutson (Eds.), Learning conversations in museums (Chapter 10, pp. 333–356). Mahwah, NJ: Lawrence Erlbaum.

Csikszentmihalyi, M. (1996). *Creativity: Flow and the psychology of discovery and invention.* New York: Harper Collins.

Csikszentmihalyi, M. (1997). *Finding flow: The psychology of engagement with everyday life.* New York: Basic Books.

Cullen, J., & St. George, A. (1996). Scripts for learning: Reflecting dynamics of classroom life. *Journal for Australian Research in Early Childhood, 1,* 10–19.

Davies, B., & Hunt, R. (1994). Classroom competencies and marginal positionings. *British Journal of Sociology of Education, 15*(3), 389–408.

de Haan, D., & Singer, E. (2003). Use your words. A sociocultural approach to the teacher's role in the transition from physical to verbal strategies of resolving peer conflicts among toddlers. *Journal of Early Years Research, 1,* 95–109.

Donaldson, M. (1992). *Human minds: An exploration.* London: Penguin.

Duncan, J. (2005). She's always been, what I would think, a perfect day-care child. Constructing the subjectivities of a New Zealand child. *European Early Childhood Education Research Journal, 13*(2), 51–62.

Duncan, J., Bowden, C., & Smith, A. B. (2005). *Early childhood centres and family resilience.* Report prepared for Centre for Research and Evaluation, Ministry of Social Development. Retrieved from www.msd.govt.nz

Duncan, J., Jones, C., & Carr, M. (2008). Learning dispositions and the role of mutual engagement: Factors for consideration in educational settings. *Contemporary Issues in Early Childhood, 9*(2), 107–117.

Dweck, C. S. (1985). Intrinsic motivation, perceived control, and self-evaluation maintenance: An achievement goal analysis. In C. Ames & R. Ames (Eds.), *Research on motivation in education* (Vol. 2: The Classroom Milieu). San Diego, CA: Academic Press, Inc.

Dweck, C. S. (2000). *Self-theories: Their role in motivation, personality and development.* Philadelphia: Psychology Press (Taylor & Francis group).

Dweck, C. S. (2006). *Mindset: The new psychology of success.* New York: Random House

Edwards, A., & D'Arcy, C. (2004). Relational agency and disposition in sociocultural accounts of learning to teach. *Educational Review, 56*(2), 147–155.

Eisner, E. W. (2005). *Reimagining schools: The selected works of Elliot W. Eisner.* London: Routledge/Taylor & Francis.

Ennis, R. H. (1989). Critical thinking and subject specificity: Clarification and needed research. *Educational Researcher, 18,* 4–10.

Feldman, C. F., & Wertsch, J. V. (1976). Context dependent properties of teachers' speech. *Youth and Society, 7*(3), 227–256.

Filer, A., & Pollard, A. (2000). *The Social World of Pupil Assessment: Processes and contexts of primary schooling.* London: Continuum.

Fitzgerald, R., Graham, A., Smith, A., & Taylor, N. (2010). Children's participation as a struggle for recognition: Exploring the promise of dialogue. In P. Barry-Smith & N. Thomas (Eds.), *Handbook of children and young people's participation* (293–305). London: Routledge.

Gallas, K. (2003). *Imagination and literacy: A teacher's search for the heart of learning.* New York: Teachers College Press.

Gee, J. P. (1992). *The social mind: Language, ideology, and social practice.* New York: Bergin and Garvey.

Gee, J. P. (1997). Thinking learning and reading: The situated sociocultural mind (Chapter 9, pp. 235–259). In D. Kirschner & J. A. Whitson (Eds.), *Situated cognition: Semiotic and psychological perspectives.* Mahwah NJ: Erlbam.

Gee, J. P. (2000–2001). Identity as an analytic lens for research in education. *Review of Research in Education, 25,* 99–125.

Gee J. P. (2003a). Literacy and social minds. In G. Bull & M. Anstey (Eds.), *The literacy lexicon* (2nd ed., Chapter 1, pp. 4–14). French's Forest, NSW: Prentice Hall.

Gee, J. P. (2008). A sociocultural perspective on opportunity to learn. In P. A. Moss, D. C. Pullin, J. G. Gee, E. H. Haertel, & L. Jones Young (Eds.), *Assessment, equity, and opportunity to learn* (Chapter 4, pp. 76–108). Cambridge, UK: Cambridge University Press.

Gellert, G. (2002). Resilience in children. *The first years: Nga tau tuatahi, 4*(1), 21–24.

Gilligan, R. (2001). *Promoting resilience: A resource guide on working with children in the care system.* London: British Agencies for Adoption and Fostering.

González, N., Moll, L. C., & Amanti, C. (2005). *Funds of knowledge: Theorizing practices in households, communities and classrooms.* Mahwah, NJ: Lawrence Erlbaum Associates.

Goodenow, C. (1992). Strengthening the links between educational psychology and the study of social contexts. *Educational Psychologist, 27*(2), 177–196.

Goodnow, J. (1977). *Children's drawing.* London: Fontana/Open Books.

REFERENCES

Goodnow, J. (1990). The socialization of cognition: What's involved? In J. W. Stigler, R. A. Shweder, & G. Herdt (Eds.), *Cultural psychology: Essays on comparative human development* (pp. 259–286). New York: Cambridge University Press.

Greene, M. (1988). What happened to imagination? In K. Egan & D. Nadaner (Eds.), *Imagination and Education* (Chapter 3, pp. 45–56). New York: Teachers College Press.

Greene, M. (1995). *Releasing the imagination: Essays on education, the arts, and social change.* San Francisco: Jossey-Bass.

Greeno, J. G. (2006). Authoritative, accountable positioning and connected, general knowing: Progressive themes in understanding transfer. *The Journal of the Learning Sciences, 15*(4), 537–547.

Greeno, J. G. (2007). Toward the development of intellective character. In E. W. Gordon & B. L. Bridglall (Eds.), *Affirmative development: Cultivating Academic Ability* (Chapter 2, pp. 17–47). Lantham, MD: Rowman & Lttlefield.

Greeno, J. G., & The Middle School Mathematics Through Applications Project Group. (1998). The situativity of knowing, learning and research. *American Psychologist, 58*, 5–26.

Greeno, J. G., & The Middle School Mathematics Through Applications Project Group. (1998). The situativity of knowing, learning and research. *American Psychologist, 58*, 5–26.

Gresalfi, M. S. (2009). Taking up opportunities to learn: Constructing dispositions in mathematics classrooms. *The Journal of the Learning Sciences, 18*, 327–369.

Guttierrez, K. (2007). Commentary. In C. Lewis, P. Enciso, & E. Birr Moje (Eds.), *Reframing sociocultural research on literacy: Identity and agency and power* (pp. 115–120). Mahwah, NJ: Lawrence Erlbaum Associates.

Hamilton, L. (2002). Constructing pupil identity. *British Educational Research Journal, 28*(4), 591–602.

Handel, G., Cahill, S. E., & Elkin, F. (2007). *Children and society: The sociology of children and childhood socialization.* Los Angeles: Roxbury Publishing Company.

Hanna, J. L. (2008). A nonverbal language for imagining and learning: Dance education in K-12 curriculum. *Educational Researcher, 37*(8), 491–506.

Harris, P. L. (1989). *Children and emotion: The development of psychological understanding.* Oxford, UK: Blackwell.

Harris, P. L. (2000). *The Work of the Imagination.* Oxford, UK: Blackwell.

Haste, H. (2001). Are all key competencies measurable? An education perspective. In D. S. Rychen & L. H. Salganik (Eds.), *Defining and selecting key competencies* (pp. 222–227). Gottingen, Germany: Hogrefe & Huber.

Hattie, J. (2009). *Visible learning: A synthesis of over 800 meta-analyses relating to achievement.* London: Routledge.

Hedegaard, M. (2009). Children's development from a cultural-historical approach: Children's activity in everyday local settings as foundation for their development. *Mind, Culture and Activity, 16*, 64–81.

Holland, D., Lachicotte, W., Skinner, D., & Cain, C. (1998). *Identity and agency in cultural worlds.* Cambridge, MA: Harvard University Press.

Hull, G. A., & Nelson, M. E. (2005). Locating the semiotic power of multimodality. *Written Communication, 22*(2), 224–226.

James, A. (2007). Giving voice to children's voices: Practices and problems, pitfalls and potentials. *American Anthropologist, 109*(2), 261–272.

Jewitt, C. (2006). *Technology, Literacy, Learning: A multimodal approach.* London: Routledge.

Jewitt, C. (2008). Multimethodology and literacy in school classrooms. *Review of Research in Education, 32*, 241–267.

Johnston, P. (2004). *Choice words: How our language affects children's learning.* Portland, ME: Stenhouse Publishers.

Jones, C. (2009). Being reflective and responsive in early childhood research: A technology episode example. In A. T. Jones & M. J. de Vries (Eds.), *International handbook of research and development in technology education* (pp. 747–757). Rotterdam, The Netherlands: Sense Publishers.

Kalil, A. (2003). *Family resilience and good child outcomes: A review of the literature.* Wellington, NZ: Ministry of Social Development.

Kalliala, M. (2006). *Play culture in a changing world.* Maidenhead, Berkshire: Open University Press.

Katz, L. G., & McLellan, D. E. (1991). *The teacher's role in the social development of young children.* ERIC Clearinghouse on Elementary and Early Childhood Education, University of Illinois, Document 217-333-1386.

Kress, G. (2003). *Literacy in the new media age.* London: Routledge.

Lacan, J. (1977). *Ecrits: A selection.* London: Tavistock.

Langer, E. J. (1989). *Mindfulness.* Reading, MA: Addison-Wesley.

Langer, E. J. (1997). *The power of mindful thinking.* Reading, MA: Addison-Wesley.

Lave, J. (1996). Teaching, as learning, in practice. *Mind, Culture, and Activity, 3*(3), 149–164.

Lave, J., & Wenger, E. (1991). *Situated learning: Legitimate peripheral participation.* Cambridge, UK: Cambridge University Press.

Lee, Y-J, Brown, B., Brickhouse, N., Lottero-Perdue, P., Roth, W-M., & Tobin, K. (2007). Discursive constructions of identity. In W-M. Roth & K. Tobin (Eds.), *Science, learning, identity: Sociocultural and cultural-historical perspectives* (Chapter 13, pp. 325–337). Rotterdam, The Netherlands: Sense Publishers.

Lemke, J. L. (2000). Across the scales of time: Artifacts, activities, and meanings in ecosocial systems. *Mind, Culture, and Activity, 7*(4), 273–290.

Lewis, C., Enciso, P., & Birr Moje, E. (Eds.). (2007). *Reframing sociocultural research on literacy: Identity and agency and power.* Mahwah, NJ: Lawrence Erlbaum Associates.

Lobato, J. (2003). How design experiments can inform a rethinking of transfer and vice versa. *Educational Researcher.* 32(1), 17-20

Lobato, J. (2006). Alternative perspectives on the transfer of learning: History, issues, and chanllenges for future research. *The Journal of the Learning Sciences.* 15(4), 431-449

Luke, A. (2005). Curriculum, ethics, metanarrative: Teaching and learning beyond the nation. In Y. Nozaki, R. Openshaw, & A. Luke (Eds.), *Struggles over Difference: Curriculum, texts, and pedagogy in the Asia-Pacific* (Chapter 1, pp. 11–24). State University of New York Press.

McNaughton, S. (2002). *Meeting of the minds.* Wellington, NZ: Learning Media.

Markus, H., & Nurius, P. (1986). Possible selves. *American Psychologist, 41*(9), 954–969.

Masten, A. S. (2001). Ordinary magic. Resilience processes in development. *American Psychologist, 56*(3), 227–238.

Mayall, B. (2002). *Towards a sociology for childhood: Thinking from children's lives.* Buckingham, UK: Open University Press.

Meier, D. (1995). *The power of their ideas: Lessons for America from a small school in Harlem.* Boston: Beacon Press.

Meier, D. (2002). *In schools we trust: Creating communities of learning in an era of testing and standardization.* Boston: Beacon Press.

Mercer, N., & Littleton, K. (2007). *Dialogue and the development of children's thinking: A sociocultural approach.* London: Routledge.

Mercer, N. (2008). The seeds of time: Why classroom dialogue needs a temporal analysis. *The Journal of the Learning Sciences.* 17. 33-59.

Miller, P. J., & Goodnow, J. J. (1995). Cultural practices: Towards an integration of culture and development. In J. J. Goodnow, P. J. Miller, & F. Kessel (Eds.), *Cultural practices as contexts for development* (pp. 5–17). *New Directions in Child Development, 67.* San Francisco: Jossey-Bass.

Ministry of Education. (1996). *Te whāriki. He whāriki mātauranga mö ngā mokopuna o Aotearoa: Early childhood curriculum.* Wellington, NZ: Learning Media.

Ministry of Education. (2007). *The New Zealand curriculum: The English-medium teaching and learning in years* (1–13). Wellington, NZ: Learning Media.

Moore, C., & Dunham, P. J. (Eds.). (1995). *Joint attention: Its origins and role in development.* Hillsdale, NJ: Lawrence Erlbaum Associates.

Morss, J. R. (1996). *Growing critical: Alternatives to developmental psychology.* London: Routledge.

Nasir, N. S., & Saxe, G. B. (2003). Ethnic and academic identities: A cultural practice perspective on emerging tensions and their management in the lives of minority students. *Educational Researcher, 32*(5), 14–18.

REFERENCES

Nelson, K., & Fivush, R. (2004). The emergence of autobiographical memory: A social cultural developmental theory. *Psychological Review, 111*(2), 486–511.
New London Group. (1996). A pedagogy of multiliteracies: Designing social futures. *Harvard Educational Review, 66,* 60–92.
Packer, M., & Goicoechea, J. (2000, Fall). Sociocultural and constructivist theories of learning: Ontology not just epistemology. *Educational Psychologist, 35*(4), 227–242.
Packer, M., & Greco-Brooks, D. (1999). School as a site for the production of persons. *Journal of Constructivist Psychology, 12,* 133–151.
Packer, M. J., & Tappan, M. B. (2001). Introduction. In M. J. Packer & M. B. Tappan (Eds.), *Cultural and critical perspectives on human development* (Chapter 1, pp. 1–37). New York: State University of New York.
Paley, V. (1992). *You can't say you can't play.* Cambridge, MA: Harvard University Press.
Paley, V. (1997). *The girl with the brown crayon: How children use stories to shape their lives.* Cambridge, MA: Harvard University Press.
Paley, V. (2001). *In Mrs Tully's room: A childcare portrait.* Cambridge, MA: Harvard University Press.
Paley, V. (2004). *A child's work: The importance of fantasy play.* Chicago: University of Chicago Press.
Papert, S. (1993). *Mindstorms: Children, computers and powerful ideas.* New York: Basic Books Inc.
Perkins, D. N. (2000, May/June). Schools need to pay more attention to "intelligence in the wild". *Harvard Education Letter,* 1–3.
Perkins, D. N. (2001, January). *Intelligence in the wild.* Paper presented at 'Breakthroughs' Ninth International Conference on Thinking. Auckland.
Perkins, D. N., Jay, E., & Tishman, S. (1993). Beyond abilities: A dispositional theory of thinking. *Merrill-Palmer Quarterly, 39*(1), 1–21.
Perkins, D., Tishman, S., Ritchhart, R. Donis, K., & Andrade, A. (2000). Intelligence in the Wild: A dispositional view of intellectual traits. *Educational Psychology Review, 12*(3), 269–293.
Perrenoud, P. (2001). The key to social fields: Competencies of an autonomous actor. In D. S. Rychen & L. H. Salganik (Eds.), *Defining and selecting key competencies.* (Chapter 6, pp. 121–150). Gottingen, Germany: Hogrefe & Huber.
Pitri, E. (2004). Situated learning in a classroom community. *Art Education.* 57(6). 6-12.
Pollard, A., & Filer, A. (1999). *The social world of pupil career: Strategic biographies through primary school.* London: Cassell.
Resnick, L. B. (1987). *Education and learning to think.* Washington DC: National Academy Press.
Rinaldi, C. (2006). *In dialogue with Reggio Emilia: Listening, researching and learning.* Oxford, UK: Routledge.
Ritchhart, R. (2002). *Intellectual character: What it is, why it matters, and how to get it.* San Francisco: Jossey-Bass.
Rogoff, B. (1990). *Apprenticeship in thinking: Cognitive development in social context.* New York: Oxford University Press.
Rogoff, B. (2003). *The cultural nature of human development.* Oxford and New York: Oxford University Press.
Roth, W.-M. (2001). Situating cognition. *The Journal of the Learning Sciences, 10*(1 & 2), 27–61.
Rychen, D. S., & Salganik, L. H. (Eds.). (2001). *Defining and selecting key competencies.* Gottingen, Germany: Hogrefe & Huber.
Rychen, D. S., & Salganik, L. H. (2003). *Key competencies for a successful life and well functioning society.* Cambridge, MA: Hogrefe & Huber.
Schaffer, H. R. (1992). Joint involvement episodes as context for development. In H. McGurk (Ed.), *Childhood social development: Contemporary perspectives* (pp. 99–129). Hove, UK: Lawrence Erlbaum Associates.
Sfard, A. (2008). *Thinking as communicating: Human development, the growth of discourses, and mathematizing.* Cambridge, UK: Cambridge University Press.
Sfard, A., & Prusak, A. (2005). Telling identities: In search of an analytic tool for investigating learning as a culturally shaped activity. *Educational Researcher, 34*(4), 14–22.

Siraj-Blatchford, I. (2004). Educational disadvantage in the early years: How do we overcome it? Some lessons from research. *European Early Childhood Research Journal, 12*(2), 5–20.

Siraj-Blatchford, I., & Manni, L. (2008). 'Would you like to tidy up now?' An analysis of adult questioning in the English Foundation Stage. *Early Years, 28*(1), 5–22.

Siraj-Blatchford, I., Sylva, K., Taggart, B., Sammons, P., Melhuish, E., & Elliot, K. (2003). *Intensive case studies of practice across the Foundation Stage. Technical Paper 10*. London: Institute of Education, University of London.

Sizer, H. R. (1992). *Horace's school: Redesigning the American high school*. Boston: Houghton Mifflin.

Smiley, P. A., & Dweck, C. S. (1994). Individual differences in achievement goals among young children. *Child Development, 65*, 1723–1743.

Smith, A. B. (1999). Quality childcare and joint attention. *International Journal of Early Years Education, 7*(1), 85–98.

Smith, A. B. (2008). Rethinking childhood: The inclusion of children's voice. In Y. Ronen & C. W. Greenbaum (Eds.), *The case for the child: Towards a new agenda* (pp. 15–27). Antwerp-Oxford-Portland: Intersentia.

Smith, A. B. (2009). A case study of learning architecture and reciprocity. *International Journal of Early Childhood, 41*(1), 33–49.

Smith, A. B., & Barraclough, S. (1999). Young children's conflicts and teachers' perspectives on them. *New Zealand Journal of Educational Studies, 34*(2), 335–348.

Smith, A. B., Duncan, J., & Marshall, K. (2005). Children's perspectives on their learning: Exploring methods. *Early Child Development and Care, 175*(6), 473–487.

Smith, A. B., Taylor, N. J., & Gollop, M. (2001). What children think separating parents should know. *New Zealand Journal of Psychology, 30*(1), 23–30.

Stephen, C., & Cope, P. (2003). An inclusive perspective on the transition to primary school. *European Educational Research Journal, 2*(2), 262–276.

Sylva, K., Roy, C., & Painter, M. (1980). *Childwatching at playgroup and nursery school*. Ypsilanti, MI: High/Scope Press.

Sylva, K., Sammons, P., Melhuish E. C., Siraj-Blatchford, I., & Taggart, B. (1999). The *effective provision of preschool education (EPPE) project. Technical paper 1. An introduction to EPPE*. London: DfEE/Institute of Education, University of London.

Thomas, N. (2007). Towards a theory of children's participation. *International Journal of Children's Rights, 15*, 199–218.

Thomson, P., & Hall, C. (2008). Opportunities missed and/or thwarted? 'Funds of knowledge' meet the English national curriculum. *The Curriculum Journal, 19*(2), 87–103.

Timperley, H. (2003). School improvement and teachers' expectations of student achievement. *New Zealand Journal of Educational Research, 38*, 73–78.

Tomasello, M. (1999). *The cultural origins of human cognition*. Cambridge, MA: Harvard University Press.

Tomasello, M., & Rakoczy, H. (2003). What makes human cognition unique? From individual to shared to collective intentionality. *Mind and Language, 18*(2), 121–147.

Ungar, M. (2000). The myth of peer pressure: Adolescents and their search for health-enhancing identities. *Adolescence, 35*(137), 167–180.

Ungar, M. (2004a). A constructionist discourse on resilience: Multiple contexts, multiple realities among at-risk children and youth. *Youth and Society, 35*(3), 341–365.

Ungar, M. (2004b). *Nurturing hidden resilience in troubled youth*. Toronto, ON: University of Toronto Press.

van Oers, B., & Hannikainen, M. (2001). Some thoughts about togetherness: An introduction. *International Journal of Early Years Education, 9*(2), 101–124.

Voloshinov, V. N. (1973). *Marxism and the philosophy of language* (L. M. Matejka & I. R. Titunik, Trans.). New York: Seminar Press. (Originally published in 1929)

Vygotsky, L. (1978). *Mind in society: The development of higher psychological processes*. Cambridge, MA: Harvard University Press.

REFERENCES

Wagner, J. F. (2006). Transfer in pieces. *Cognition and Instruction, 24*(1), 1–71.

Walker, D., & Nocon, H. (2007). Boundary-crossing competence: Theoretical considerations and educational design. *Mind, Culture, and Activity, 14*(3), 178–195.

Walsh, F. (1996). The concept of family resilience: Crisis and change. *Family Process, 35*(3), 261–281.

Walsh, F. (1998). *Strengthening family resilience*. New York: The Guilford Press.

Wells, G. (2002). Inquiry as an orientation to learning. In G. Wells & G. Claxton (Eds.), *Learning for life in the 21st century: sociocultural perspectives on the future of education* (pp. 197–210). Oxford, UK: Blackwell.

Wenger, E. (1998). *Communities of practice: Learning, meaning and identity*. Cambridge, UK: Cambridge University Press.

Wertsch, J. V. (1991). *Voices of the mind: A sociocultural approach to mediated action*. Cambridge, MA: Harvard University Press.

Wertsch, J. V. (1998). *Mind as action*. Oxford, UK: Oxford University Press.

Wertsch, J. V., Tulviste, P., & Hagstrom, F. (1993). A sociocultural approach to agency. In E. Forman, N. Minick, & C. Stone (Eds.), *Contexts for learning: Sociocultural dynamics of children's development* (Chapter 14, pp. 336–356). New York: Oxford University Press.

Whalley, M. (1994). *Learning to be strong: Setting up a neighbourhood service for under-twos and their families*. Sevenoaks, Kent: Hodder & Stoughton.

Wertsch, J. V., Tulviste, P., & Hagstrom, F. (1993). A sociocultural approach to agency. In E. Forman, N. Minick, & C. Stone (Eds.), *Contexts for learning: Sociocultural dynamics of children's development*. New York: Oxford University Press.

White, B., Kahan, B., & Attamucci, J. (1979). *The origins of human competence*. Lexington, MA: D. C. Heath.

Wiliam, D. (2008). What should education research do, and how should it do it? *Educational Researcher, 37*(7), 432–438.

Zachner, J. (2008). Social hierarchies and identity politics. In J. Albright & A. Luke (Eds.), *Pierre Bourdieu and Literacy Education* (Chapter 13, pp. 252–278). London: Routledge.

INDEX

LaVergne, TN USA
03 January 2011
210774LV00003B/129/P